Paris

Paul Vannier
Photographs by Philippe Moulu

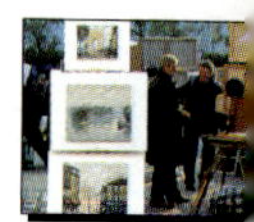
Place du Tertre

Montmartre p. 4

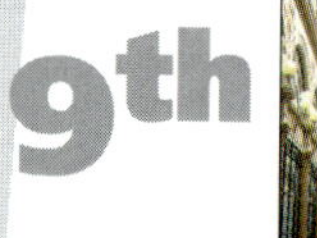
Grands Boulev

Opéra p. 37

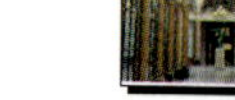

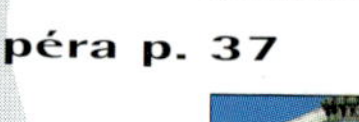
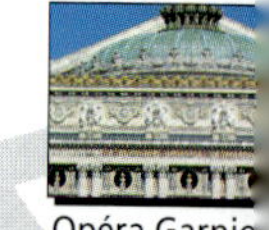
Opéra Garnie

Louvre –
Palais-R
p. 50

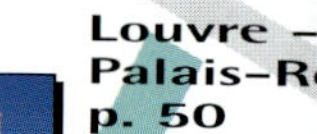

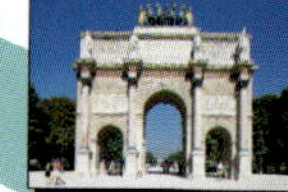
Place de
la Concorde

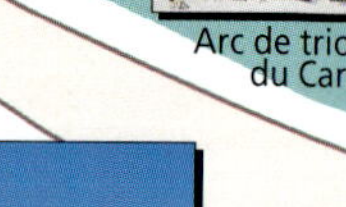
Arc de triomphe
du Carrousel

Champs–Élysées p. 61

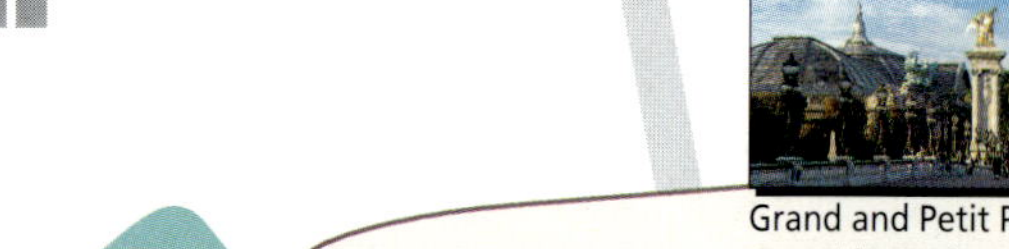
Grand and Petit Palais
pont Alexandre-III

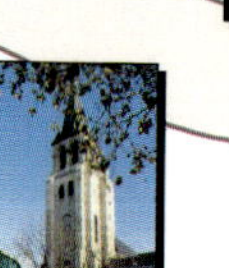
Musée d'Orsay

Invalides –
Orsay p. 79

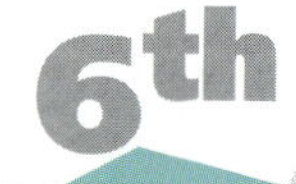
Saint-Germain-des-Prés churc

Saint-Germain-des-Prés p. 87

Luxembourg p.

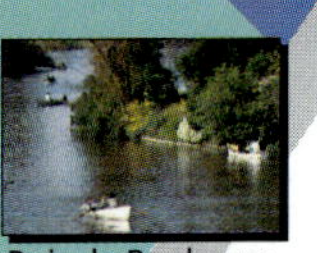
Bois de Boulogne

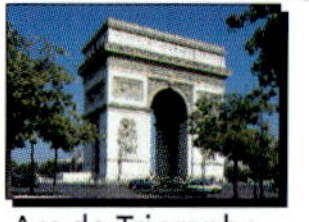
Arc de Triomphe

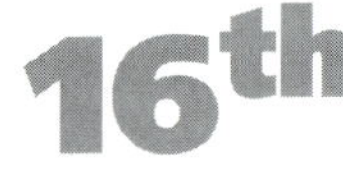
Le palais de Chaillot

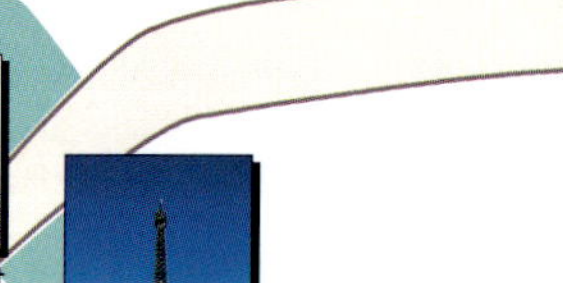
La tour Eiffel

Tour Eiffel p. 71

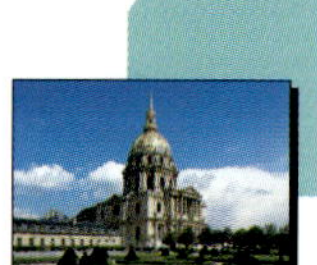
Les Invalides

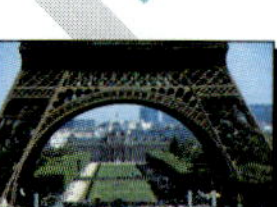
Champ-de-Mars
École militaire

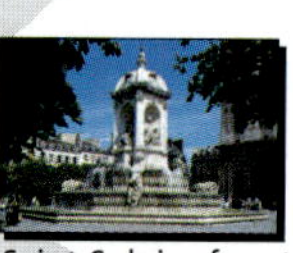
Saint-Sulpice fountain

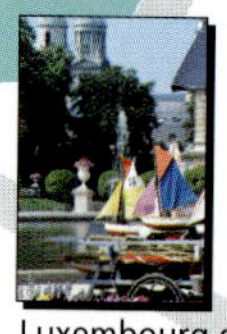
Luxembourg gar-
dens

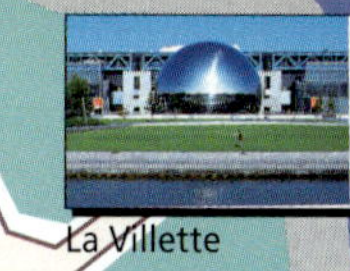
La Villette

18th

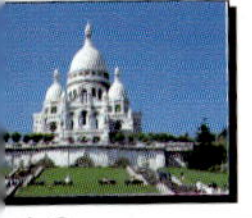
ré-Cœur

19th

10th

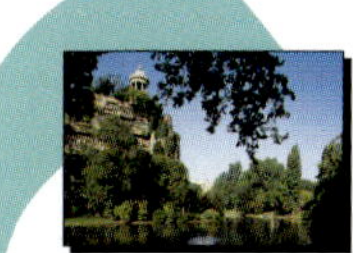
Buttes-Chaumont Park

2nd

20th

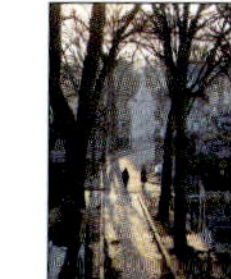
Père-Lachaise Cemetery

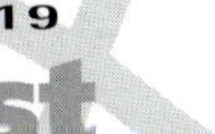
âtelet –
s Halles
19

Georges-Pompidou
Centre

3rd

1st

Tour Saint-Jacques

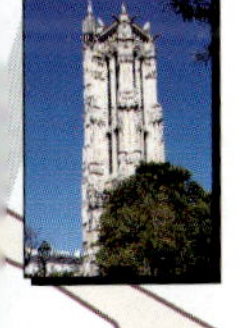
Notre-Dame p. 9

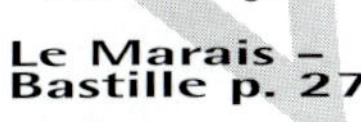
Place des Vosges

4th

11th

Le Marais –
Bastille p. 27

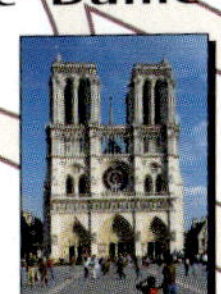
Notre-Dame

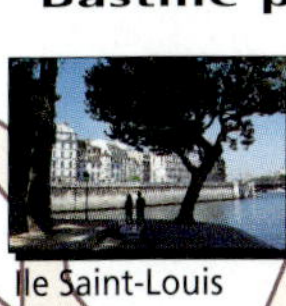
Île Saint-Louis

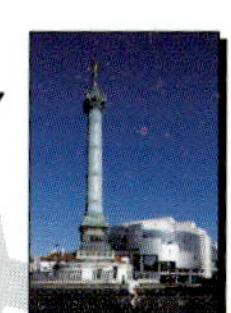
Place de la Bastille

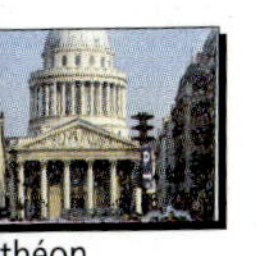
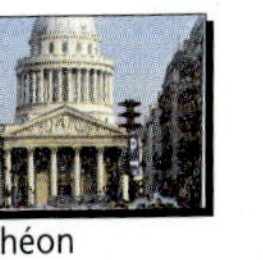
théon

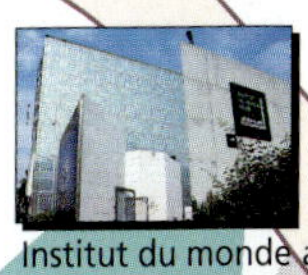
Institut du monde arabe

Jardin des Plantes p. 103

5th

12th

Jardin des Plantes

13th

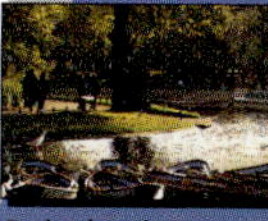
Bois de Vincennes

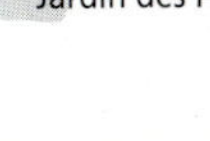

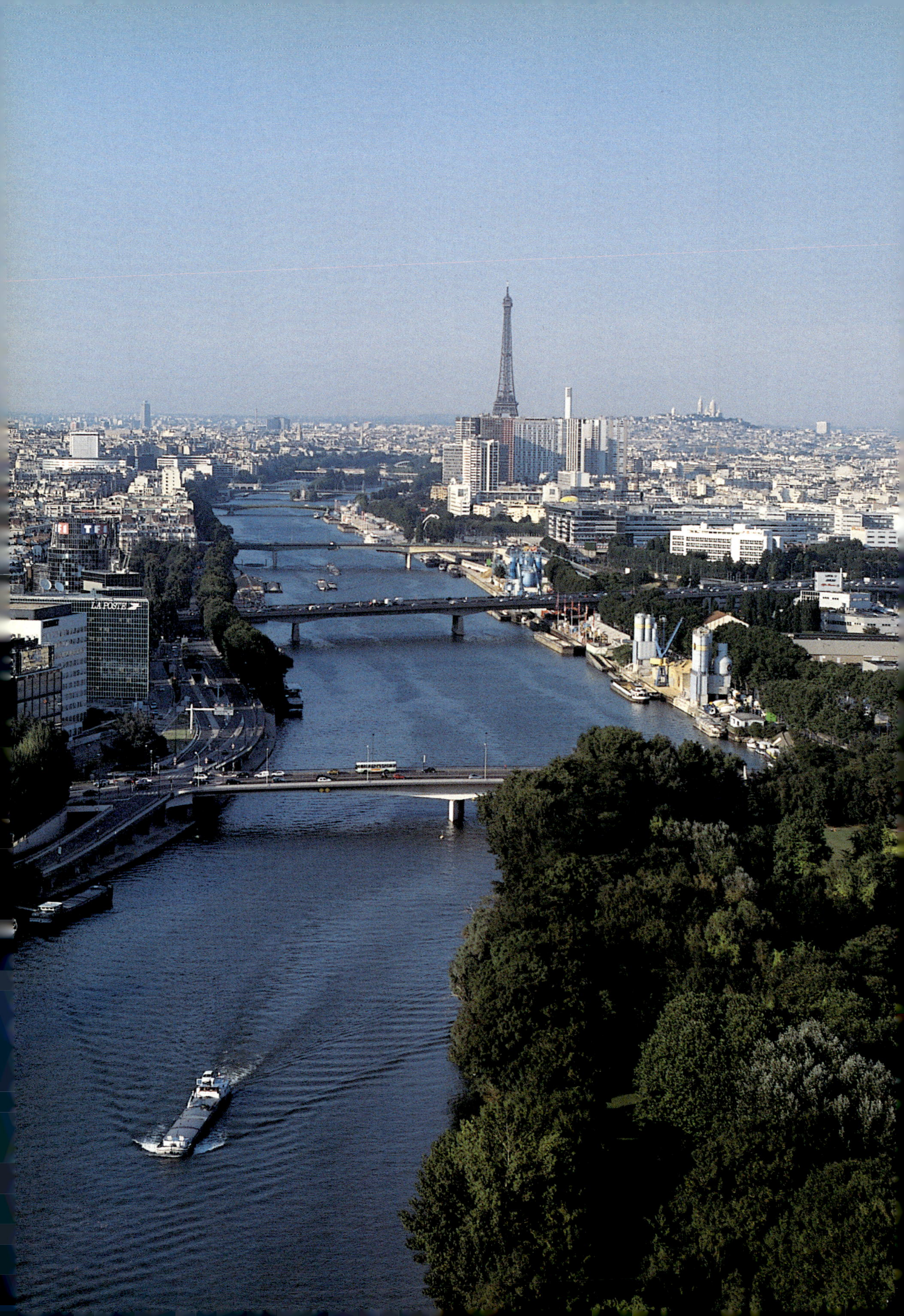

Contents

Preface

The Seine, the river which feeds Paris and led to its creation,
crosses the city from east to west along thirteen kilome-
ters... and holds the key to the secrets of the capital.
From the Ile de la Cité, which was once home to fishermen
and boatmen in prehistoric times, the town soon expanded
onto the surrounding banks and hills. However, its close
link with the river always remained. Not only is the city's
coat of arms the mark of the river merchants - a boat -
but its motto Sic fluctuat nec mergitur means "it floats and
does not sink".

Time, like water, passes beneath the bridges: today, Paris
has no less than thirty-three which join the right bank to
the left. Because in this city, where you are or where you
live implies one or the other. You might be Parisian, but are
you left bank or right?

So keep the Seine in sight to discover the capital's many
monuments, gardens, squares and roads and of course, the
river's bridges and quaysides.
Just about every period in history has left its mark on one
or other of the city's districts. But Paris is no museum... you
won't find yourself wandering through Pompeiian streets
or stumbling upon a Roman forum. Every era has managed
to adopt the cultural heritage of its predecessors, to cher-
ish, re-energise and in some way enrich it. Even if each city
feature has a date and historical significance, all are a living part of the Paris of today. Where the Seine has flowed
for over two thousand years...

Paul VANNIER

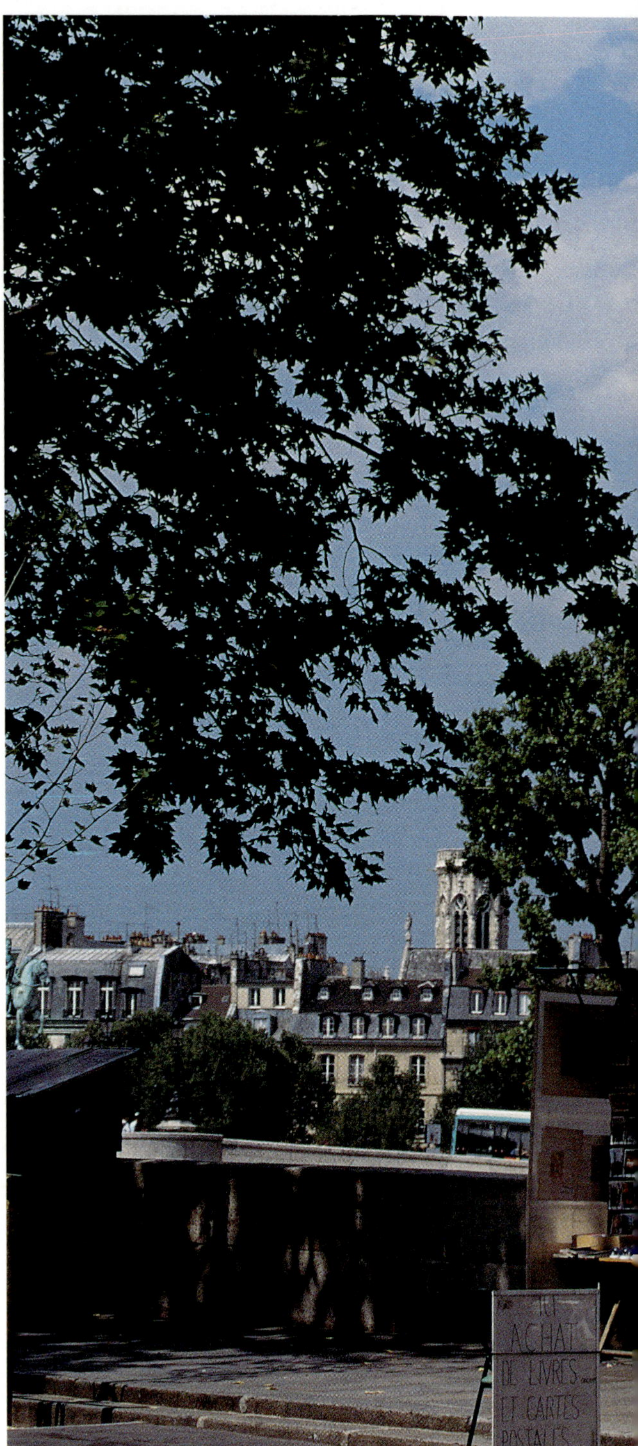

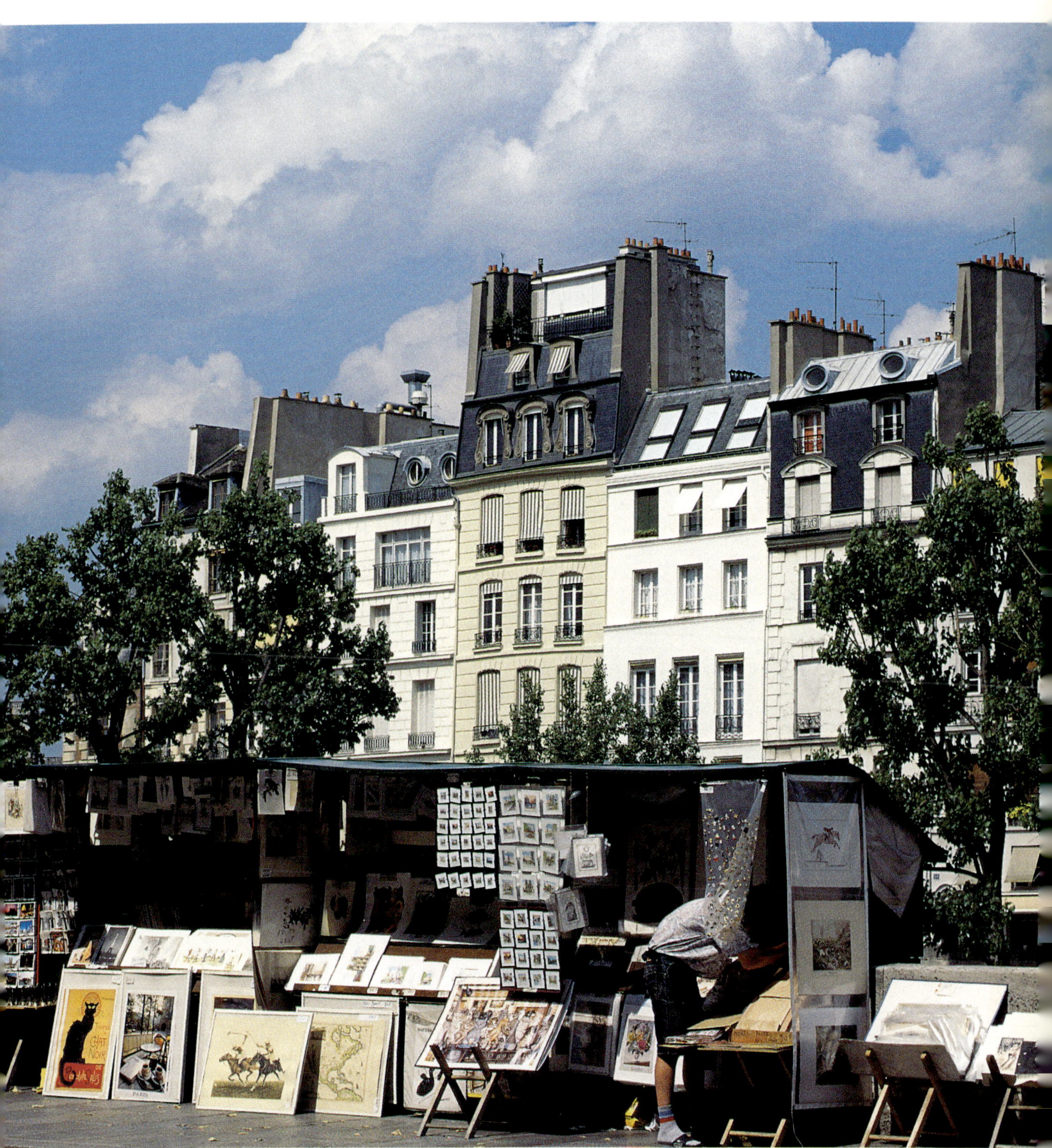

Monument

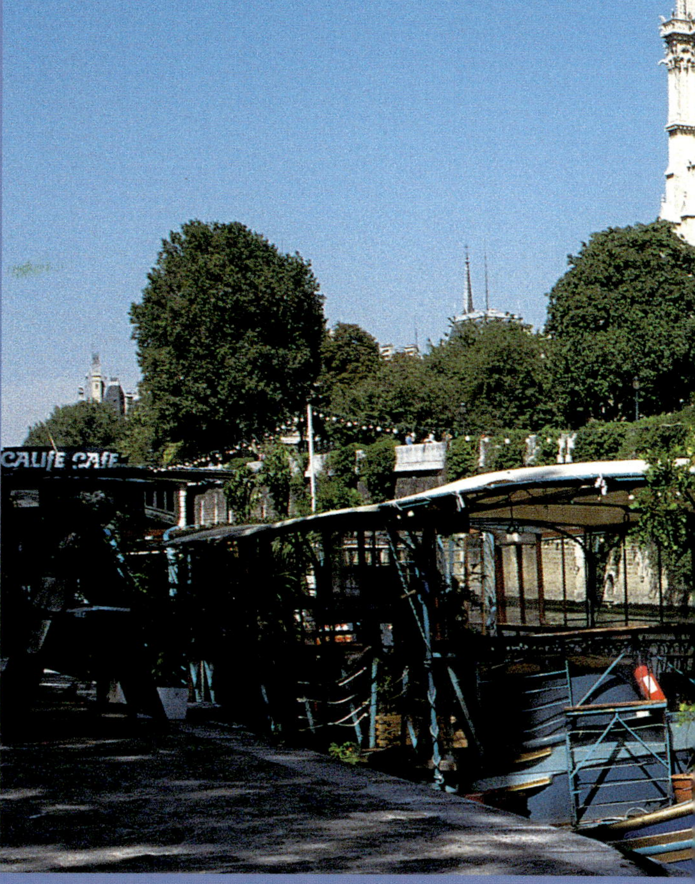

1ˢᵗ and 4ᵗʰ arrondissements

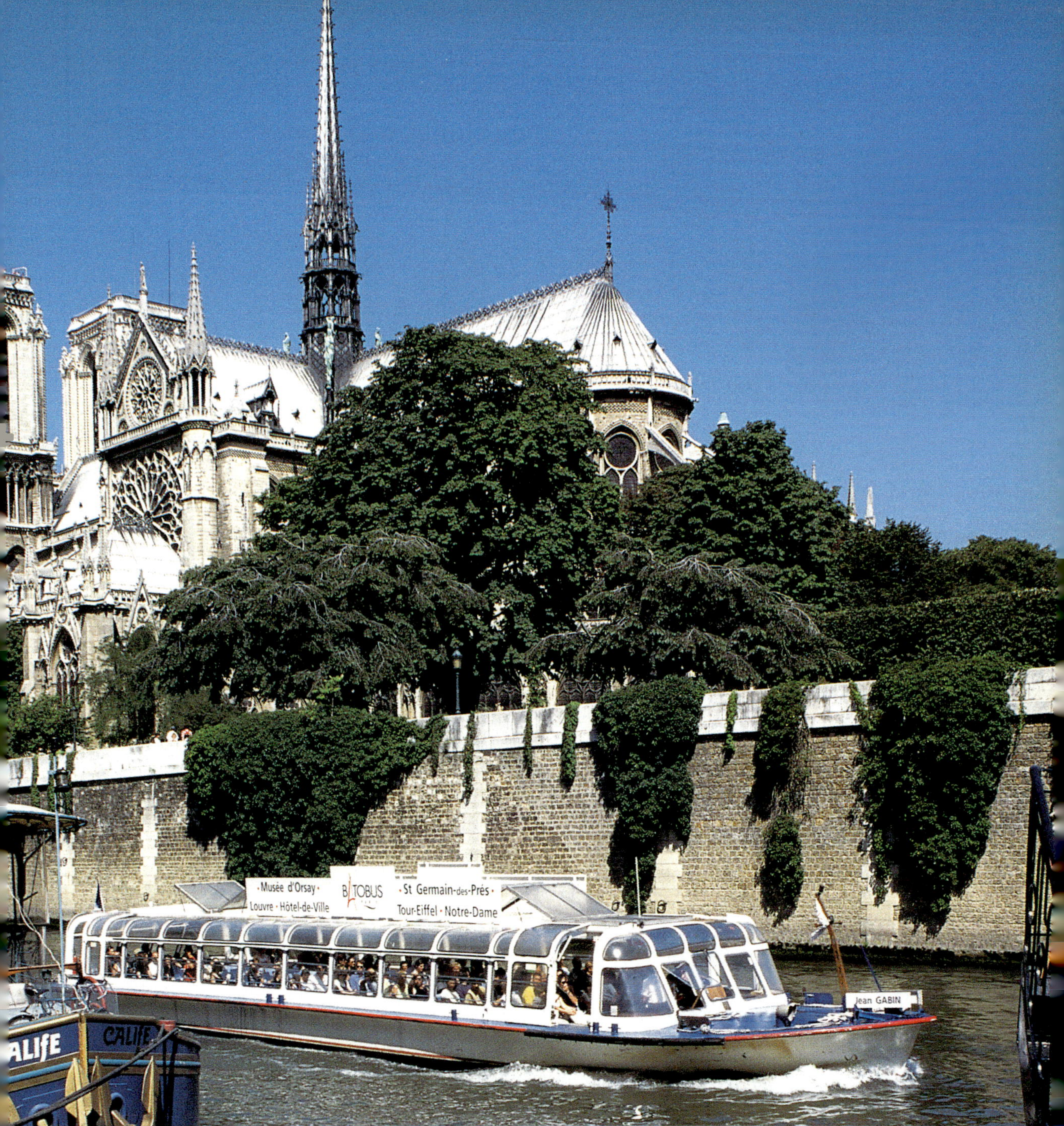

Notre-Dame

Notre-Dame
Conciergerie
Sainte-Chapelle
Pont-Neuf
Ile Saint-Louis

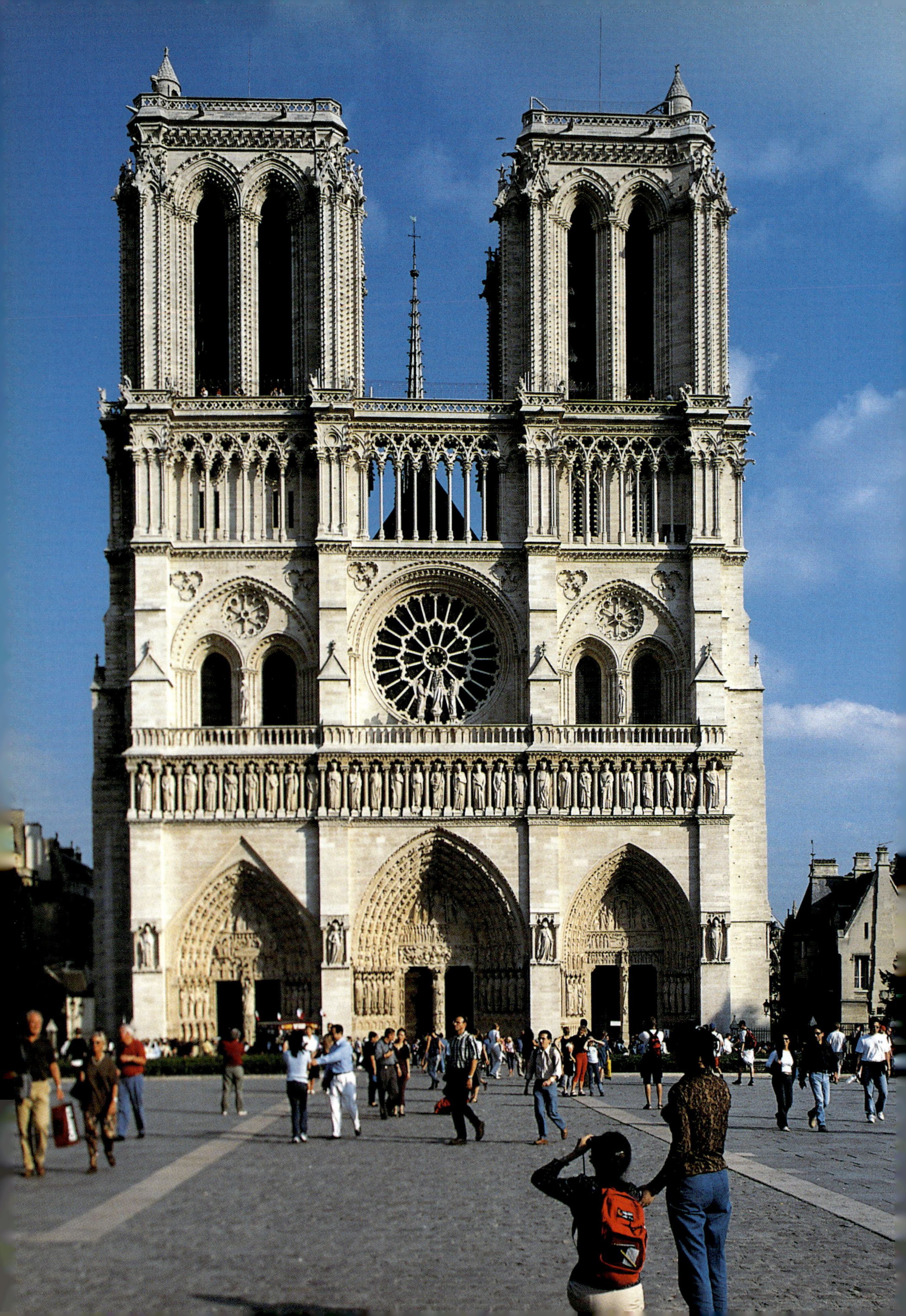

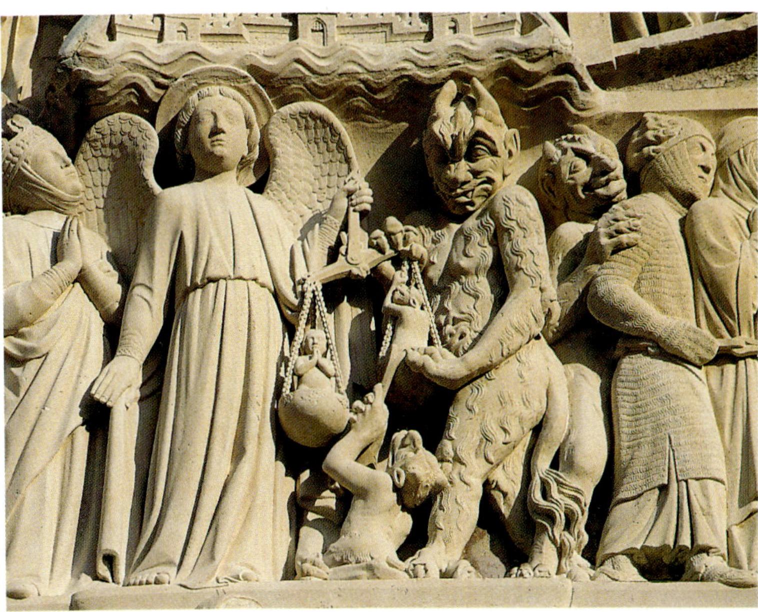

The façade of Notre-Dame
is impressive for its unity and
size (opposite).
This detail from the tympanum
of the Last Judgement, in the centre
of the West façade, evokes Heaven
and Hell (left).

Notre-Dame

At the very heart of the Ile de la Cité, the magnificent towers of Notre-Dame reach up to the skies. The site of the cathedral was formerly occupied by a temple dedicated to Jupiter in Roman times and a basilica placed under the patronage of Saint Etienne in the 5th century. In 1163, the Bishop of Paris, Maurice de Sully, decided to build a new cathedral. It took seventy five years to complete, under the successive reigns of Louis VII, Philippe Auguste, Saint Louis and Philippe VI. Its impressive size - 130 m long, 108 m wide and 35 m high under the arches - makes it the largest edifice constructed since Roman times.

Notre-Dame has seen darker days. It was pillaged during the Revolution, religious objects were confiscated and melted down to make canons and the statues of the Kings of Juda which decorate its façade were defaced. It narrowly escaped being destroyed by fire during the Paris Commune in 1871. Then during the 1914-1918 war, a bomb fell through its roof but miraculously failed to cause any damage.

On its almost square front façade are three doors: on the left, the Portal of the Virgin, in the centre, the Portal of the Last Judgement and on the right, the Portal of Saint Anne. Above the three doors is the gallery of the 28 Kings of Juda which was restored in the 19th century. On the upper level, surmounted by a gallery of interlaced arcatures are two twin windows which frame the large rose window. The latter is over 10 m in diameter and some parts have been in place for over seven centuries. The two towers, illuminated by tall windows, are almost 70 m high. The right tower houses the famous 13 ton bell which was cast during the reign of Louis XIV and named Emmanuelle-Marie-Thérèse. Traditionally, the bells of Notre-Dame ring out to mark the city's major historical events. The famous gargoyles which grimace under the grand gallery and on the top of the towers, are the work of Viollet-le-Duc who restored the monument between 1844 and 1864. He is also responsible for the 90 m spire, a unique structure consisting of an oak frame covered in 250 tons of lead.

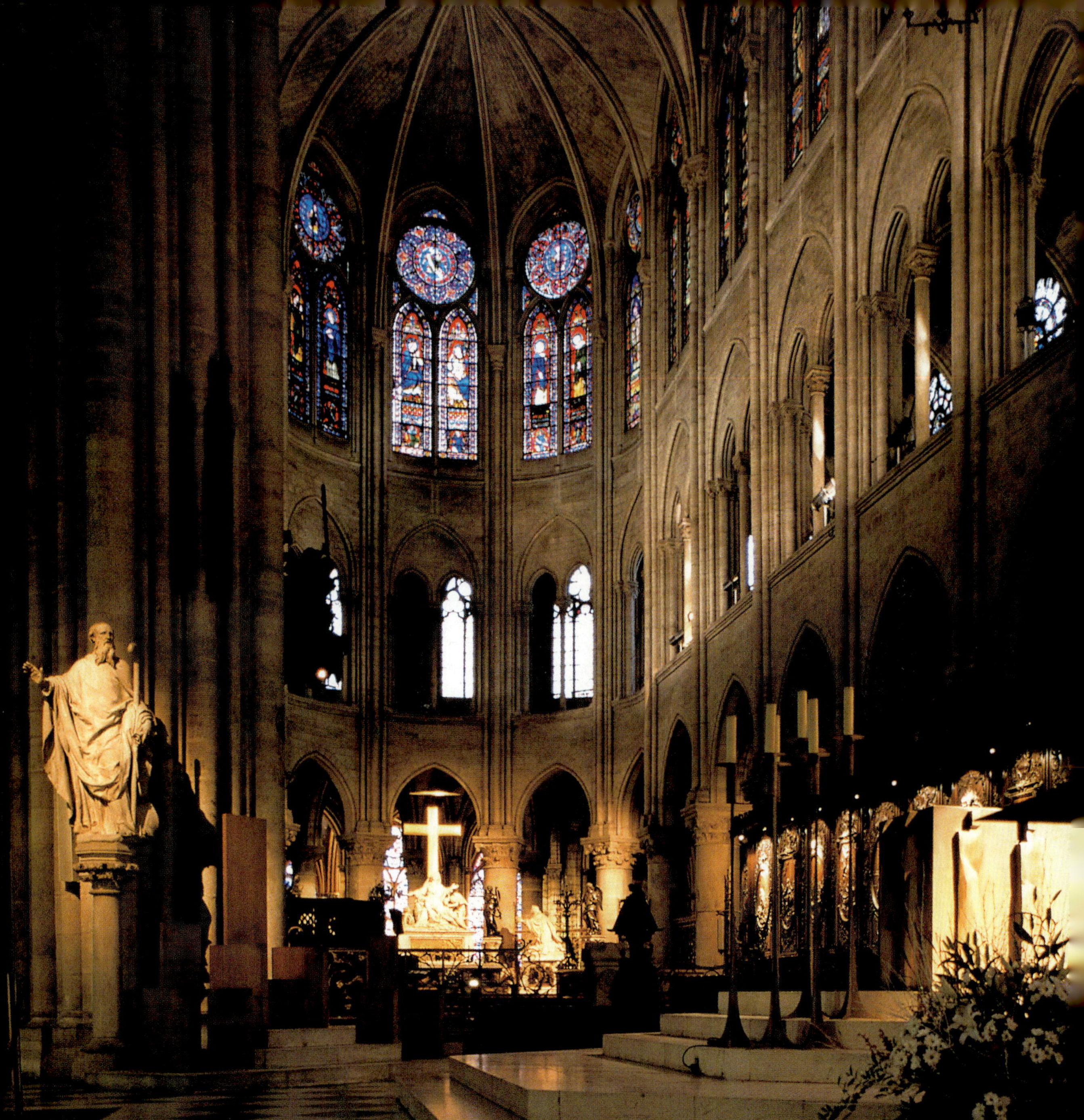

Inside the cathedral, under the high vaults with their ribbed casements is a vast nave composed of five double bays flanked by side aisles. The transept and chancel, which lead onto a round seven-sided apse, are surrounded by an ambulatory. On each side of the nave are chapels dating from the 13th and 14th centuries. The large hall of the nave is illuminated by huge stained glass windows, by the North rose window with its blue tones and central figure of the Virgin and Child and the South rose window with its dominant red colours, which radiate around the figure of a majestic Christ. In the chancel, around the main altar composed of Egyptian marble, a group piece designed by Robert de Cotte and Mansart illustrates the "Vœu de Louis XIII" (The Wish of Louis XIII). The latter, who still had no heir after twenty three years of marriage, wished to dedicate France to the Virgin as thanks for the gift of a son. The wish became

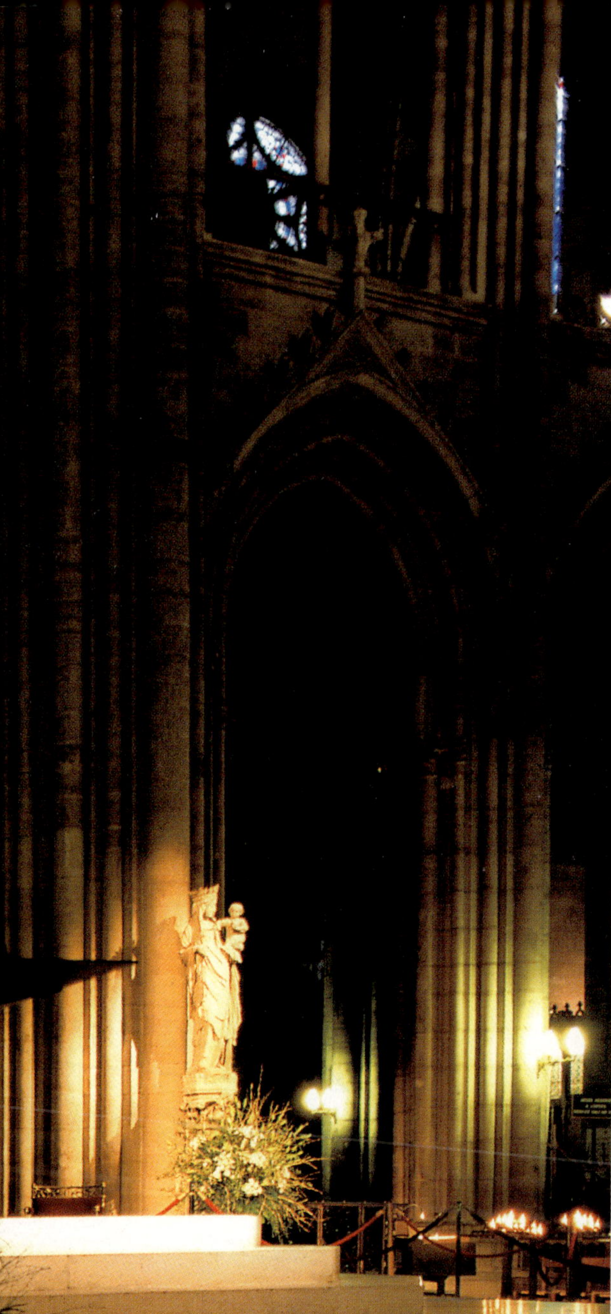

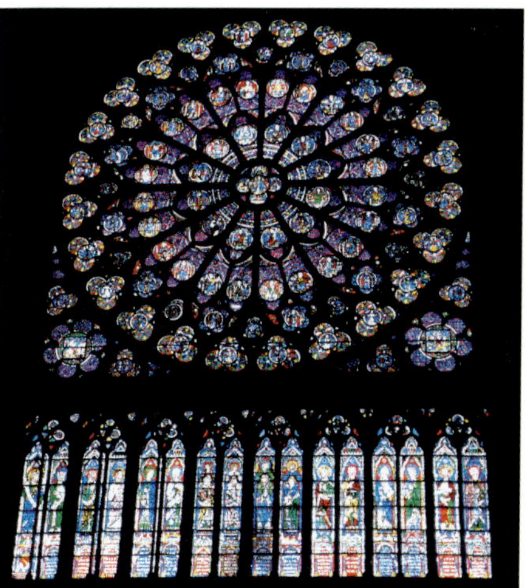

The transept is decorated with two statues representing Saint-Denis and Notre-Dame de Paris (left).
The stained-glass of the north rose window represents 80 characters from the Old Testament gathered around the Virgin (above).

Mansart and Cotte and created between 1711 and 1715. Overlooking the nave under the blue-toned rose window of the West façade are the Cliquot organs. Composed of 6,000 pipes, 110 registers, 5 keyboards and 113 organ stops, they comprise the largest instrument of this type in France.

Notre-Dame was the inspiration for the famous figures of Quasimodo and Esmeralda from Victor Hugo's novel *Notre-Dame de Paris*, characters who are now inseparable from the monument itself. In fact it was the publication of this book in 1831 which drew public and state attention to the dilapidated state of the cathedral and led to its restoration.

The vast square in front of the cathedral was enlarged during the large-scale city development work carried out by Haussman in the 19th century. Here, you can find a bronze star on the ground which marks the centre of Paris. Under the Ancien Régime, this was also the point used to measure road distances between the capital and provincial towns.

reality in the person of his son, the future Louis XIV, who was born in 1638. Around the work of the burial of Christ by Girardon, are the statues of Louis XIII by Coustou, who also created the Pietà, and the statue of Louis XIV by Coysevox. Both are offering their crown and sceptre to the Virgin as a token of their esteem, under the watchful eyes of bronze angels carrying the instruments of the Passion. The stalls, which occupy three aisles, were designed by

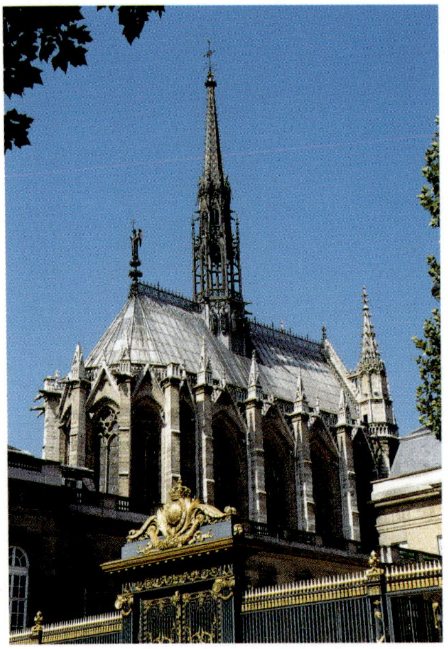

The Conciergerie is all that remains of the first palace of the Capetian kings, when the Ile de la Cité was the bustling centre of Paris (right).
The Sainte-Chapelle, a royal church which stands out for its elegant architecture, is located in the grounds of the Paris Law Courts (above).

Conciergerie

The Palais de Justice de Paris (Paris Law Courts) now occupies the site of the first Palace-Fortress of the French kings. It was gradually taken over by the Royal Administration during the 14th century, in particular the French Parliament, and today, the only original buildings which remain are the Sainte-Chapelle (Holy Chapel) and the northern part of the fortress called the "Conciergerie", which served as both the Palace Administrator's accommodation and a prison. Following a fire, some of the buildings were reconstructed in 1782 and the majority date from the 19th century. The entrance to the Conciergerie on the Quai de l'Horloge is located between two massive towers and leads to three large halls, the vestiges of the former Palais de la Cité.

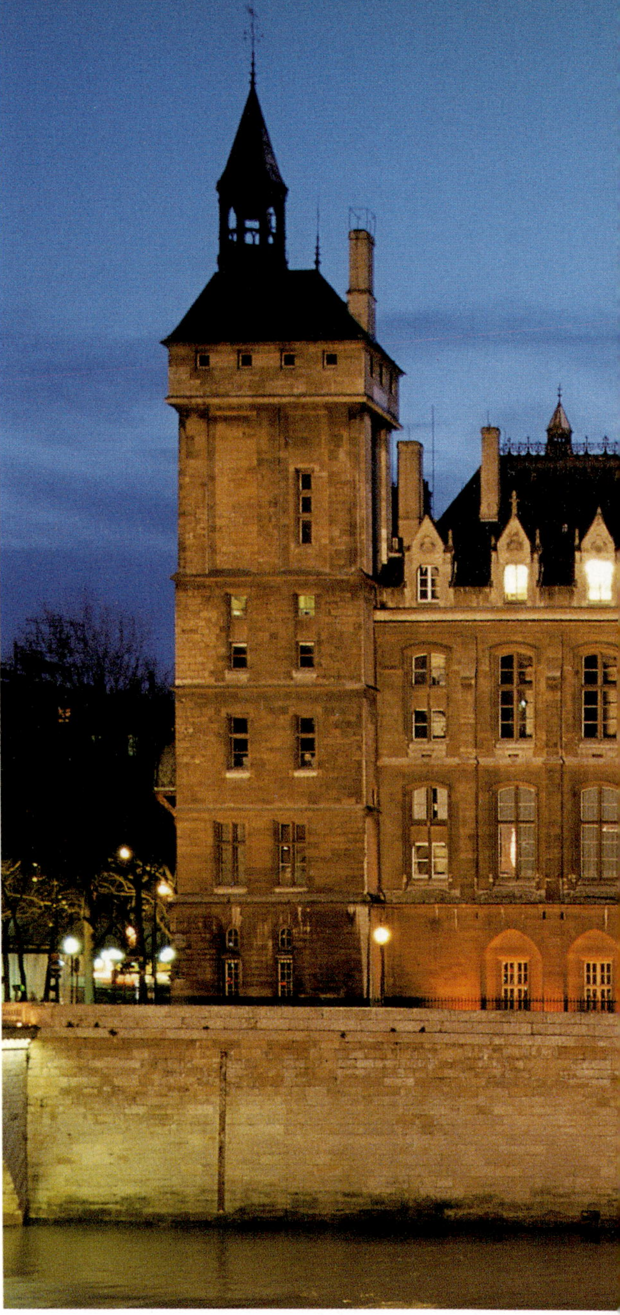

The Salle des Gardes (Guardroom) was built during the reign of Philippe le Bel at the beginning of the 14th century and is divided into two naves composed of four aisles: two stairways lead to the Tour d'Argent (Silver Tower) and Tour de César (Caesar's Tower), formerly known as the Tournelle Criminelle and Tournelle Civile (the Criminal and Civil Towers). The square shaped kitchen hall, built around 1353, consists of twelve columns and four monumental chimneys. The Salle des Gens d'Armes, (Police Hall) which

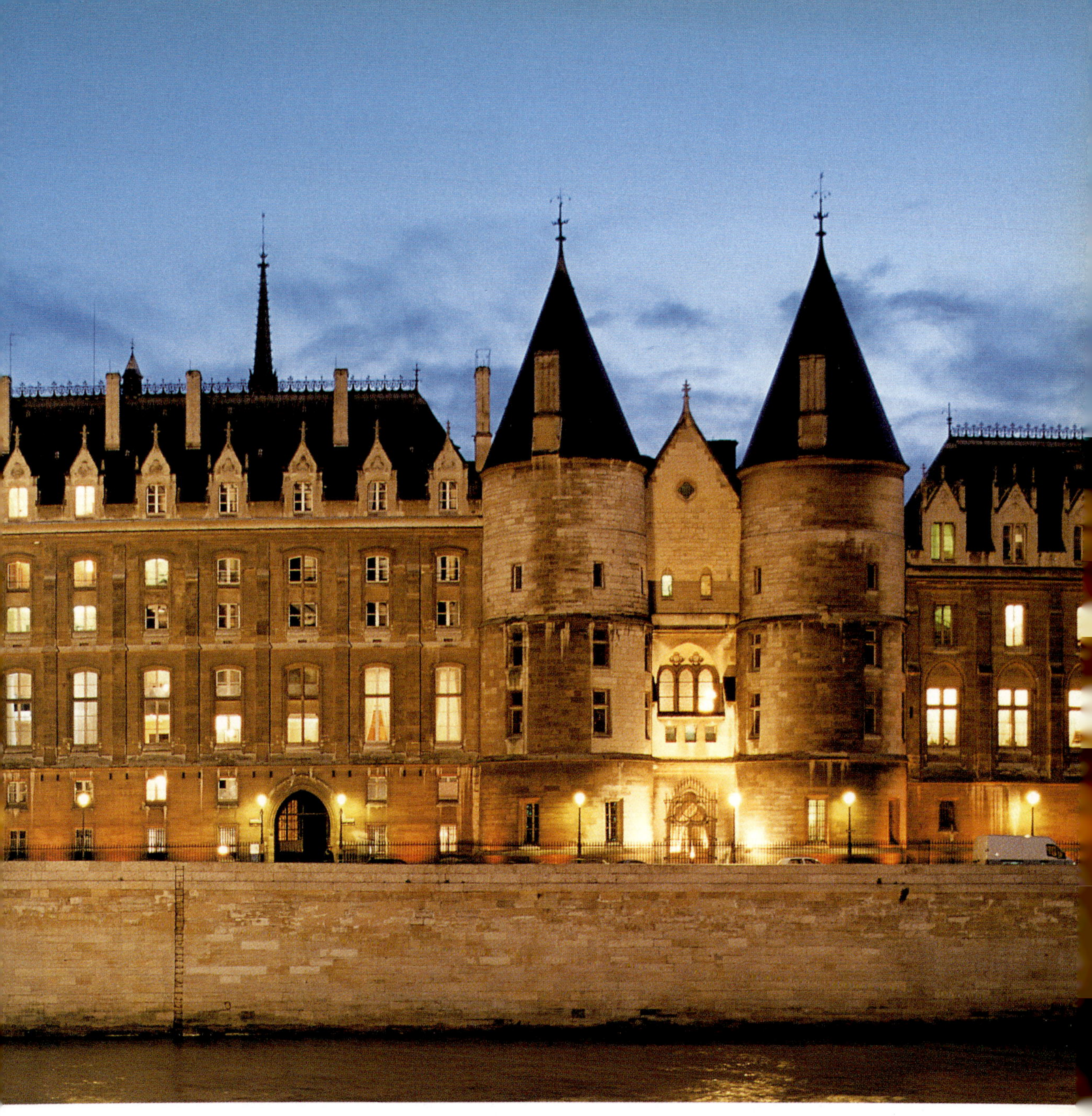

also dates from the 14th century, is a beautiful Gothic structure. The four Western aisles form a corridor which was
known as the "Road of Paris" during the Revolution and
led to the dungeons. The Conciergerie, where those con-
demned to the guillotine were kept, held many famous prisoners during the French Revolution, including Queen
Marie-Antoinette, the wife of Louis XVI.

In 1914, the Conciergerie officially stopped being a prison
and became a historical monument open to the public.

Sainte-Chapelle

King Louis IX, decided to build a chapel inside the royal
palace of the Ile de la Cité to house the relics from the
Passion of Christ. The chapel was built from 1241 to 1248.
The presence of projecting instead of flying buttresses to
support the thrust of the vaults, gives the whole structure
an unrivalled elegance. This is further accentuated by the
tall, perforated 75 m spire. Each architectural element seems
to have been designed to highlight the chapel's beautiful

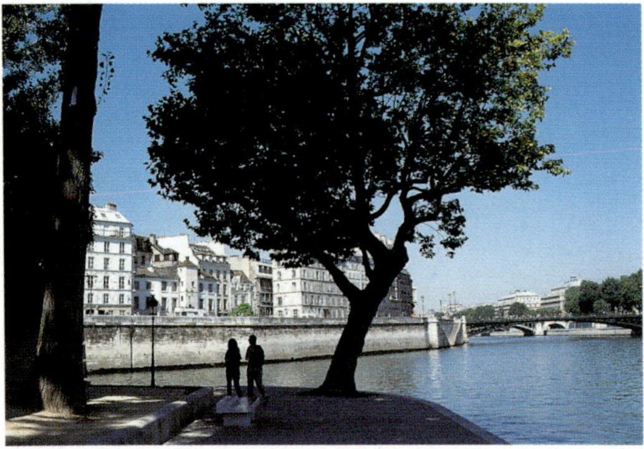

At 278 m long and 38 m wide, the Pont-Neuf remains one
of the largest bridges in Paris (right).
On the Ile Saint-Louis, the beautifully shaded Quai de Bourbon
is lined with the elegant façades of private mansions from the
17th and 18th centuries (above).

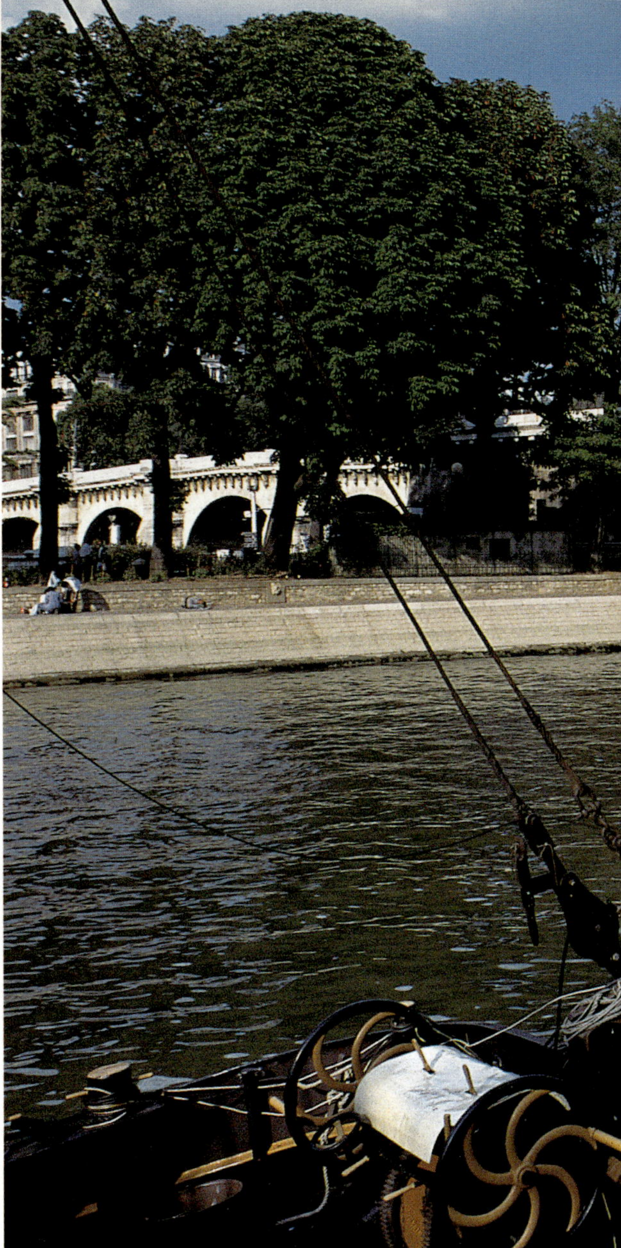

rose windows and enormous stained-glass windows The
upper chapel is exceptional for its pure, elegant lines. "On
entering", said Saint Louis, "one feels transported to the
skies". In fact the King was able to enter the upper chapel
directly from his chambers without having to pass through
the lower one. The main altar and gallery were restored
in the 19th century, but the most beautiful aspect of the
upper chapel is without doubt its wonderful polychrome
decoration. The majority of its enormous 15 m wide stained-
glass windows, with their dominant reds and blues, illuminated by golden yellows, are some of the oldest in Paris.

Pont-Neuf

The Pont-Neuf is the oldest bridge in Paris. It was built
following a decision made by Henry III in 1577 and was the
first bridge not to involve the construction of houses The
first stone was laid in 1578 but it was not until 1607 that
the bridge was finally opened by Henry IV, who crossed it
on horseback. From its earliest days, the Pont-Neuf has
been a hive of activity. It was not only occupied by book-
seller stalls but popular with gangs of conmen and com-
panies of jugglers and acrobats, including the company
of "Tabarin", one of the "masters" of Molière. The bridge
is still an inspiration for artists today. In 1985, the American
artist Christo covered the whole bridge in an enormous
golden plastic canvas.

The statue of King Henry IV which stands in the middle of the Pont-Neuf, was commissioned from Jean de Bologne
by Marie de' Medici. It was destroyed during the Revolution
and replaced by a work by Frédéric Lemot in 1818.

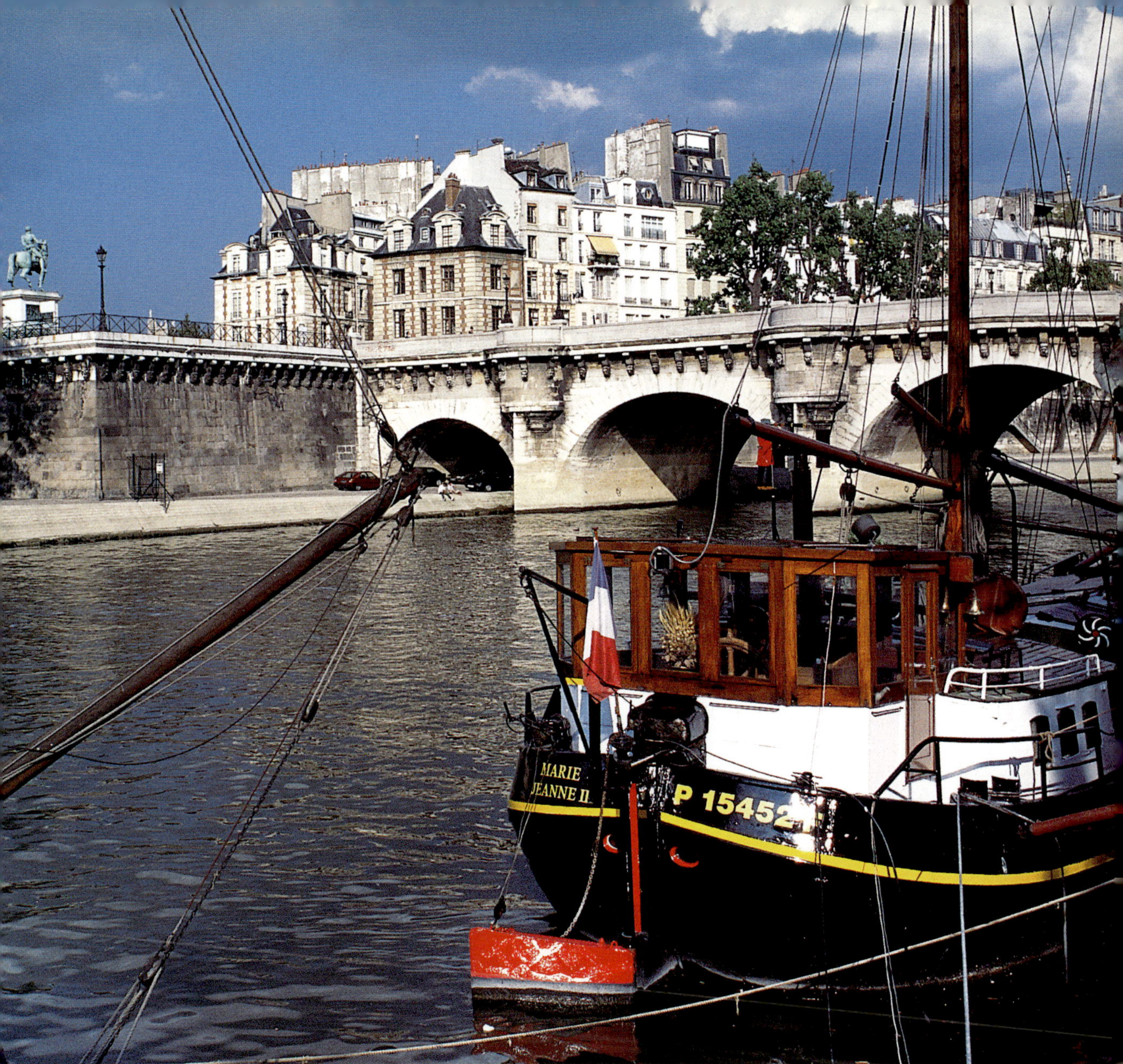

Ile Saint-Louis

In the Middle Ages, the Ile Saint-Louis - which did not take this name until 1726 - was divided into two small islands, the Ile aux Vaches (Cow's Island) and ile Notre-Dame. During the 17th century, under the reigns of Henry IV and Louis XIII, work was carried out to join the two and create just a single island, linked to the two banks of the Seine by bridges. The quays were faced with stone to raise the island above flood levels, roads were marked out and houses and private mansions were built. The latter, designed by famous architects and artists such as Le Vau and Le Brun, are quite exceptional. The originality of the structures is due to the use of dressed stone instead of brick, the material traditionally used in the 17th century.

In spite of work carried out at the end of the 19th century, the Ile Saint-Louis has preserved its original character and boasts some of the most beautiful architecture in Paris. Today, you can still stroll along its quays and lose yourself in a labyrinth of quiet streets, admiring the façades, doorways and balconies of the island's beautiful 17th century homes.

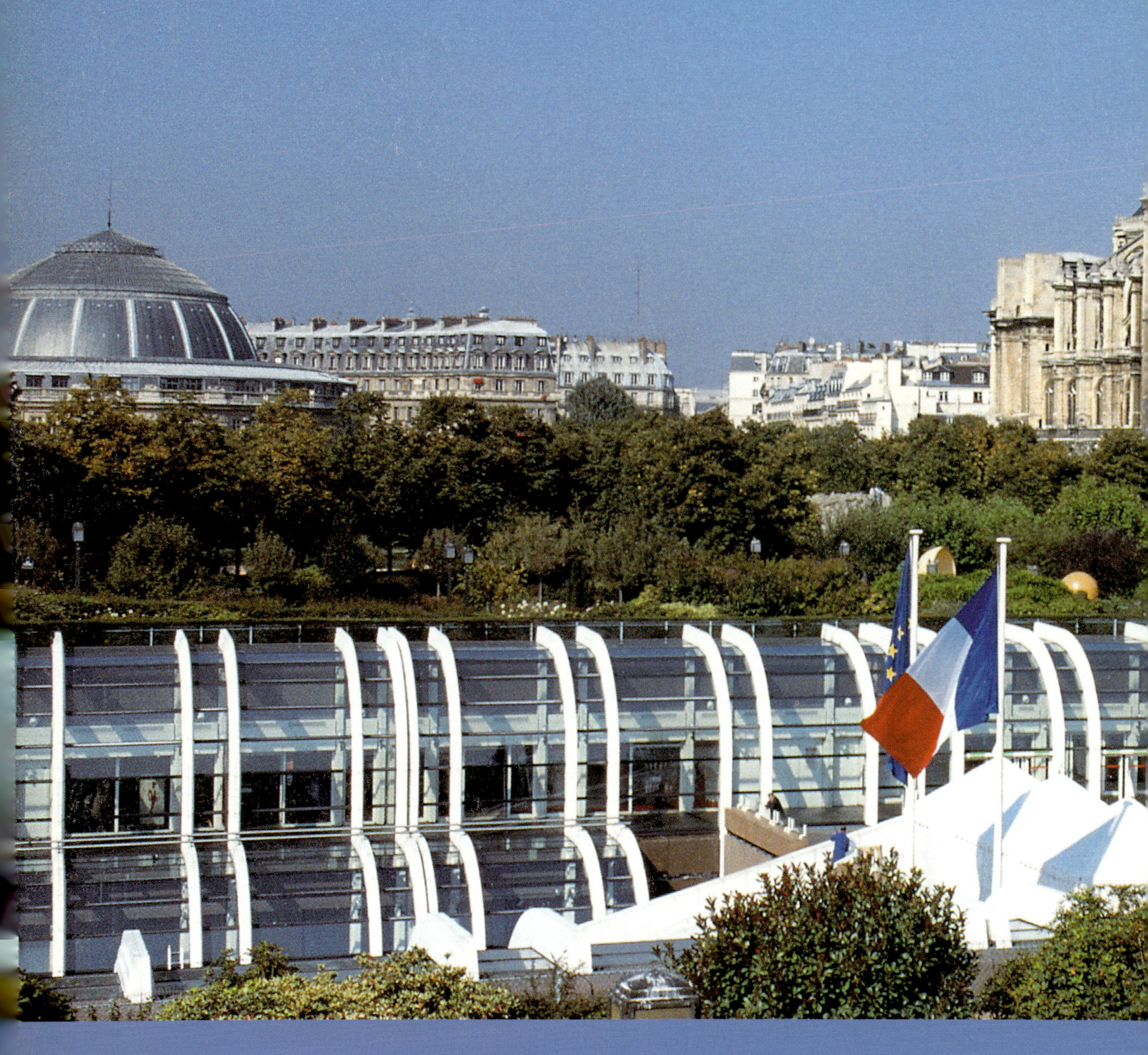

City life

1st and 4th arrondissements

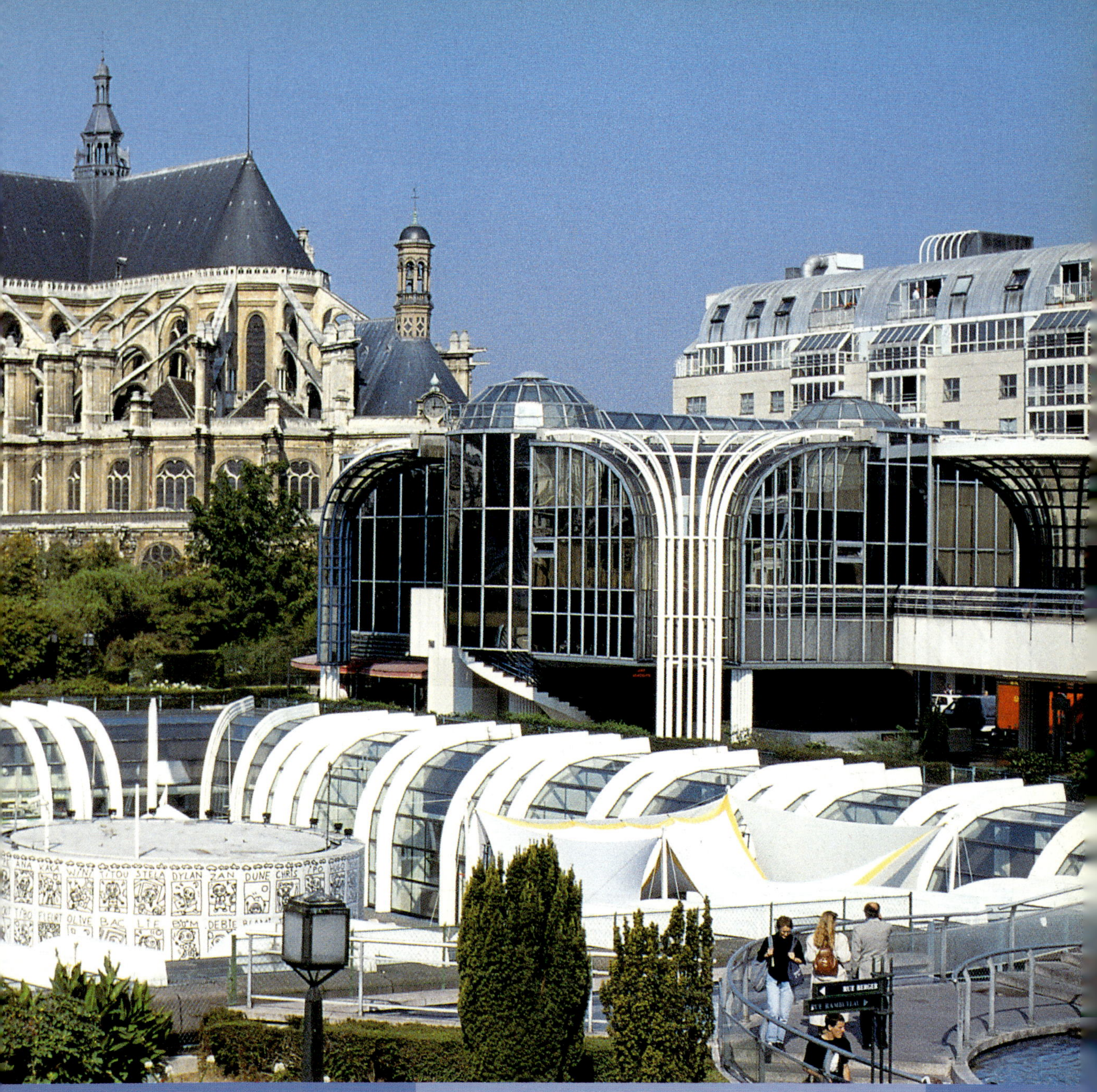

Châtelet – Les Halles

Hôtel de Ville
Tour Saint-Jacques
Place du Châtelet
Forum des Halles
Georges Pompidou Centre

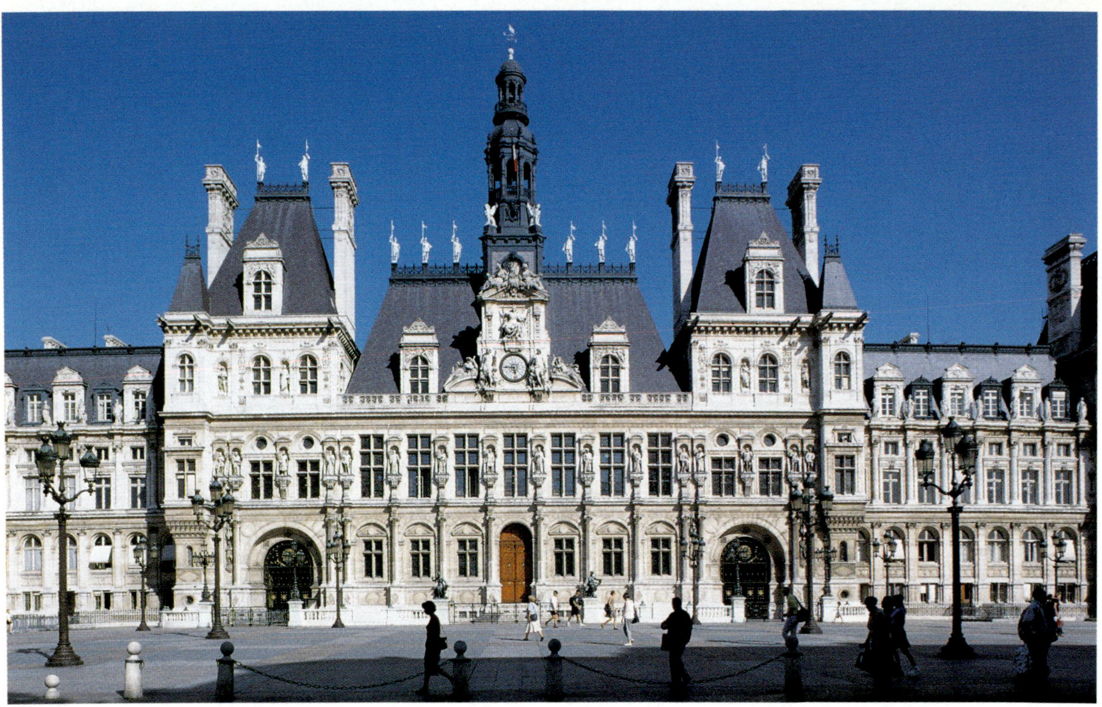

Hôtel de Ville

In 1357, Étienne Marcel, Provost of the merchants of Paris - the representative of the city's middle class population - bought the "Maison aux Piliers" on the Place de Grève in Paris. This became the venue for the meetings of local town councillors. The southern part of the first Hôtel de Ville (Town Hall) was rebuilt on the orders of Francis I by an architect from Verona, known as "Boccador", between 1533 and 1551. The northern part was completed during the reigns of Henry IV and Louis XIII from 1660 to 1628. It was extended and improved under Louis-Philippe and became the seat of the Revolutionary government during the Commune before being burnt to the ground by the rebels on 24 May 1871. It was then rebuilt from 1874 to 1882 following the plans and in the style of the original Renaissance construction - a main building flanked by two wings at the back, with two corner pavilions on each side. Its sumptuous interior decoration is a vivid reminder of the pomp and splendour of the 3rd Republic. On its four façades are alcoves housing 108 statues of important figures from the capital, and above the coping are another 30 statues representing allegories of 30 provincial towns. On the pediment of the clock are other allegories, one of which represents the City of Paris itself.

Tour Saint-Jacques

This is all that remains of the Saint-Jacques-de-la-Boucherie church, one of the most important churches in Paris in the Middle Ages and a stopover on the Saint-Jacques-de-Compostelle pilgrimage route. The tower is built in the purest flamboyant Gothic style and on the top, 52 m from the ground, is a small steeple at the north-west corner which supports a large statue of Saint-Jacques le Majeur. At the other corners are symbols of the Evangelists. From top to bottom are alcoves surmounted by spires and pinnacles which alternate with narrow windows containing other statues.

It was at the top of this tower that Pascal repeated the barometric experiments he had originally carried out at the summit of the Puy de Dome in 1648, which explains why his effigy can be seen under the arch on the ground level. In the Square Saint-Jacques is a stele erected in 1959 to commemorate the poet Gérard de Nerval, who was hung nearby.

Since 1982, there has been a vast pedestrian esplanade in front of the Hôtel de Ville (top). Located on the pilgrim route of Saint-Jacques-de-Compostelle, the tower is dedicated to the apostle Jacques le Majeur (right).

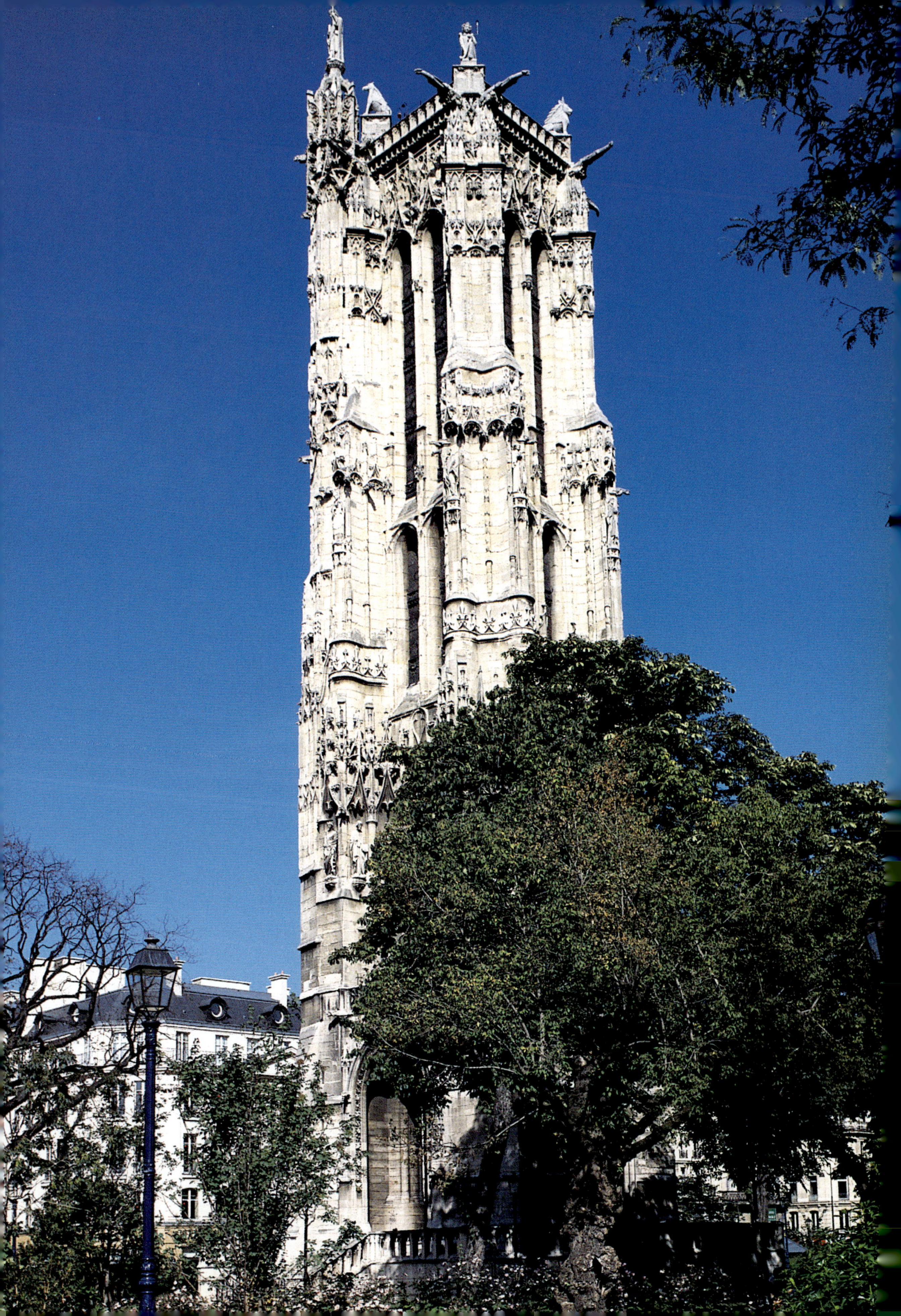

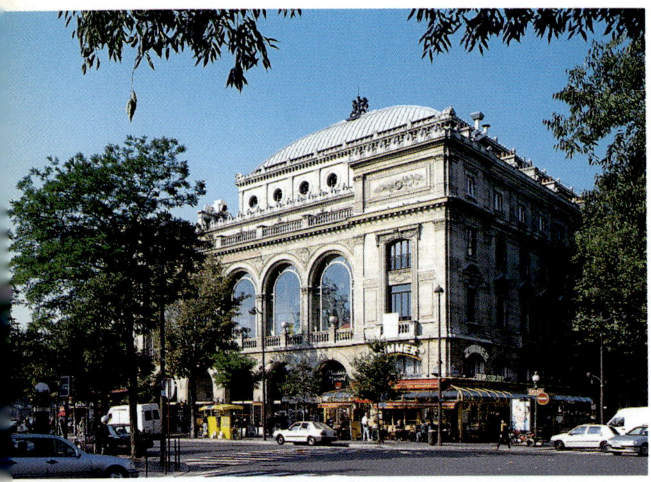

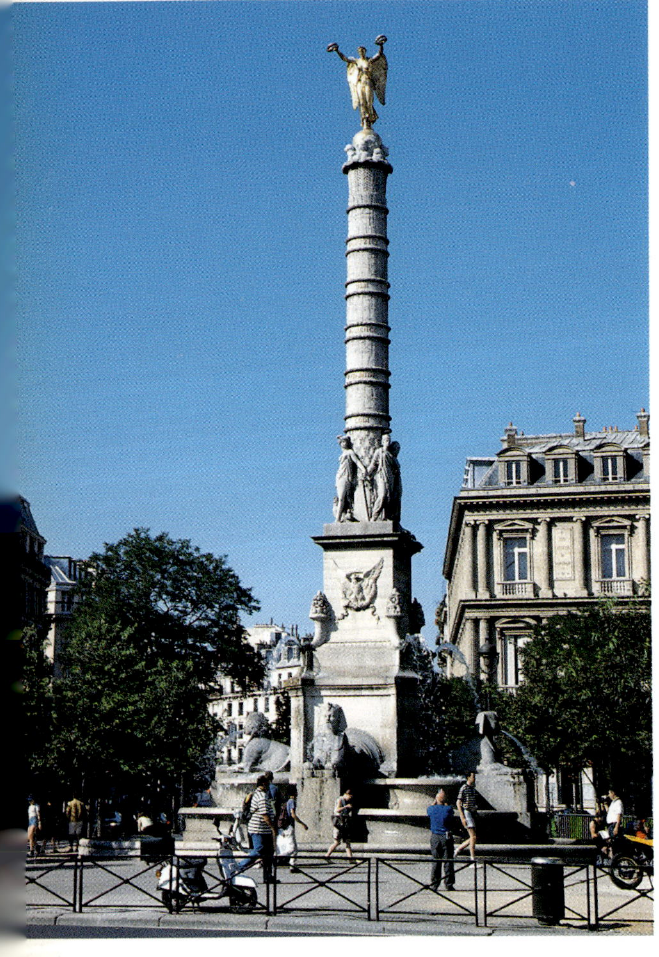

Place du Châtelet

Situated in the heart of Paris, the Place du Châtelet is one of the most lively areas of the city. Until its demolition from 1802 to 1810, it was occupied by the Grand Châtelet, a fortress built by Louis VI in 1130 to guard the entry to the Ile de la Cité which was later transformed into a prison at the end of the 12th century. Today, the site is occupied by two theatres constructed by Davioud in 1862: the Théâtre Musical de Paris, formerly the Théâtre de Châtelet, which was once the venue for operas but now hosts concerts and contemporary dance shows and the Théâtre de la Ville, where the famous actress Sarah Bernhardt used to perform. It was here that she played to great acclaim in *L'Aiglon* by Edmond Rostand in 1900. In the middle of the square is the Fontaine de la Victoire or Fontaine du Palmier, the work of the sculptor Bralle which he created in 1806. In 1856, the piece was remounted on a pedestal flanked by four sphinxes and is a souvenir of the Egyptian craze which took hold of Paris after Bonaparte's expedition.

Forum des Halles

As far back as the Middle Ages, this was the site of a large covered public market built in stone. Over the centuries, this district has remained the city's busy central market, frequented by many colourful characters. Napoleon III decided to redevelop the area and between 1854 and 1912, ten glass and steel pavilions were built on the plans of the architect Baltardin, to house the City of Paris' wholesale market, the "Ventre de Paris", celebrated by Emile Zola in his novel of the same name. From 1930 it was felt necessary to transfer the market outside the city walls, as Les Halles was not linked by any road or rail station. It was not until 1962 that the Rungis site was finally adopted. Baltard's pavilions were dismantled and all but two destroyed. These were rebuilt, one at Nogent-sur-Marne and the other in Japan. This left an enormous hole 25 m deep and cover-

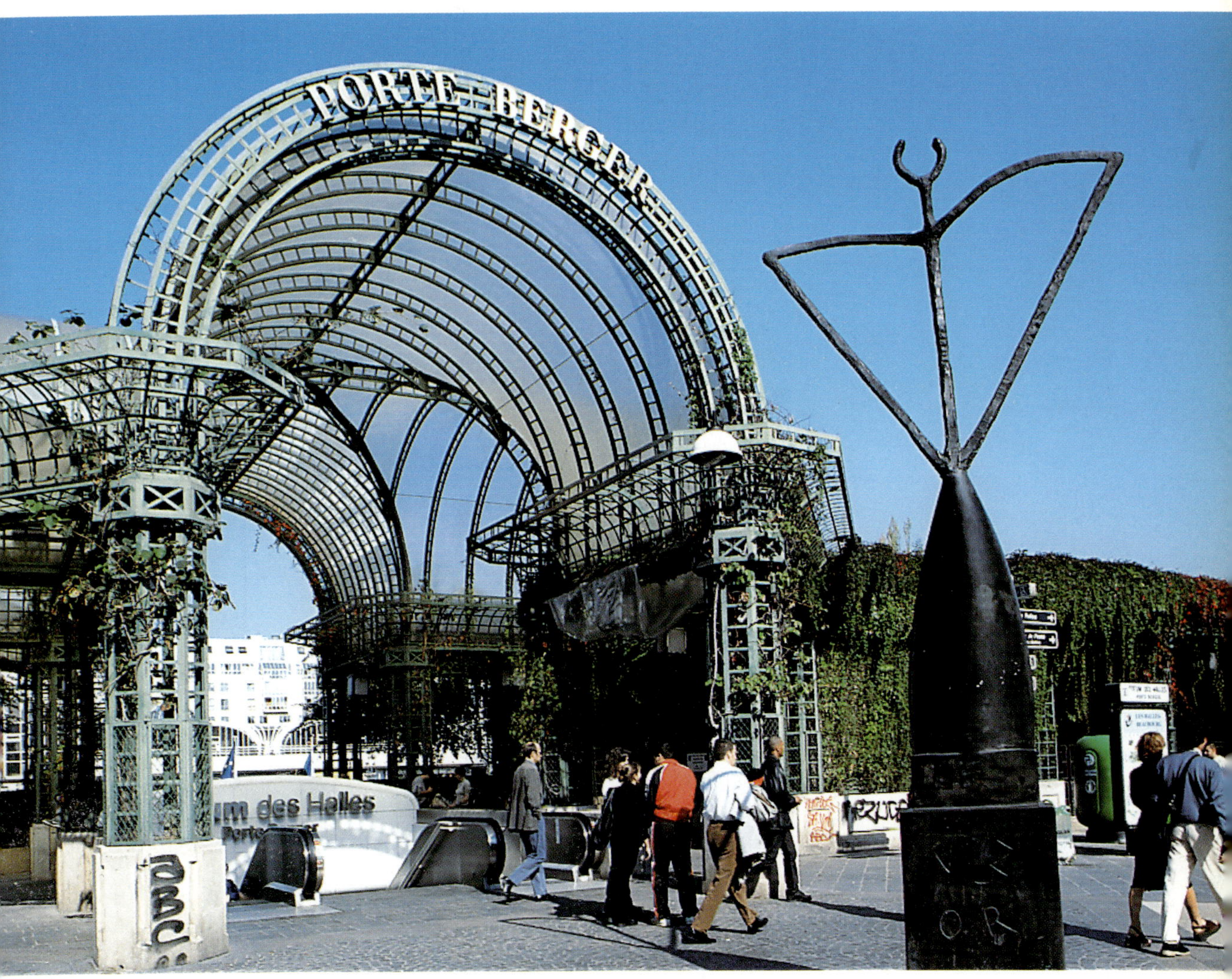

Left: the celebrated actress Sarah Bernhardt bought the Théâtre de la Ville in 1899. Her lodge can still be found here (top). The Fontaine du Châtelet stands on the site of the Parloir aux Bourgeois, the first municipal organisation in Paris (bottom).
The Porte Berger leads to the Forum des Halles (above).

ing 10 hectares which needed to be developed. In 1977, the R.E.R. metro station of Châtelet-les-Halles was opened. The vast underground shopping complex of the Forum des Halles was completed in 1979 and has 5 levels of shopping space. The Forum is not only an enormous shopping centre but also a cultural and leisure centre, which includes the Centre for Music and Dance, a video and music lending library, a swimming pool and tropical greenhouse. Over 200,000 people visit the Forum des Halles every day.

Nearby is the Fontaine des Innocents by Jean Goujon dating from 1549, a reminder that this was once the site of a cemetery closed in 1786.

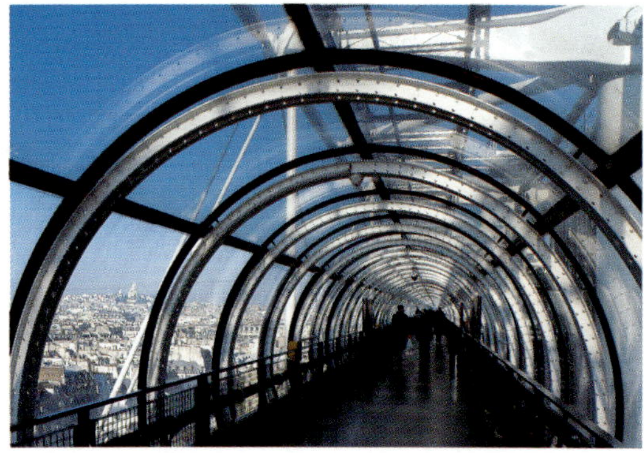

Georges-Pompidou Centre

In 1969, the president Georges Pompidou decided to create a new National Centre for Art and Culture. From among the 681 projects presented, that of Renzo Piano, Richard Rogers and their associates was adopted. Opened on 31 January 1977, the 166 m long, 60 m wide and 42 m high building was revolutionary to say the least. Familiarly known as "Beaubourg" rather than the "Centre Georges Pompidou" by Parisians, its striking modern architecture in the heart of old Paris, has led to some rather unflattering comparisons, including that of a refinery or boat covered in chimneys.

All the structural elements - its stairways, ventilation and heating shafts and support girders - have been placed on the outside of the building, in order to increase the available space inside. Its whole design as well as the materials used - metallic frames, glass and coloured plastics - aim to create maximum transparency and clarity, both from an architectural point of view and regarding the functions of its equipment. Furthermore, each colour is associated with a particular function: blue for air-conditioning, white for fresh air, green for liquids, red for circulation passages and yellow for electricity.

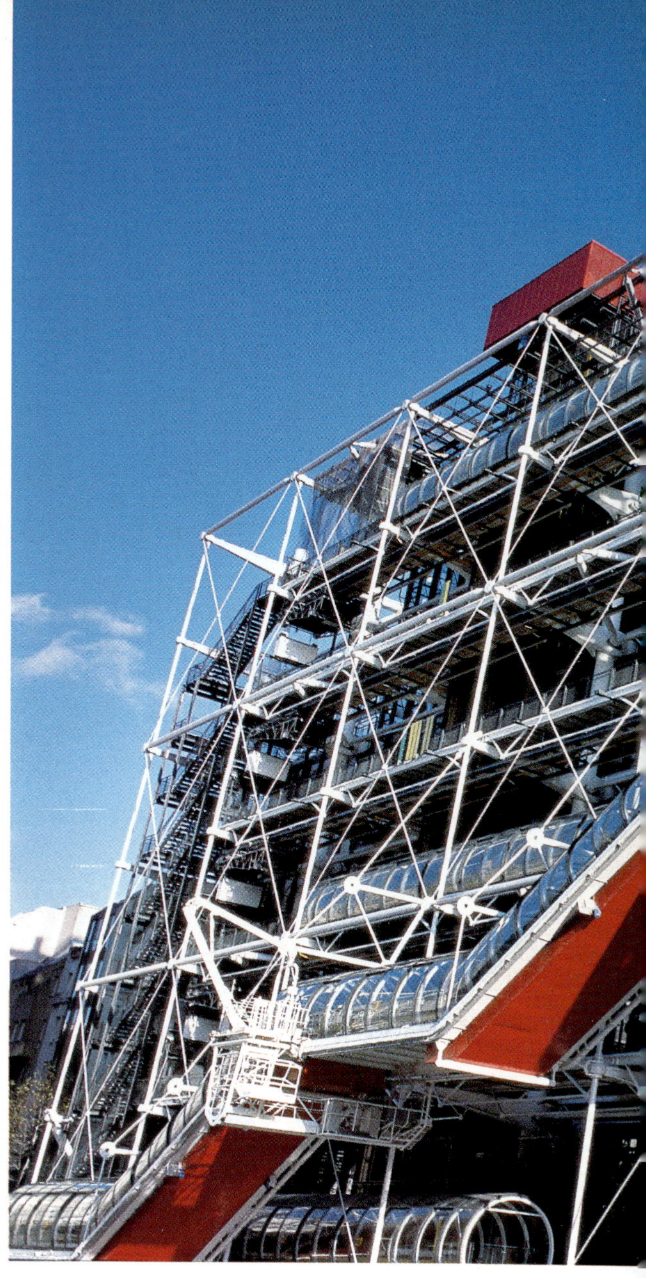

The interior has been designed to enable the Centre to fulfil its multi-purpose function as both a museum and creative centre. In the basement are rooms for conferences, shows and meetings, while on the ground floor visitors can find a central information point, a press room and areas reserved for children. The mezzanine on the first floor is occupied by exhibition galleries, the Industrial Creation room and a cinema. The public information library consists of three floors and gives visitors direct access to reading materials. They can also consult films, tapes and slides and use various com-

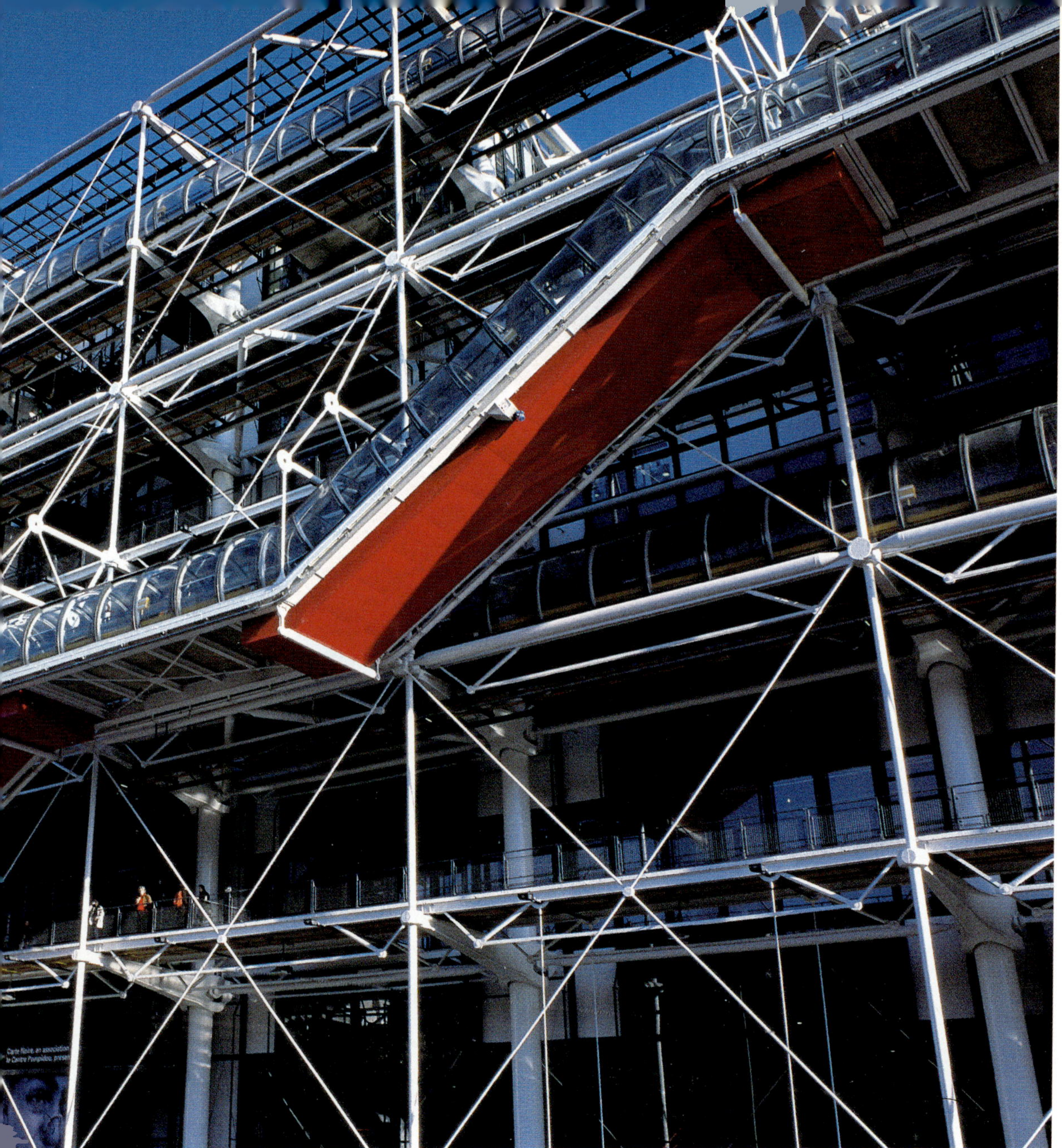

puter tools. The National Museum of Modern Art occupies the fourth and fifth floors, and the centre is also home to Ircam and the Institute of Acoustic and Musical Research and Co-ordination which are located on the Place Stravinski.

With its impressive collection of 44,000 works, the National Museum of Modern Art offers visitors a vast panorama of the history of art from the beginning of the 20th century up to the present day, and follows on from the collection exhibited in the Musée d'Orsay. The works take up two floors and include the art of Fauvism, Cubism, major movements of the First World War up to 1965 and pieces of contemporary art.

On the fifth floor are a café and restaurant, which offer a spectacular view over the city.

The whole interior of the Georges Pompidou Centre is devoted to culture and exhibitions. Visitors move around by escalators and corridors placed on the outside of the building (above). On the fifth floor, which houses a café and restaurant and temporary exhibitions, visitors can enjoy a spectacular view of Paris (left).

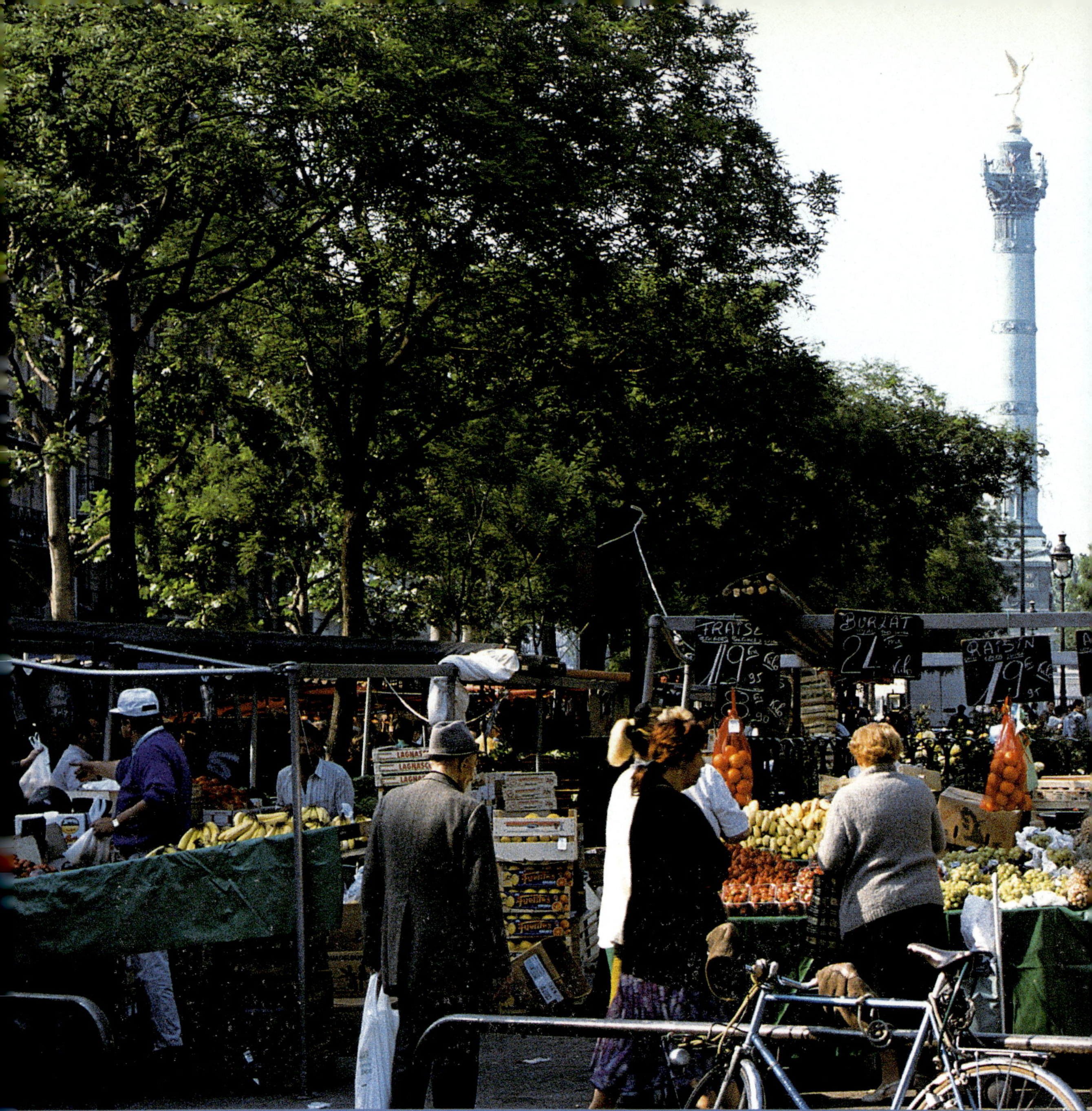

City life

3rd-4th and 11th-12th arrondissements

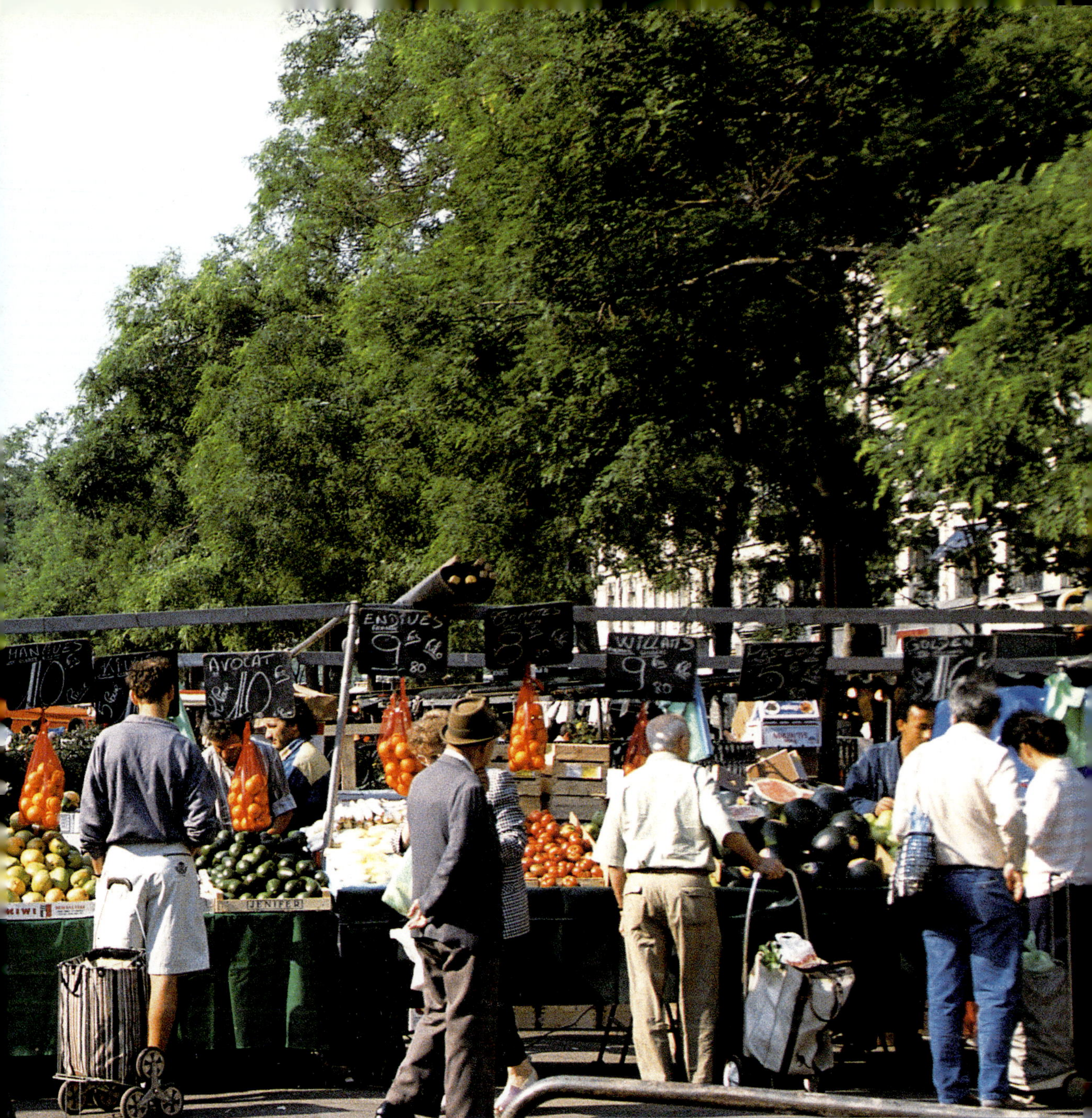

Le Marais – Bastille

**Private mansions
of the Marais**

Carnavalet Museum

Picasso Museum

Place des Vosges

Place de la Bastille

Opéra Bastille

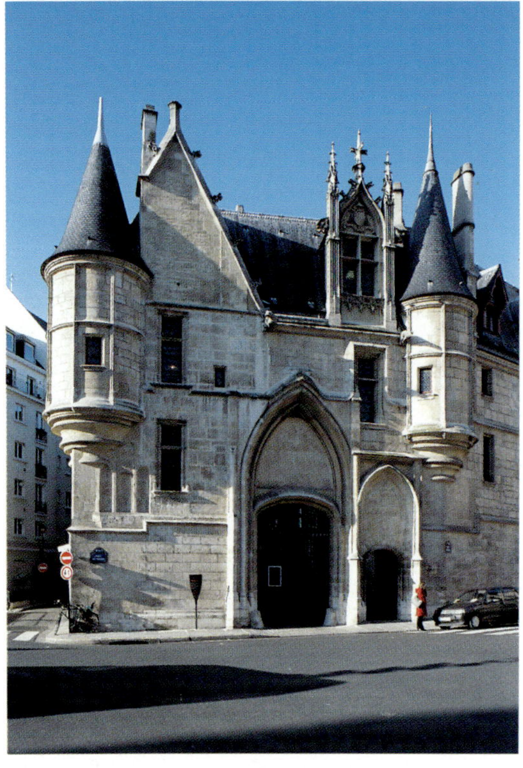

Mansions (Hôtels)
of the Marais

Some beautiful historical mansions can still be admired today in the winding streets of the Marais district. The Hôtel of the Archbishops of Sens at No.1, Rue du Figuier, today houses the Forney library of decorative arts. Although almost entirely rebuilt in 1940, it remains one of the Marais' oldest mansions. Built in the 15th century, it was once occupied by Queen Marguerite de Navarre. The Hôtel d'Aumont at No.7, Rue de Jouy, was built in the 17th century following the plans of Le Vau and today houses the head office of the civil law courts. At No.68, Rue François-Miron is the 17th century Hôtel de Beauvais, where Mozart stayed during a trip to Paris in 1763. Buildings of note in the Rue des Francs-Bourgeois include the Hôtel de Sandreville at No.26, Hôtel d'Albret at No.29 bis, and Hôtel d'Almeras at No.30. The

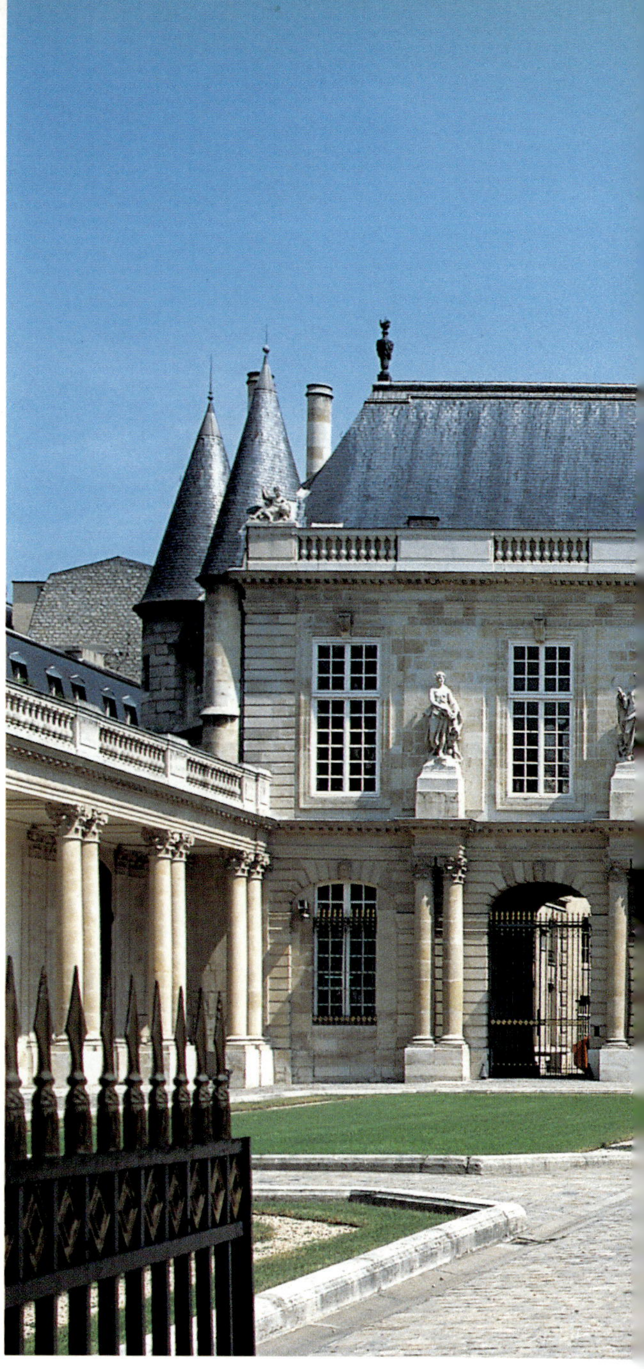

Hôtel de Marle at No.11, Rue Payenne, is currently occupied by the Swedish Cultural Centre. At No.10, the Hôtel de Vigny now houses the National Centre for Heritage Preservation. The Hôtel de Lamoignon at No.24, Rue Pavée was built in 1611-1612 for Diane de France, the legitimate daughter of King Henry II. Today it is occupied by the Historical Library of the City of Paris where visitors can admire the French-style painted ceilings of its reading room.

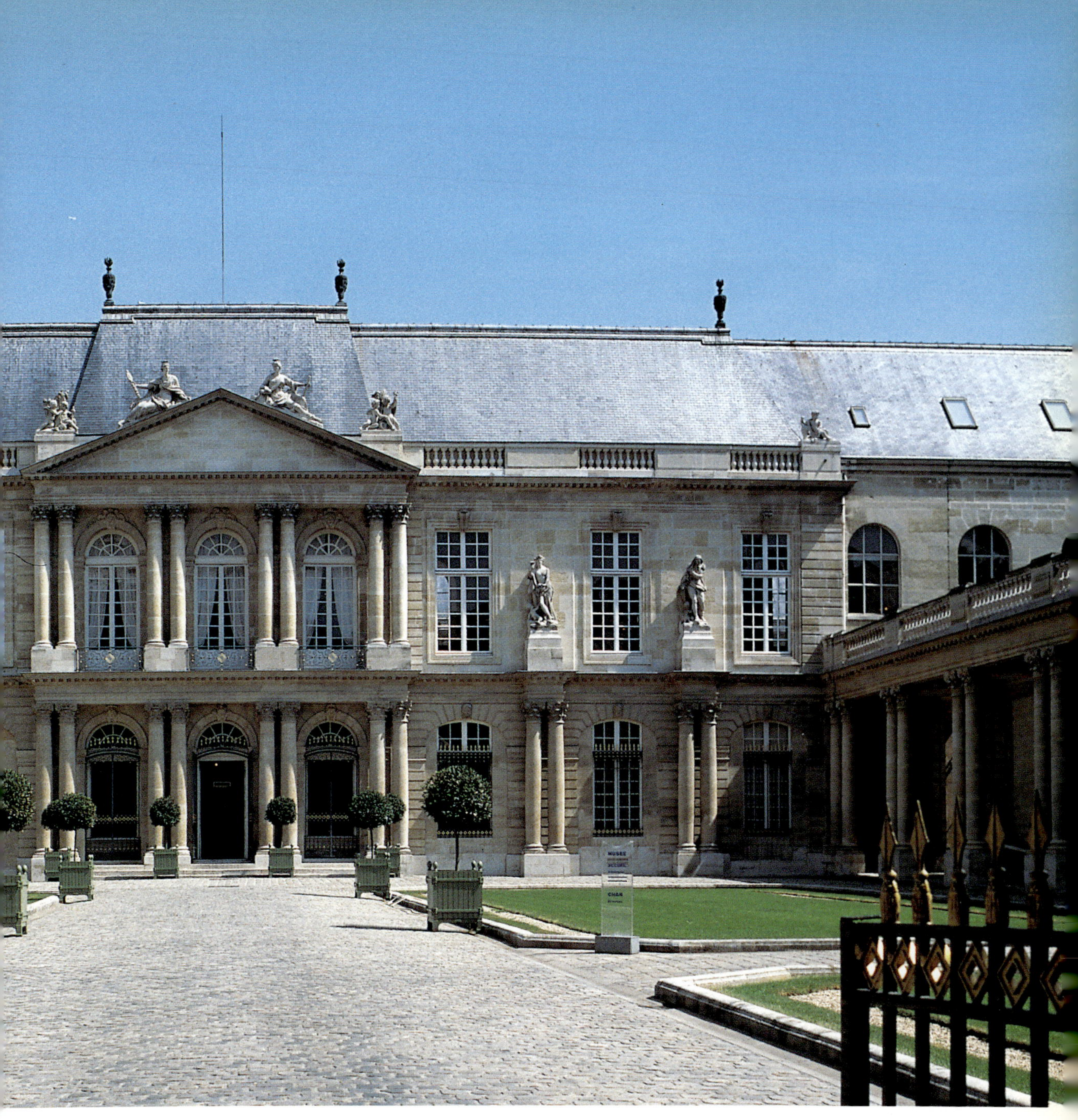

The Saint-Paul-Saint-Louis church, built from 1627-1641 and based on the design of the Gesù in Rome, is one of the oldest religious buildings in the Jesuit style in Paris. The music of Marc-Antoine Charpentier and severe sermons of Father Bourdaloue - who is buried in its crypt - once echoed under its breathtaking vaults. Inside is a painting by Delacroix, *Le Christ au Jardin des Oliviers* and the *Vierge des douleurs* by Germain Pilon.

The Hôtel de Sens, the former residence of Queen Margot, has been considerably restored (left).
The exceptionally large courtyard of the Hôtel de Soubise gives access to the Museum of the History of France located on the first floor. The façade of the Hôtel, which was acquired by François de Rohan, prince de Soubise in 1700, underwent alterations in the 18th century (above).

Carnavalet Museum

Built between 1548 and 1560 for Jacques des Ligneris, the first president of the Paris Parliament, the Hôtel Carnavalet gets its name from a deformation of the family name of Françoise de Kerneveroy, Lady of Honour to Queen Margot, who acquired the mansion in 1578. Around 1660, the mansion was modernised and extended by François Mansart at the request of the then owner, the financier Claude Boislève. But its most famous resident is without doubt the Marquise de Sévigné, who called it "ma Carnavalette" (my little Carnavalet) and who lived here from 1677 to 1694. Of the original mansion there remains the Renaissance portal, which is perfectly integrated into the façade created by Mansart and the main building with its mullion windows and bas reliefs by Jean Goujon representing the Four Seasons. In the main courtyard is a bronze statue of Louis XIV by Coysevox which miraculously escaped destruction during the Revolution.

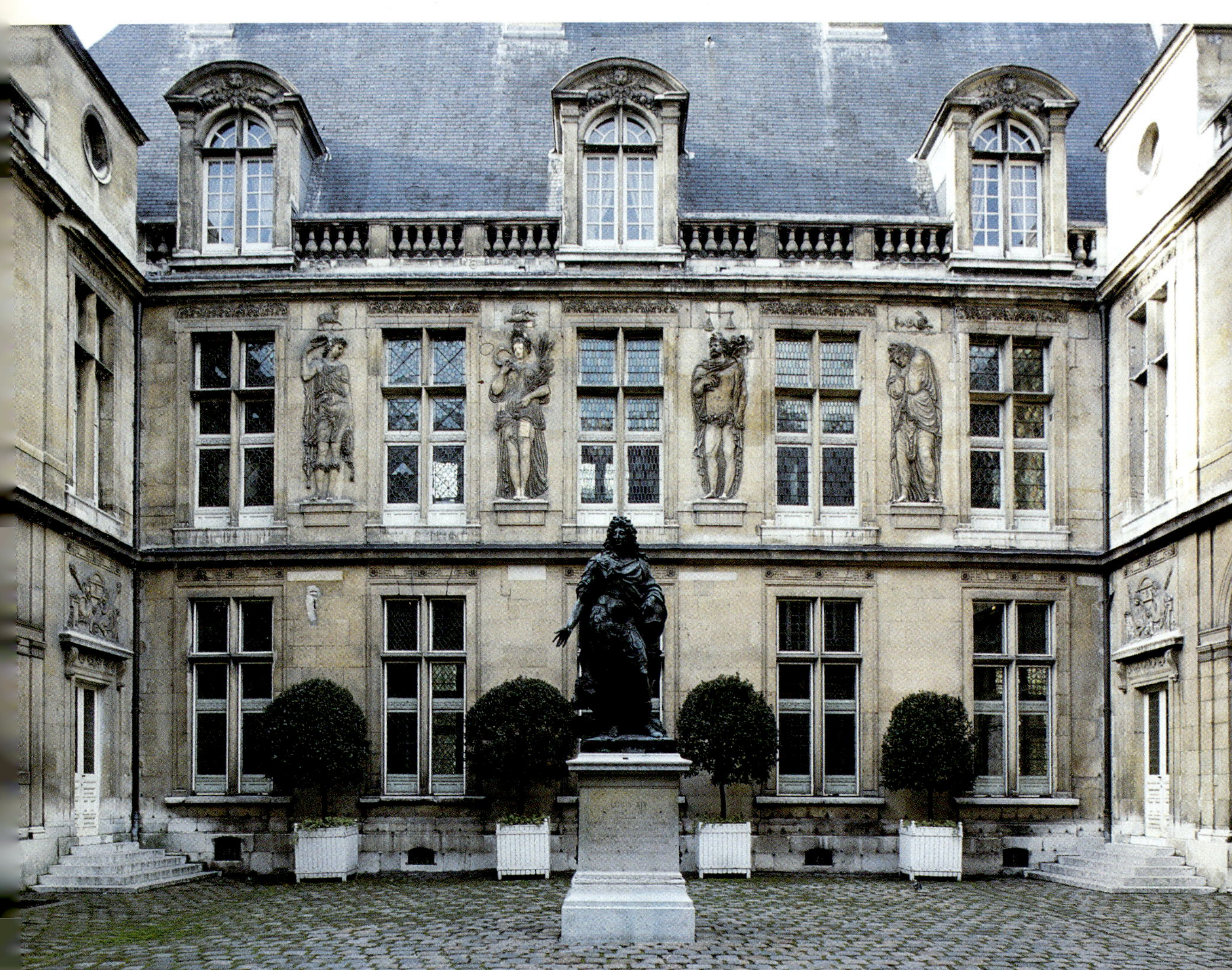

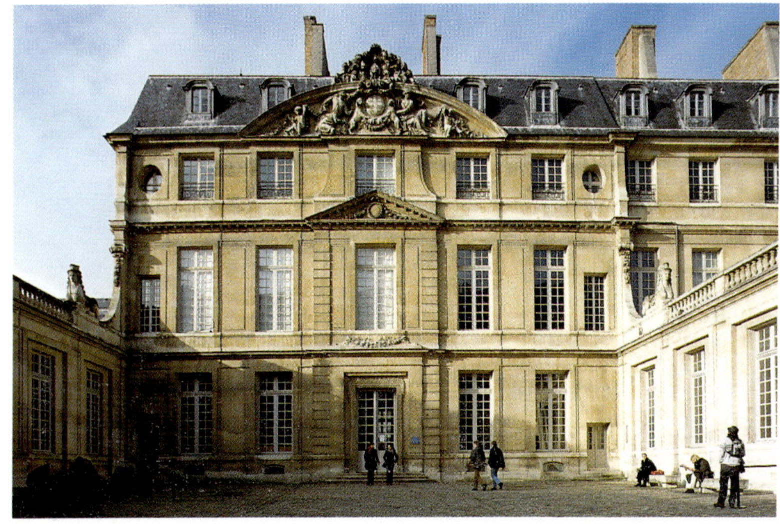

In the main courtyard of the Carnavalet Museum is a statue of Louis XIV by Coysevox (left). The semicircular courtyard of the Hôtel Salé was considered a daring architectural feature for its time (right).

Since 1880, the Hôtel Carnavalet has been linked to the Hôtel Le Peletier-de-Saint-Fargeau and houses the Historical Museum of the City of Paris. The Museum offers visitors a wide panorama of the capital's illustrious history, from the founding of the city to the present day, through a collection of some 500,000 pieces. These include various objects from archaeological excavations and collections, works of art and decorative pieces (panelling, woodwork, furniture, tapestries and decorated ceilings) taken from public or private buildings which have now disappeared. Through its many paintings, objects and documents, visitors can learn about the great figures and events that marked Paris of the 17th and 18th centuries and Paris under the reign of Louis XV, and admire the sumptuous interiors of the Louis XVI period and pieces designed by Nicolas Ledoux. Several rooms are dedicated to the French Revolution and display portraits of Danton and Marat as well as a model of the Bastille carved from one of the original stones from the famous prison. Some of its most celebrated works include *Portrait de Madame de Grignan* by Mignard, *La Partie de billard* by Chardin, *Incendie de l'Opéra au Palais-Royal* by Hubert Robert (1781) and *Portrait de Madame Récamier* by François Gérard (1805).

Picasso Museum

The Hôtel Salé, which houses the Picasso Museum, was built between 1656 and 1660 by Jean Boullier de Bourges for Pierre Aubert de Fontenay. The latter was an administrator of the "gabelle", a tax on salt under the Ancien Régime. The mansion was given the name "Salé" (Salty) in humorous reference to the origins of the owner's fortune. Over the centuries, the mansion passed through the hands of the Maréchal de Villeroy, the Ambassador of the Republic of Venice and the Marquis du Juigné. After the Revolution, it housed the Central School of Arts and Manufacture followed by the School of Artistic Professions of the City of Paris and was later restored in order to house the Picasso collection. The pediment on its beautiful façade is decorated with dogs' heads, the coat of arms of the Aubert House. Inside is a magnificent sculpted staircase leading to various exhibition rooms which are organised in chronological order and house over 250 paintings, *papier collé* and reliefs, some 3,000 drawings and prints, illustrations and manuscripts, 88 ceramics and Picasso's entire engravings collection. Also on display are works by some of Picasso's favourite artists and primitive art objects from his private collection.

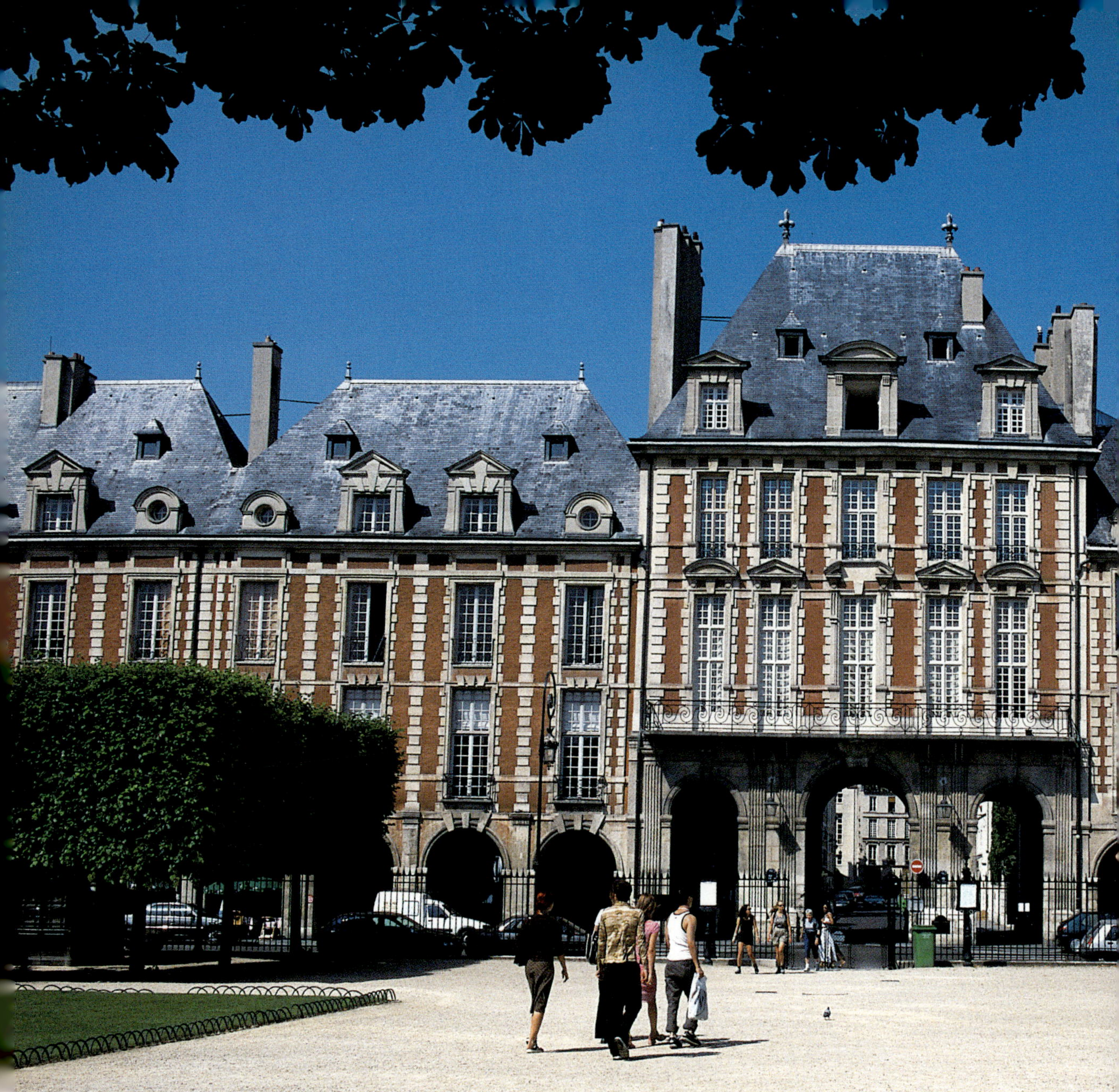

Place des Vosges

In 1605, Henry IV decided to sell off the land once occupied by the Palais de Tournelles - where Henry II was killed in 1559 during a tournament - which at the time was being used as a horse market. According to the letters patent of the King, the buildings constructed around the square had to be "symmetrical". This original architectural unity - a ground floor composed of arches, with two upper floors in brick surmounted by a sloping roof illuminated by dormer windows - is what gives the Place des Vosges its unrivalled beauty and charm. On the south side, the King's Pavilion faces that of the Queen. At No.6, the apartments of Victor Hugo have now been transformed into a museum dedicated to the celebrated novelist. In the middle of the square is a statue of Louis XIII on horseback, executed in the 19th century by Cortot and Dupaty to replace the original, which was inaugurated in 1639 and later destroyed during the Revolution. Formerly the Place Royale, the square was later renamed Place des Vosges, after the Department of the Vosges when it became the first region to send in its taxes in 1800.

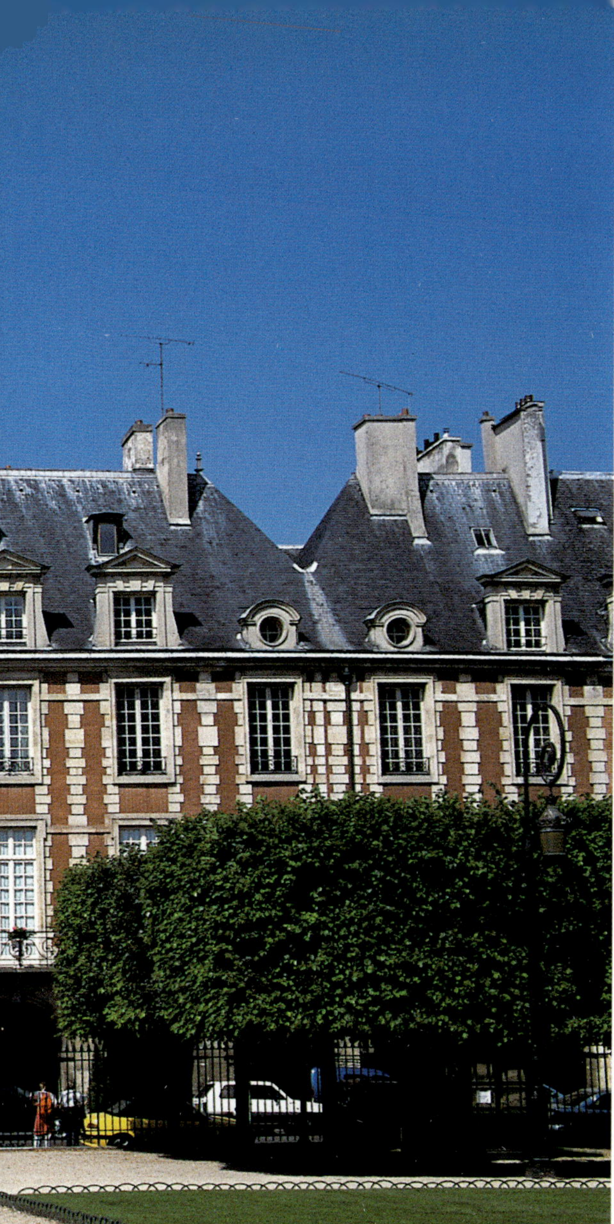

The raised King and Queen's pavilions break the monotony
of the quadrilateral Place des Vosges (above).

Place de la Bastille

The "Bastille Saint-Antoine" was constructed between
1370 and 1382 by the Provost Hugues Aubriot at the request
of King Charles, to guard one of the gates to the city. Used
as a state prison from the time of Richelieu, it quickly became
the symbol of royal despotism, since an order under the King's
private seal was all that was needed to send any undesirable
individual to prison, without trial. From the reign of Louis
XIV, the fortress never held more than fifty inmates. So, on
14 July 1789, when the crowd of rebels composed mainly of
workers and artisans from the nearby Faubourg-Saint-Antoine
district gathered before its gates, it was not to free the Bastille
prisoners but to get hold of arms. The event soon took on
a mythical dimension, as it represented a victory over absolute
Royal power. Not long after, the decision was taken to demol-
ish the stronghold, the most visible symbol of this despotism.

In 1830, it was decided to erect a monument in memory of the victims of the Three Glorious Days of the
Revolution, the 27, 28 and 29 July of the same year which
had seen the overthrow of Charles X. This is the July column which can be seen today - a bronze monument inspired
by the column of Trajan at the Roman forum standing 47
m high and weighing over 170 tons. The remains of the
victims of the 1830 and 1848 Revolutions were buried under
the column, which was completed in 1840. At the top, overlooking the gallery which visitors can reach via a staircase
of 238 steps, the golden figure of the Génie de la Liberté
created by the sculptor Dumont, takes flight into the Parisian
sky, "breaking its chains and spreading light".

The anniversary of the storming of the Bastille, the 14
July, has been a national holiday since 1880. And the square,
located between that of Nation and Republique, remains a
traditional assembly point for major political and trade union
demonstrations.

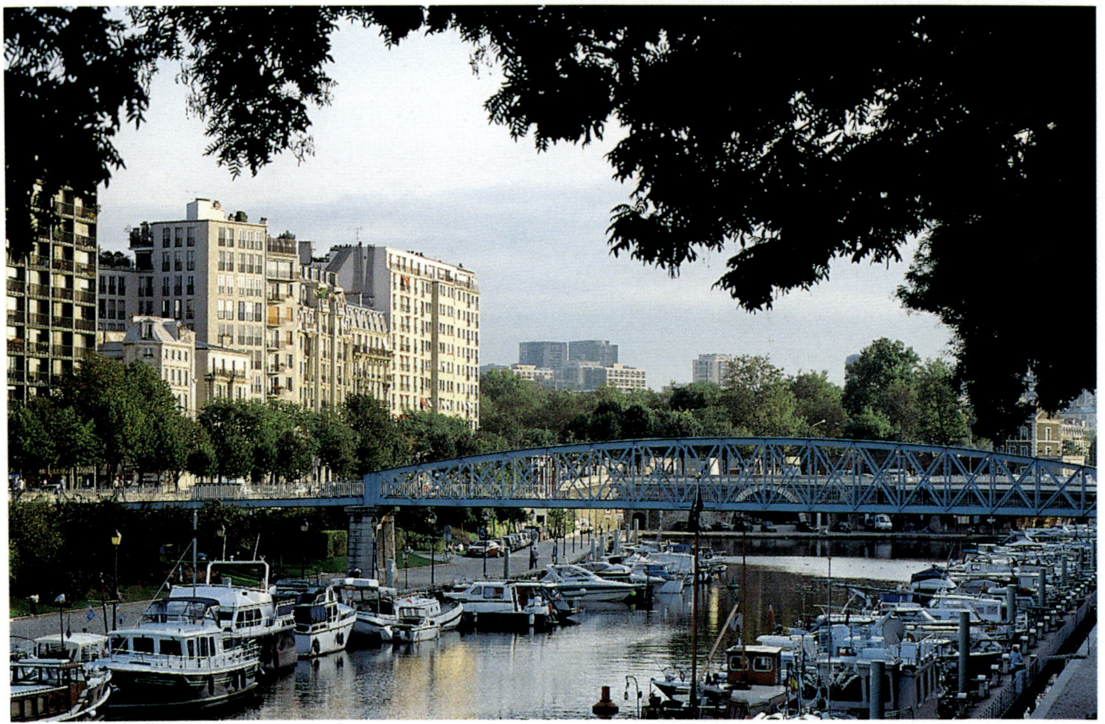

Opéra Bastille

On 14 July 1989, exactly two hundred years after the storming of the Bastille, the Opéra Bastille was opened. This new venue, dedicated to opera and erected on the site of the former Vincennes station demolished in 1985, was created to hold more spectators than the Opéra Garnier which is now devoted to ballet. The vast, austere building, with its glass façade and sombre marble portico was designed by Carlos Ott. In addition to the main hall decorated in granite and oak which can hold up to 2,700 spectators, is a multi-purpose hall, a studio with seating for 250, rehearsal rooms and an amphitheatre. Although its design was the subject of great controversy, its technical capacities are beyond reproach… even if the management of its equipment - 74 different trades work here! - sometimes causes problems.

The Bastille Opera is in fact part of an ambitious and large-scale urban plan to restructure and re-energise the East of the capital, which to date has involved the construction of the new Ministry of Finance completed in 1988, the Palais Omnisport and gardens at Bercy, the development of the Arsenal marina on part of the moat of the old fortress, the redevelopment of the Bercy warehouses and the construction of the spectacular new François-Mitterrand Library.

Situated lower down from the Place de la Bastille, the Arsenal dock has been transformed into a marina (top). **The July Column in the middle of the Place de la Bastille commemorates the 1830 and 1848 Revolutions. Despite its unconventional architecture, the Opéra-Bastille seems to blend into the various buildings that surround the square** (right).

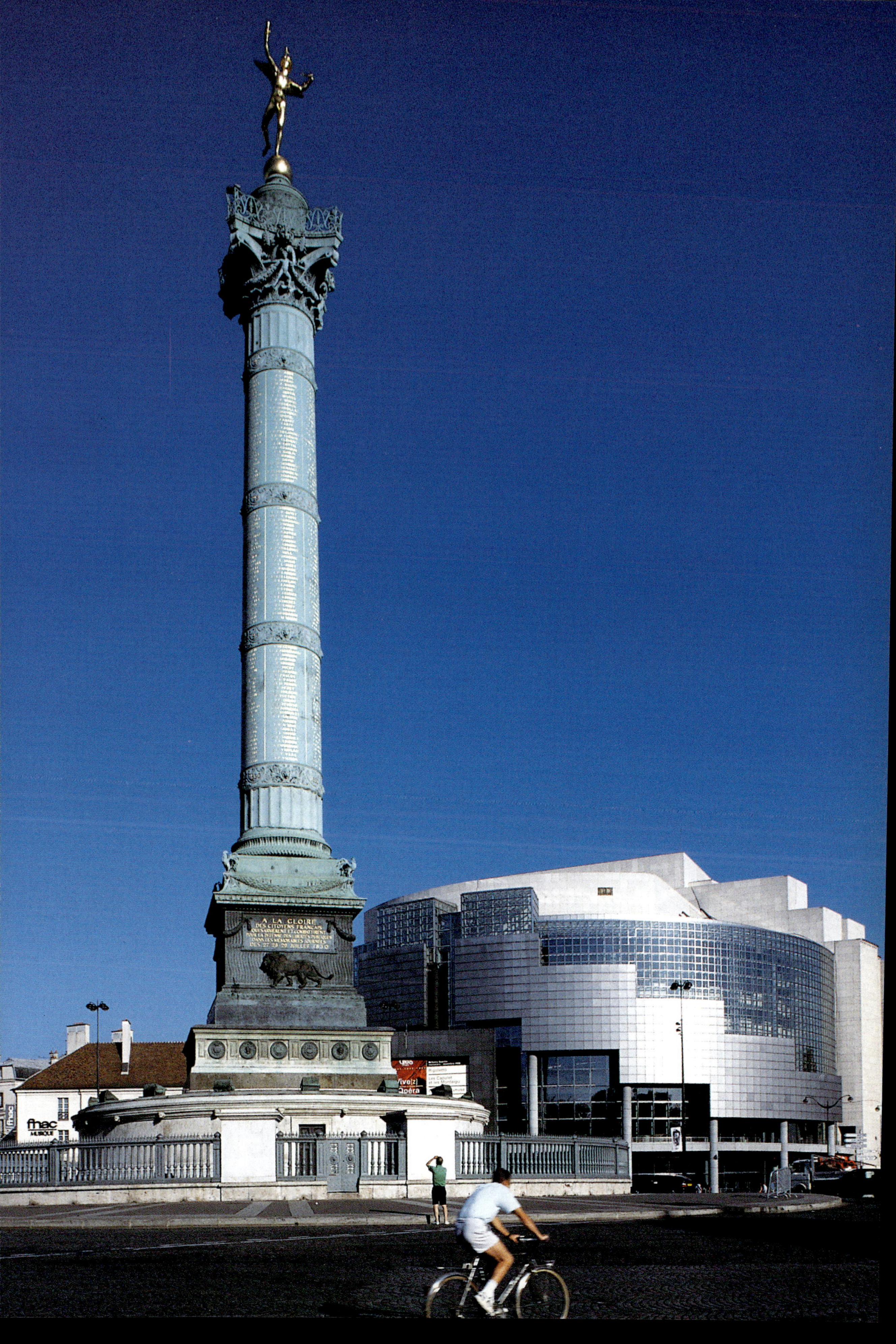

Monument

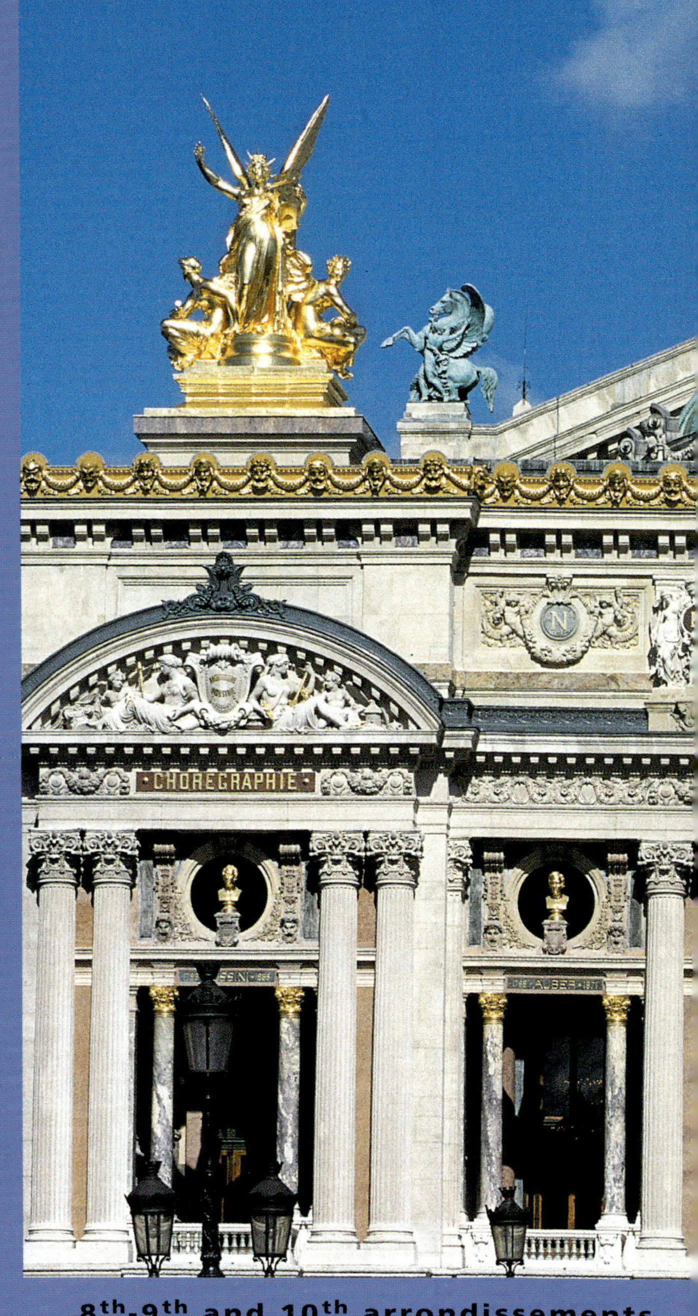

8th-9th and 10th arrondissements

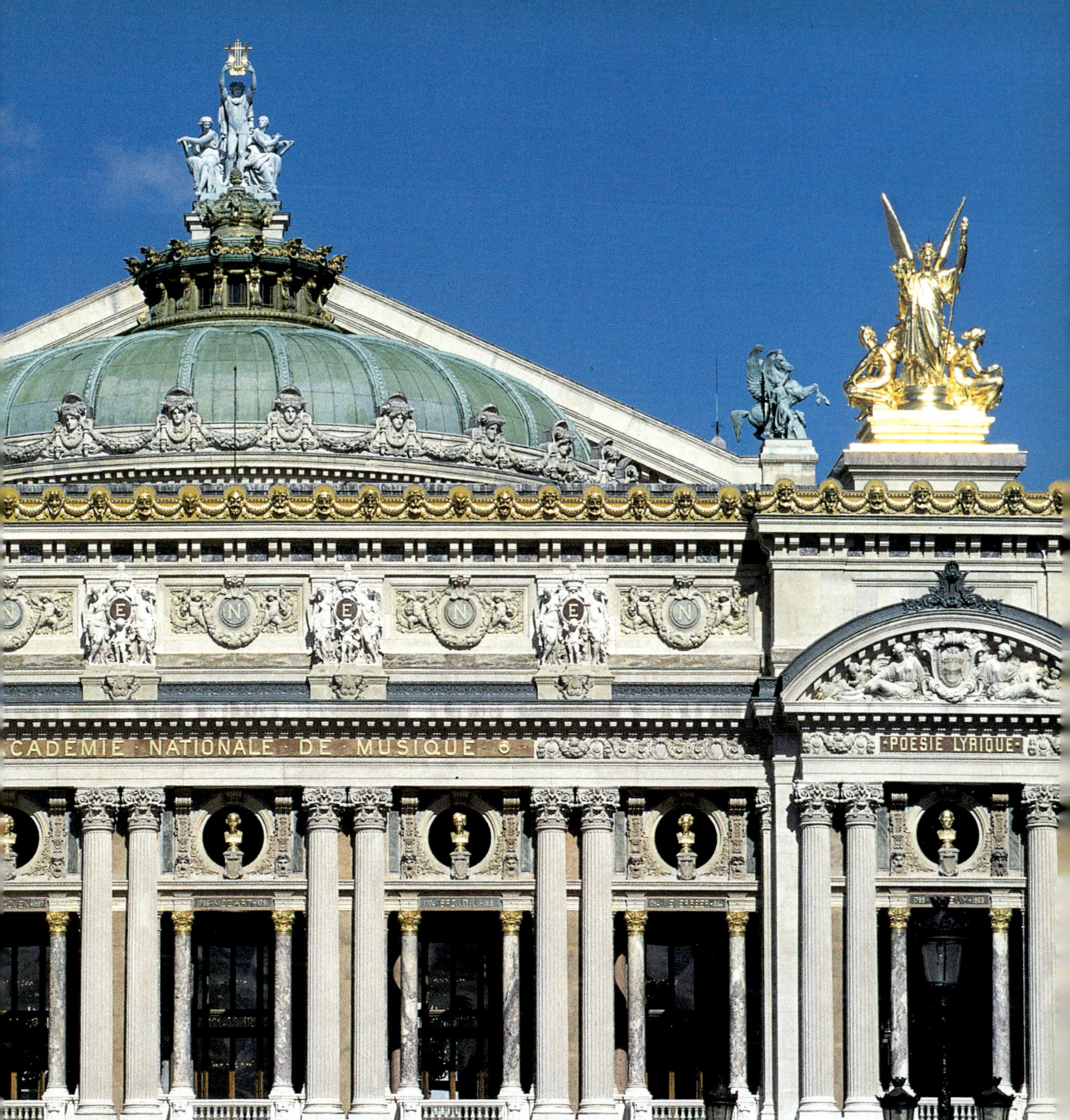

Opéra

Opéra Garnier
Place Vendôme
Madeleine Church
Grands Boulevards

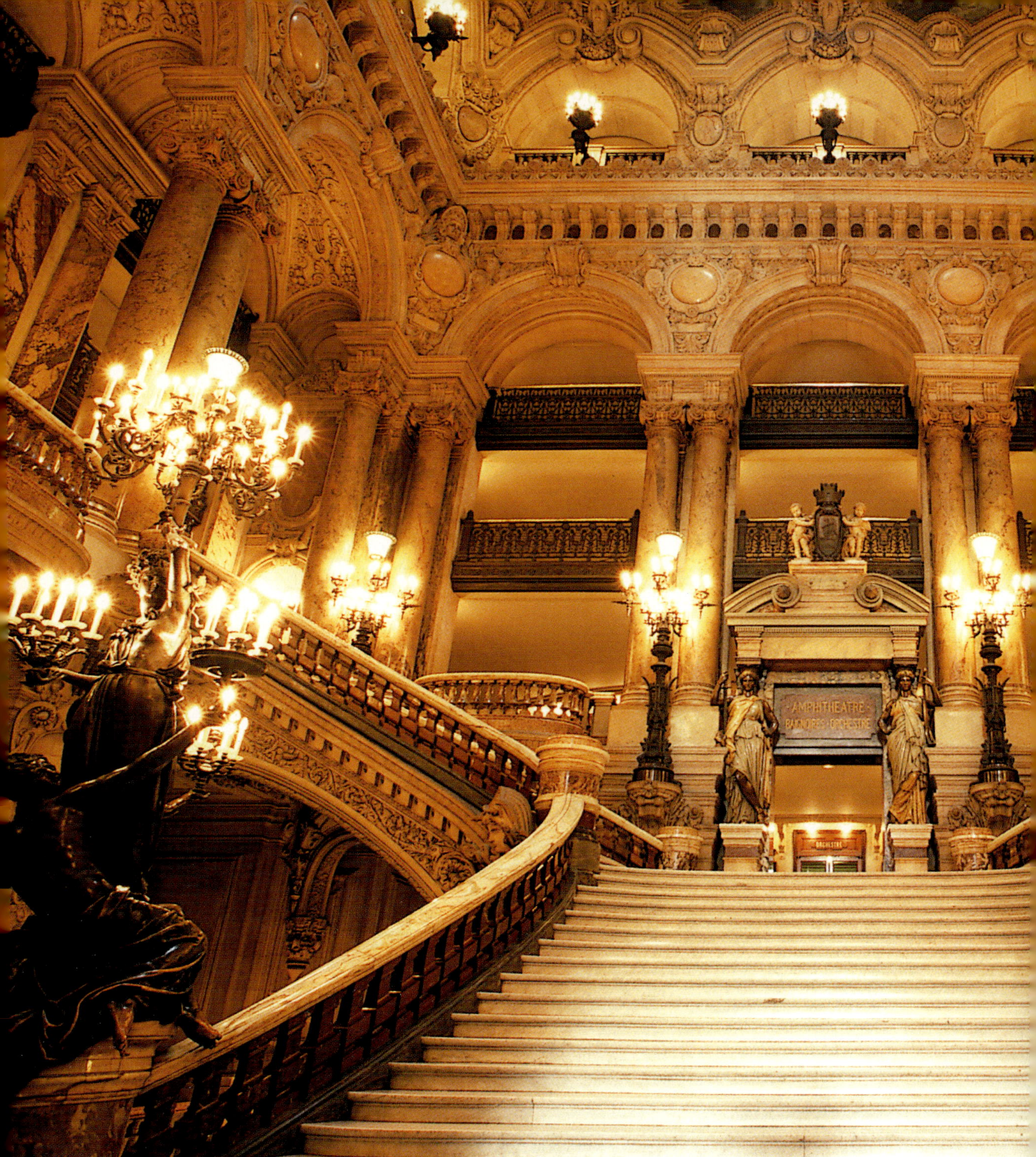

Opéra Garnier

After the assassination attempt by Orsini which nearly cost Napoleon III his life as he was leaving the Le Peltier Hall, the Emperor decided to build a new Opera in a location which was better suited for the deployment of security forces. The project was given over to Charles Garnier, who wanted to construct a "monument to art, luxury and pleasure". The location of the new opera was ideal, in the heart of the capital's bustling business and trade district. Although completed under the 3rd Republic, this "worldly

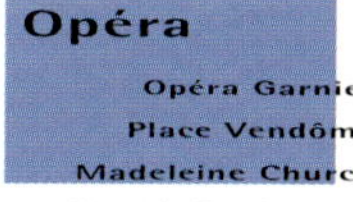

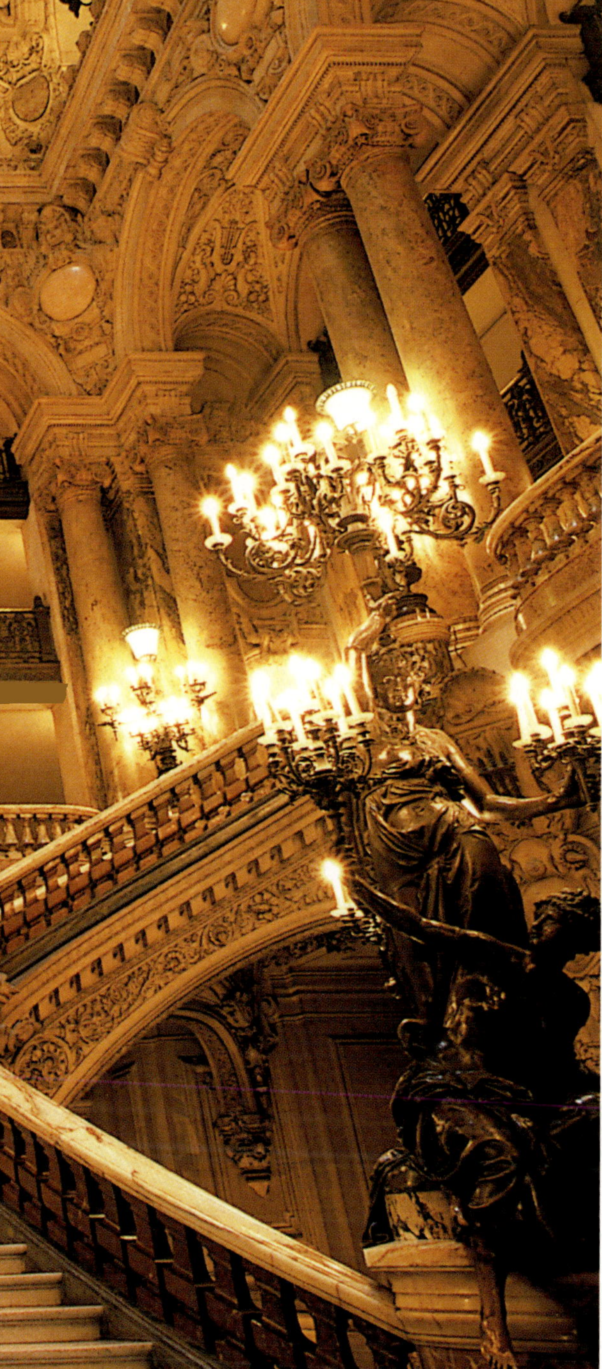

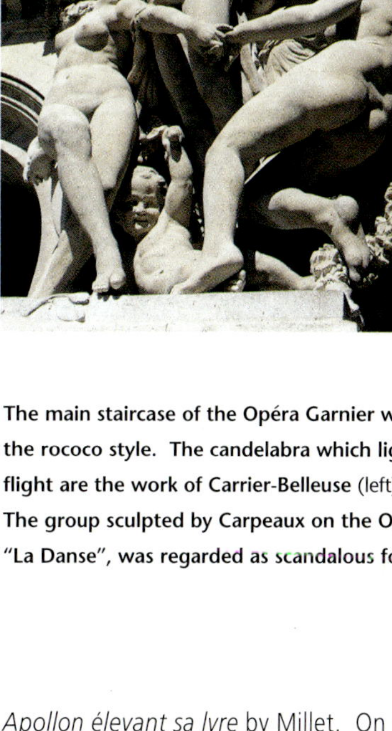

The main staircase of the Opéra Garnier was built in
the rococo style. The candelabra which light the first
flight are the work of Carrier-Belleuse (left).
The group sculpted by Carpeaux on the Opera's façade,
"La Danse", was regarded as scandalous for its time (above).

cathedral of civilisation", in the words of Théophile Gautier,
is an example of the Napoleon III style and a mixture of
Baroque and Neo-Renaissance. The seven arches on the
building's façade are surmounted by seven openings and
a loggia, which lie beneath a dome crowned with an

Apollon élevant sa lyre by Millet. On the ground floor
are several groups of statues representing Music, Poetry
and Opera, the most famous being a replica of Dance by
Carpeaux. The interior is designed to serve as a fitting
backdrop for fashionable, high society evenings, with its
grand ceremonial staircase, polychrome marble decoration, grand foyer gallery, the Moon and Sun rooms, the red
and gold room with seating for over 2,100 and its wonderful ceiling decorated by Chagall in 1964. In 1985, the
Opéra Garnier was renamed the Palais de la Danse and the
majority of operas are now held at the Opéra Bastille.

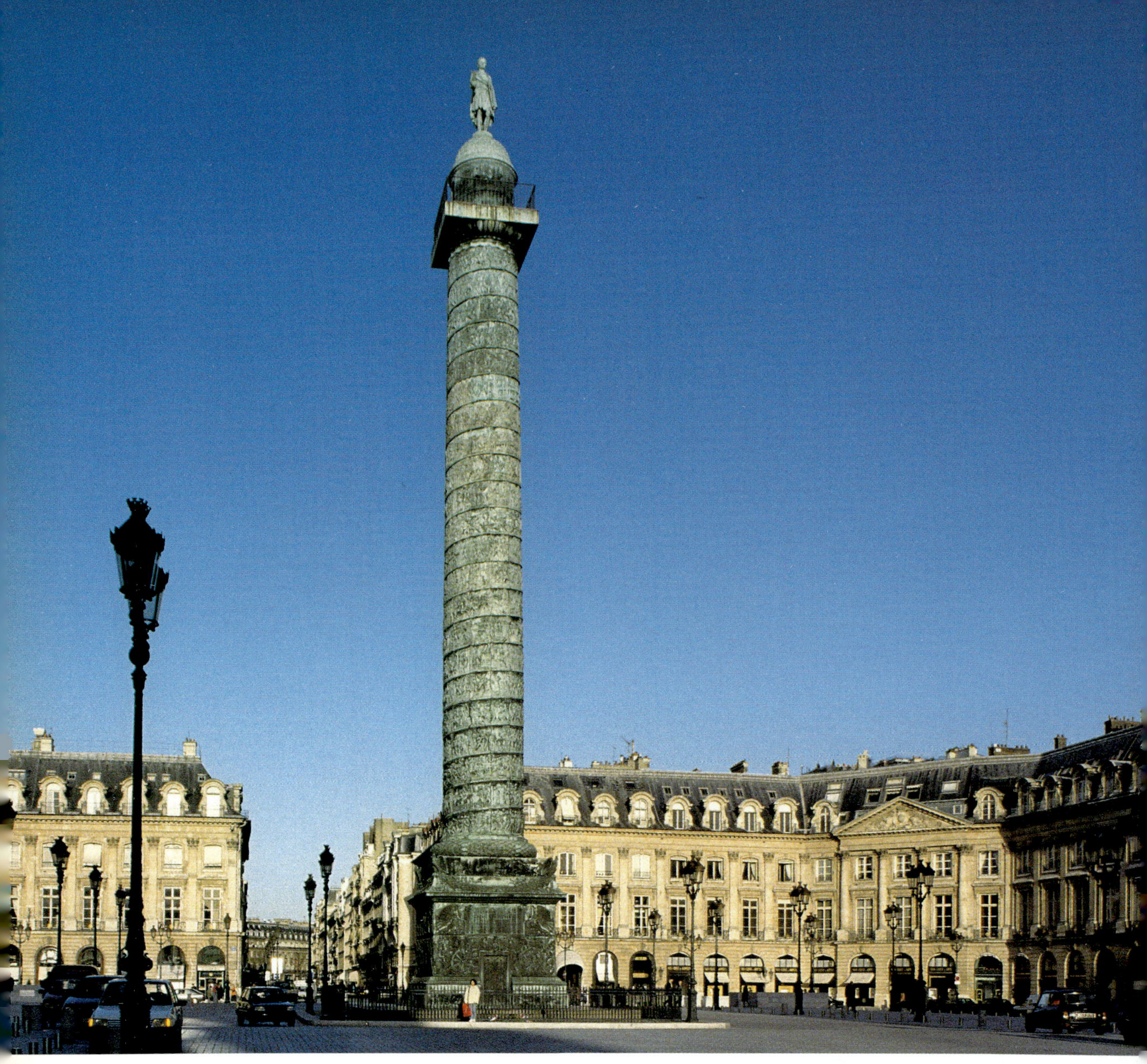

Place Vendôme and Vendôme Column

In 1686, Louis XIV, the son of Henry IV and Gabrielle d'Estrées, adopted an idea of Louvois to create a square designed to hold his own statue. The site chosen was that occupied by the Hôtel du Duc de Vendôme and it was to be named the Place des Conquêtes. Jules Hardouin Mansart was put in charge of the project. The square is octagonal in shape and on its main sides are projections supported by engaged columns. Above the blocked arches are two floors joined by Corinthian pilasters, under a large roof illuminated by dormer and bull's-eye windows. Along with the Place des Victoires, the square is one of the most beautiful examples of classical urbanism. Up to the Revolution, it was called the Place Louis-le-Grand. The equestrian statue of Louis XIV by Girardon which stood at the centre was melted down in 1792. Napoleon decided to replace it with a bronze column inspired by the Trajan column in Rome, using cannons seized from the Russians and Austrians, decorated by bas reliefs telling the story of the feats of the Great Army. Inaugurated on 15 August 1810, it was later pulled down on 16 May 1871 by the Commune rebels, incited by the painter Gustave Courbet. It was then erected again in 1873, at the artist's expense. Behind the elegant façades designed by Mansart,

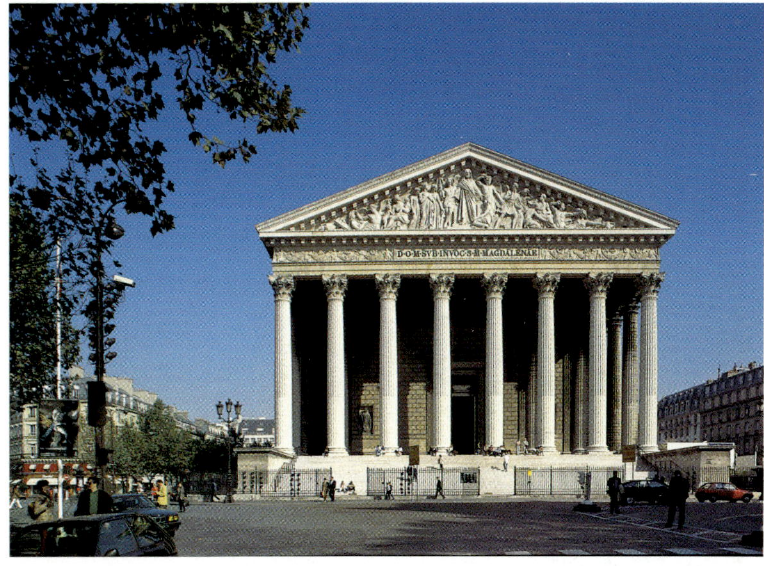

Napoleon I left his mark on the Place Vendôme which was originally designed as a tribute to the conquests of Louis XIV (left). The main pediment of the Madeleine church represents the Last Judgement (right).

the financiers of the Regency period built sumptuous mansions which can still be admired today, such as the Hôtel de Monbreton, the Hôtel Evreux currently occupied by the company Crédit Foncier, the Hôtel du Fermier Général Luillier and Hôtel de Poison de Bourvallais which house the Ministry of Justice, the Hôtel Ritz, one of the most famous hotels in Paris and the Hôtel de Nocé, the residence of the celebrated jeweller Boucheron. Today, the Place Vendôme is one of the city's major luxury business centres and home to internationally famous jewellery houses. Leading out of the square is the Rue de Paix, also famous for its exclusive jewellery boutiques.

Madeleine Church

The unusual architecture of the Madeleine church, which has no cross or bell tower and resembles more a Pagan temple, can be explained by the rather complicated story of its construction. On 13 August 1763, Louis XV laid the first stone of a new church designed by Contant d'Ivry which was to replace the chapel built in the 15th century. By 1777, only the foundations had been completed and the site was abandoned during the Revolutionary period.

In 1806, Napoleon decided to erect a temple to the glory of the Great Army on the site. By the fall of the Empire, the building was still unfinished. Louis XVIII then planned to transform it into a monument in memory of the members of the Royal family guillotined during the Revolution. The Madeleine was finally completed by Vignon under the reign of Louis-Philippe and inaugurated on 9 October, 1845.

The church is a vast edifice, surrounded by a peristyle of 52 Corinthian columns which support a sculpted frieze representing the Last Judgement. The interior has no transept or side aisles and its single nave leads to three bays each covered by a cupola and a semicircular chancel decorated with gold and marble. Among the many statues, paintings and mosaics which make up the interior decoration, there are two works of particular interest: the *Ravissement de Sainte Madeleine* by Marochetti which overlooks the main altar and the *Baptême du Christ* by François Rude, located in the vestibule. The ceiling over the chancel, composed of a semi-cupola vault, is covered in a 250 m^2 fresco entitled *Histoire et glorification du christianisme* by Ziegler. The organ, attributed to Cavaillé-Call, dates from 1846.

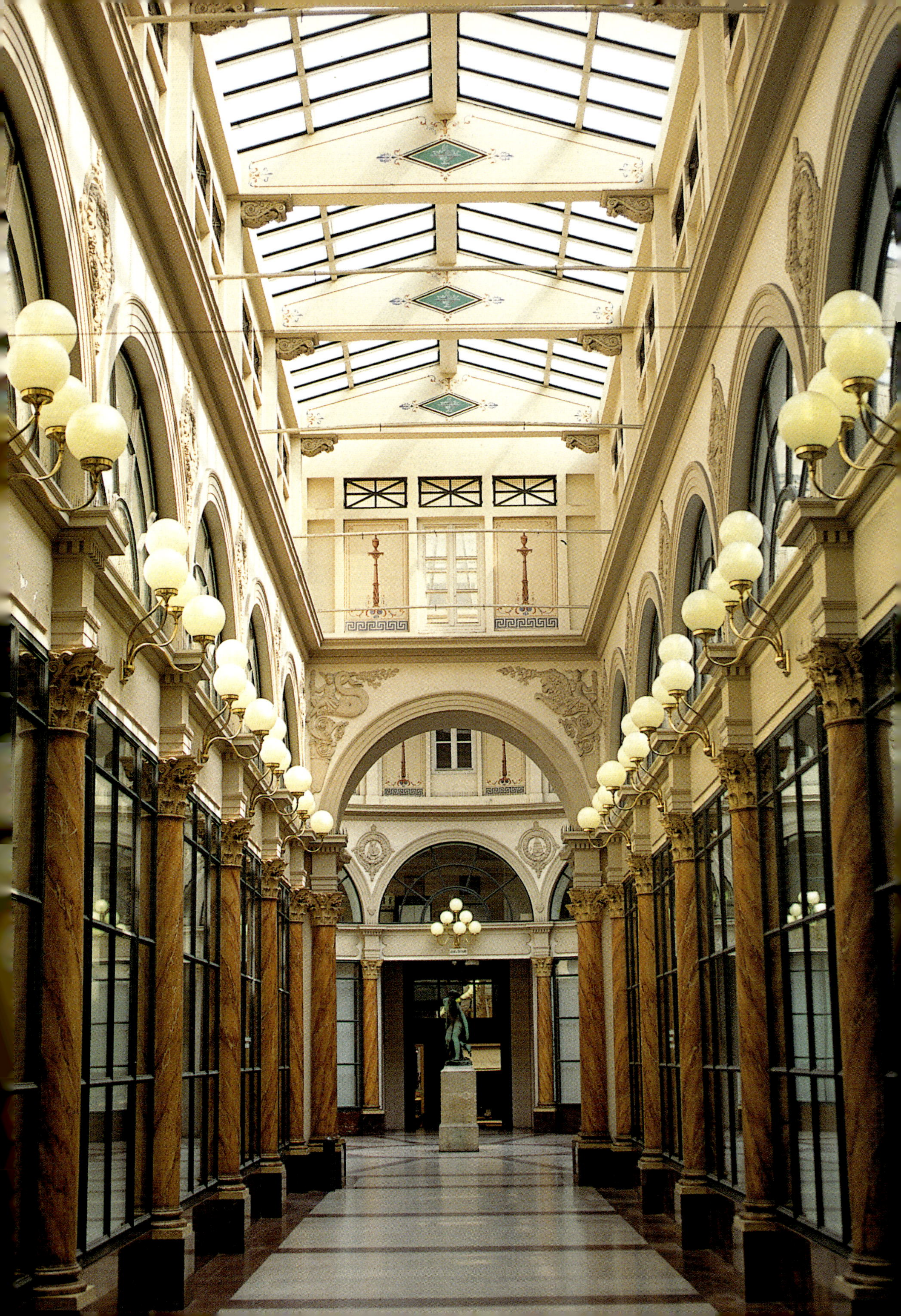

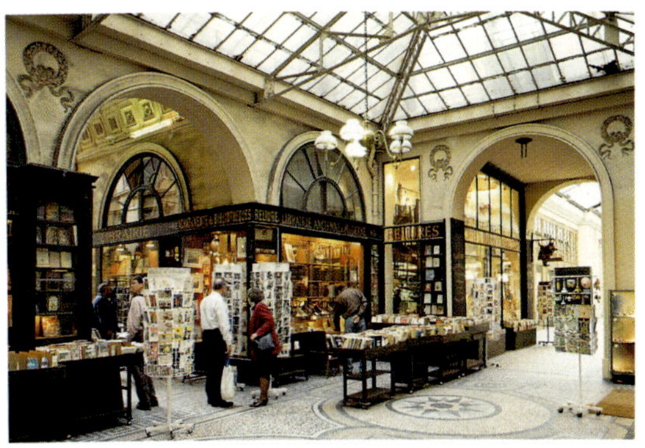

The decoration of the Galerie Colbert, opened in 1826,
is inspired by the Pompeiian style (left).
The Galerie Vivienne houses both bookshops and fashion
designer boutiques (above).
The Grévin Museum tells the history of France through
wax figures (below).

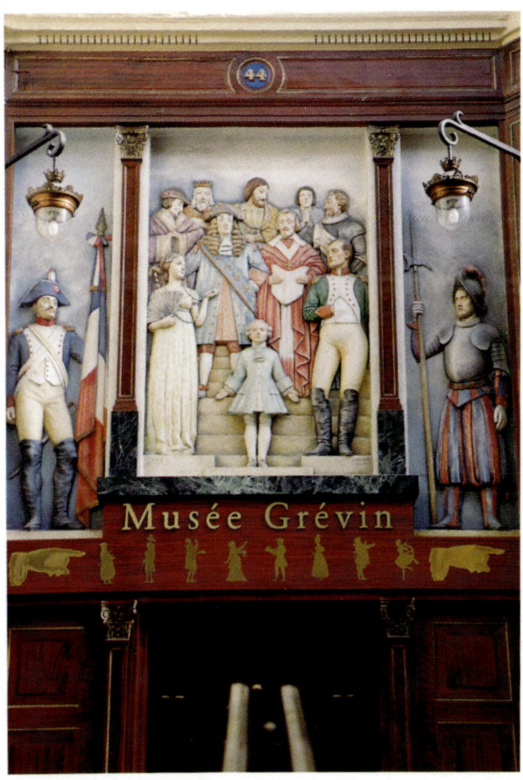

Grands Boulevards

In 1670, Louis XIV decided to replace the now obso-
lete city walls built by Charles V in the 14th century with
a roadway. And so, from the 18th century and particularly
in the following century, the Grands Boulevards which
linked the Place de la Bastille to the Place de la Madeleine
became popular for leisure activities and walking and a
whole host of theatres, shopping arcades known as the
"Passages", restaurants and cafés drew in the crowds.
Today, the operettas of Offenbach still attract audiences at
the Opéra-Comique on Rue Favart, while the Théâtre des
Variétés on the Boulevard Montmartre continues to stage
the popular Boulevard plays of Labiche. The modern entertainment of the 20th century such as music hall at the
Olympia theatre on the Boulevard des Capucines and the
cinemas which began to appear from the beginning of the
century, have also enjoyed enormous success. Built in 1932,
the Grand Rex on the Boulevard Bonne-Nouvelle is now
classed as a historical monument.

The Musée Grévin at No.10, Boulevard Montmartre
was created during the Belle Epoque of the Grands
Boulevards. It was a Parisian journalist, Arthur Meyer who,
in 1881, had the idea of creating a museum exhibiting the
famous people of his day in the form of wax figures. Alfred
Grévin was given the task of making this idea a reality.
Since then, politicians, actors and sports stars have been
added to the gallery of famous personalities. The museum
also incorporates a theatre and magic show.

The two triumphal gateways erected in honour of
Louis XIV at each end of the Boulevard Saint-Dénis are
purely decorative. The Porte Saint-Dénis, built in 1672, is
decorated with allegorical figures commemorating the
crossing of the Rhine and the capture of Maastrict by Louis
XIV, while the Porte Saint-Martin, erected in 1674, cele-
brates the victories of the King in the Franche-Comté region
of France.

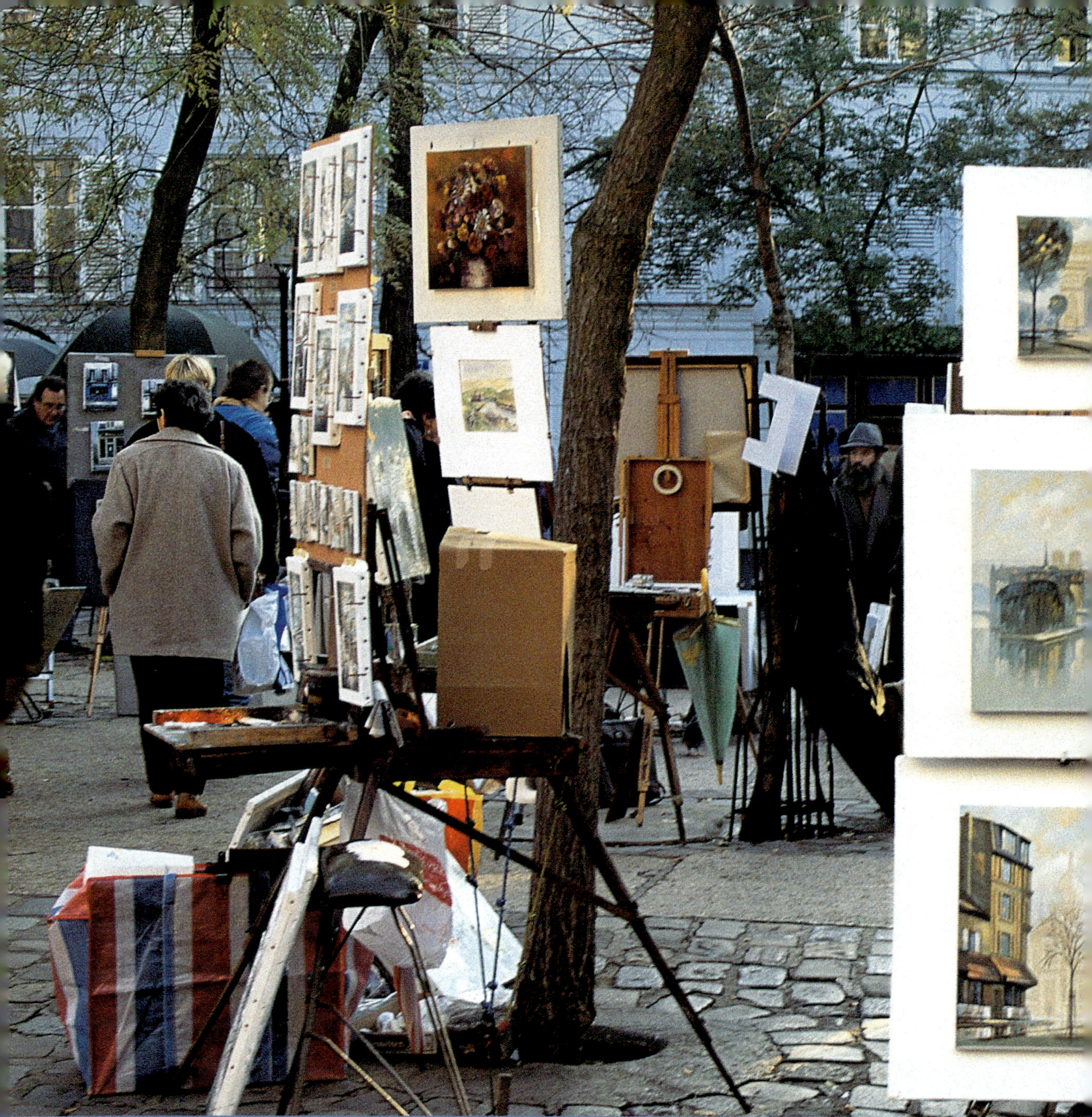

City life

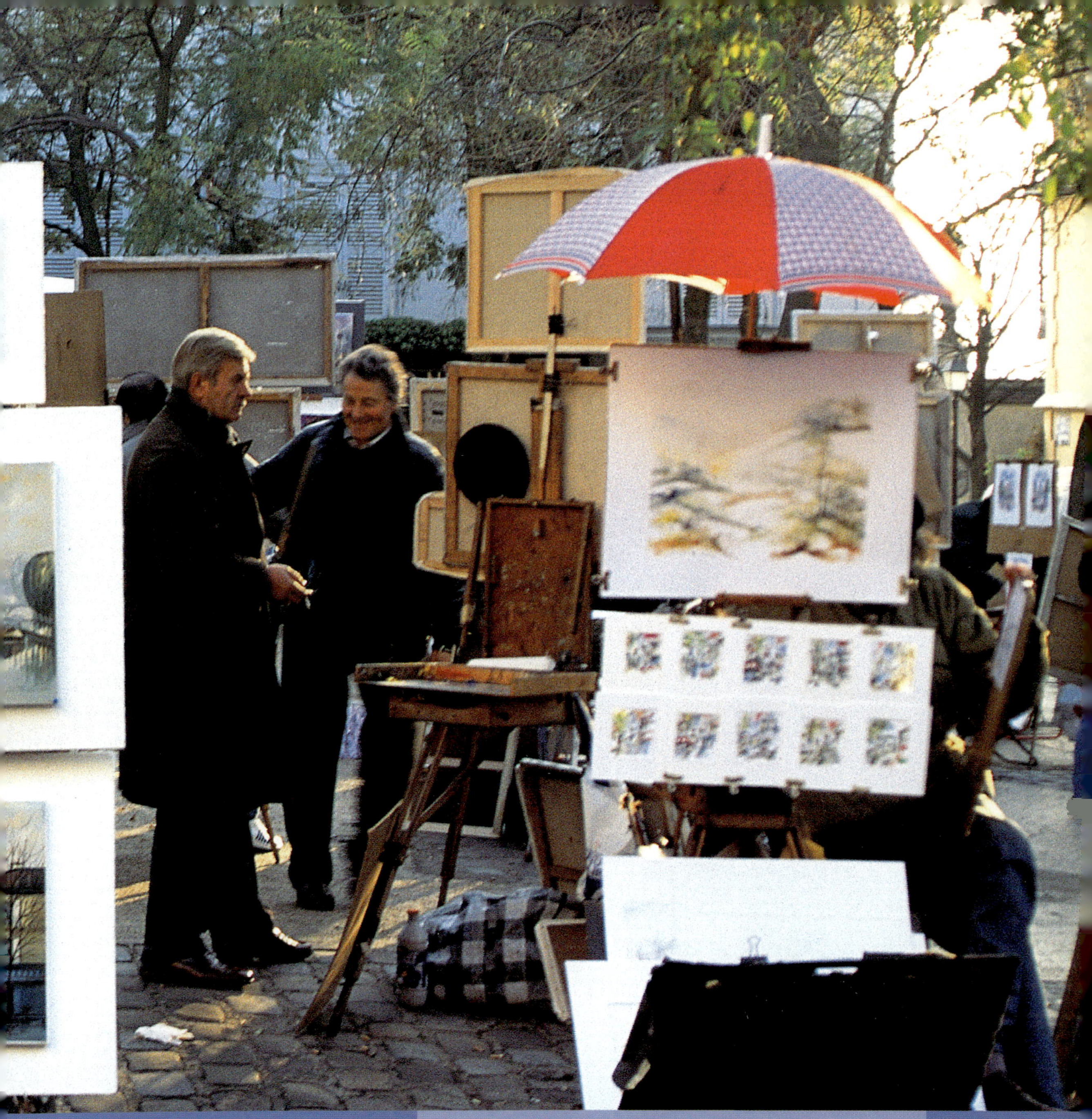

Montmartre

Montmartre
and Sacré-Cœur

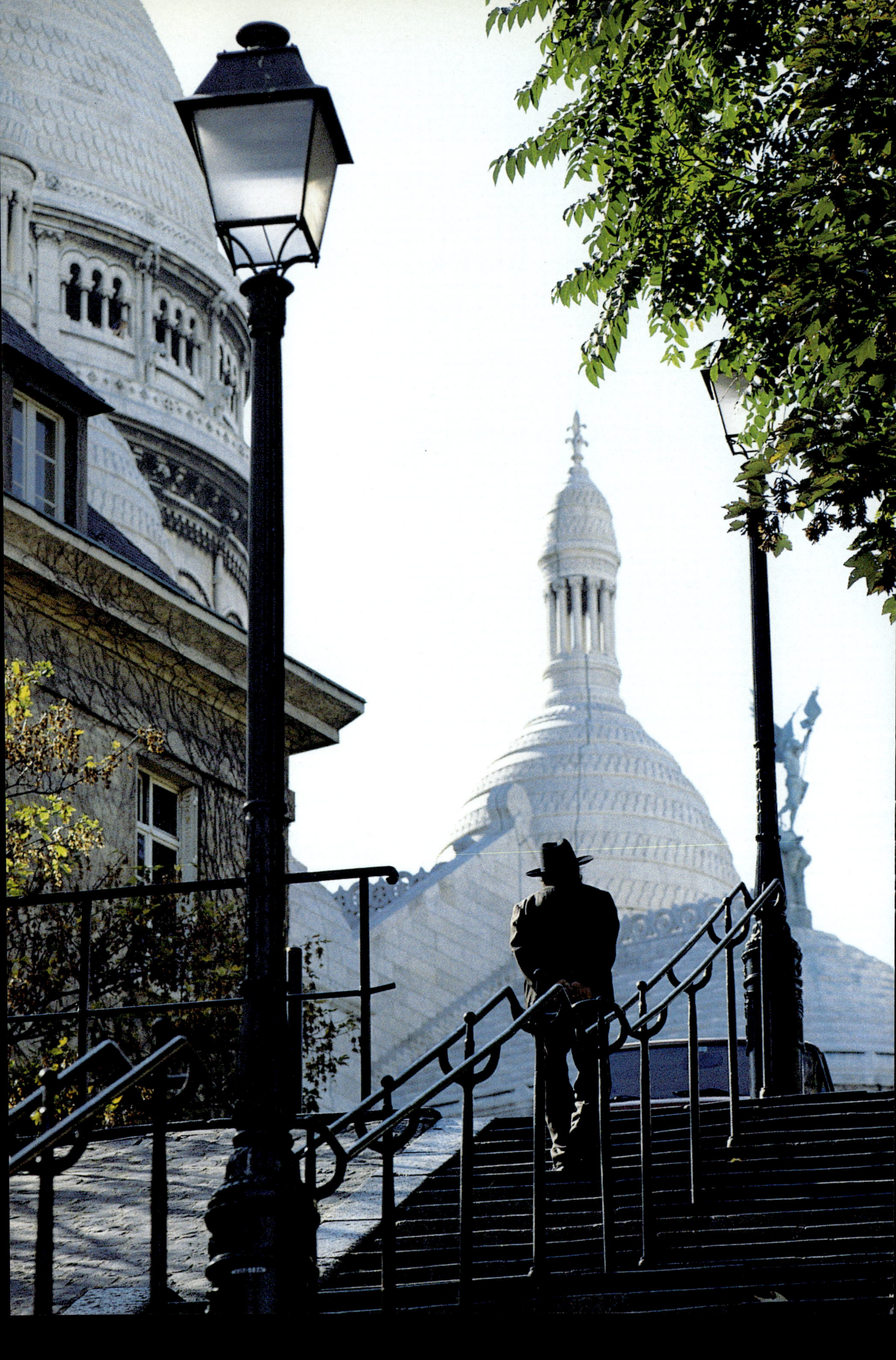

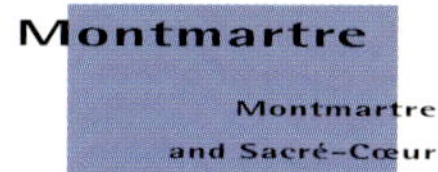

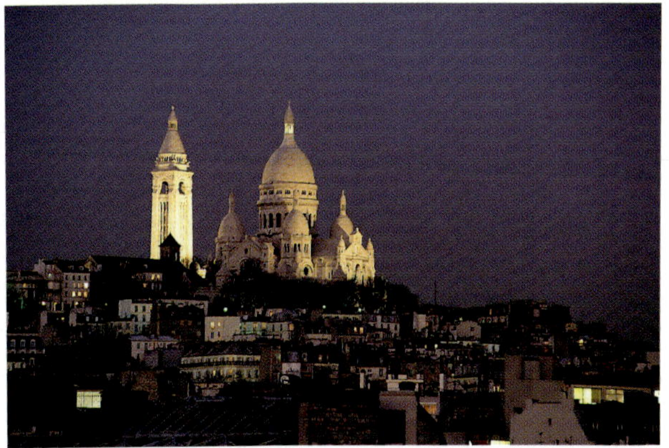

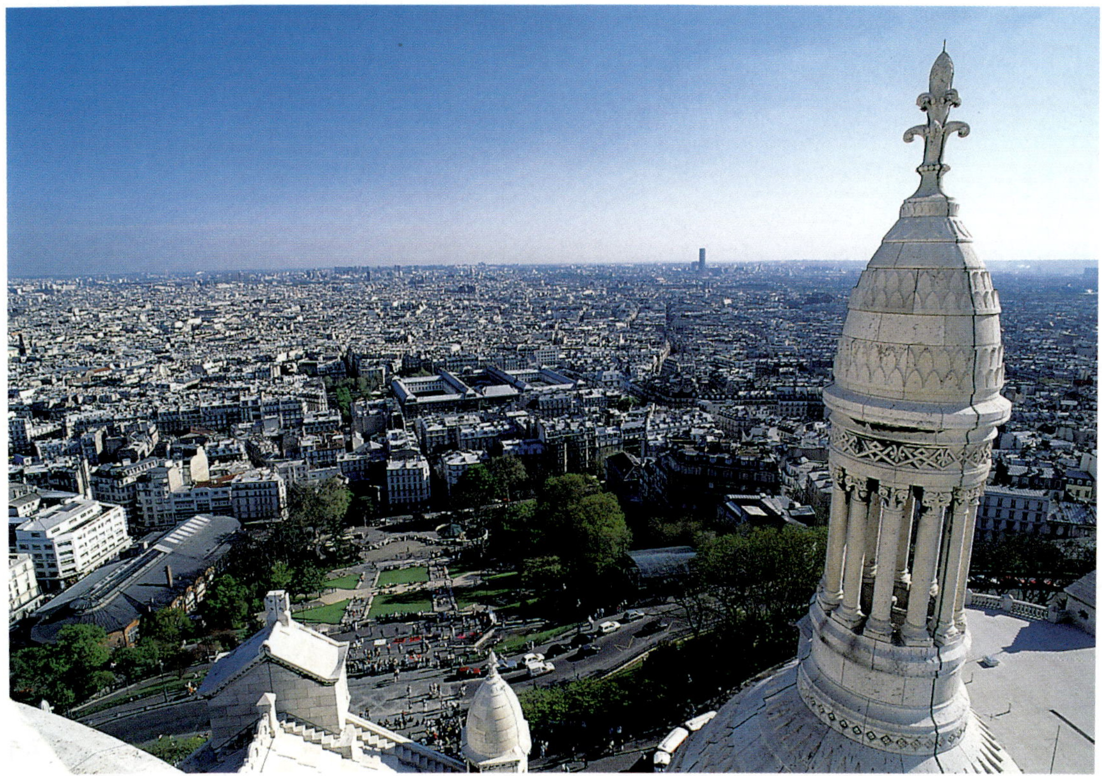

One of the charms of Montmartre is to stroll along
its characteristic winding streets, which sometimes end
in flights of stone steps (left).
The campanile of Sacré-Cœur is home to one of the largest
known bells. Cast in Savoy in 1895, it weighs an impressive
19 tons. From the Sacré-Cœur dome, the view stretches
50 km in every direction (above).

Montmartre and Sacré-Cœur

Variously known as the Mount of Mars (*Mons Martis*),
in reference to the temple dedicated to the god of war
located on the hill in Gallo-Roman times, or the Mount
of Martyrs (*Mons Martyrum*), in memory of the first martyrs of Paris (Saints Dénis, Eleuthère and Rustique) who
met their death here in the 3rd century... Montmartre
hill overlooks the city at a height of 130 m. The present
Place des Abbesses was once the site of a Benedictine convent founded in the 12th century by Queen Adélaïde de

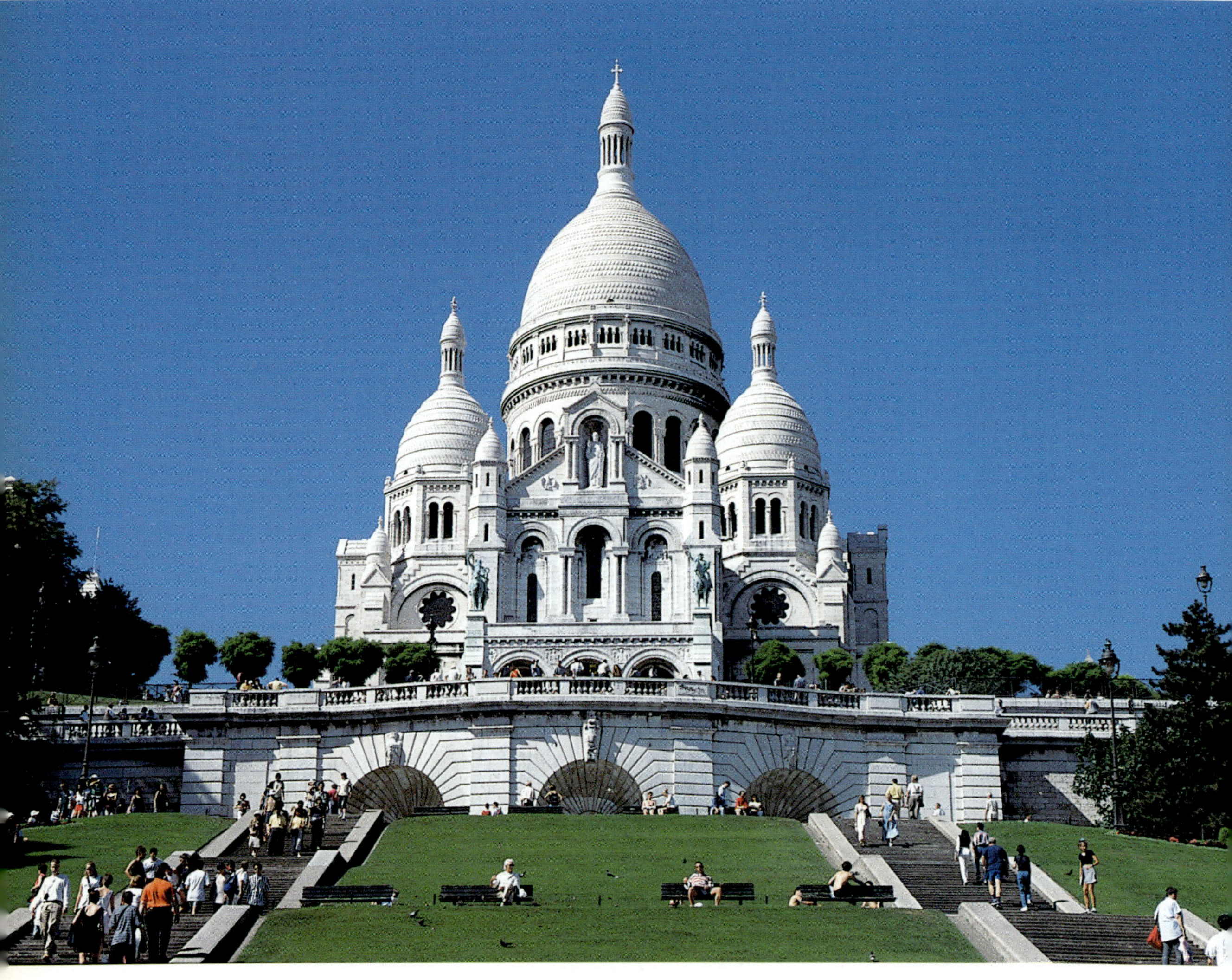

Savoie, the wife of Louis VI le Gros, which was later destroyed during the Revolution. It was not long before a number of windmills were erected on the hill - under the reign of Louis XIV there were around thirty - only two of which still stand today, the Moulin de la Galette, immortalised by Renoir and the Moulin du Radet, a favourite subject of Toulouse-Lautrec. During the siege of Paris in 1870, Montmartre was used as a base for the release of balloons for observing enemy lines. On 7 October the same year, it was also by balloon that Gambetta left the besieged capital for Orléans.

Towards the end of the 19th century, painters began to settle on the hill, attracted by the district's rustic charm. Some of the most famous include Renoir, Degas, Dufy, Toulouse-Lautrec, Pissarro, Van Dongen and Van Gogh… who were regulars of the famous Bateau-Lavoir. It was here that Picasso painted "Les Demoiselles d'Avignon". A favourite spot of this Bohemian community was Le Lapin Agile (originally Le Lapin à Gill, named after its owner), a cabaret frequented by artists such as Utrillo, Derain, Verlaine, Apollinaire, Carco, Dullin and the French cancan dancers of the Moulin Rouge. Another cabaret was Le Chat Noir

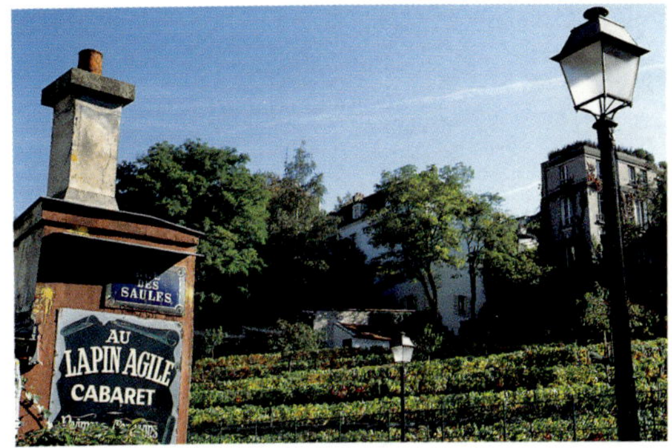

Below the parvis of the Sacré-Cœur Basilica are two squares consisting of terraces bordered by flights of steps leading to the Place Saint-Pierre (left).
The hill was once famous for its vineyards and "moulins" (mills). Now they are just picturesque souvenirs, such as the vineyard replanted in 1933 (above) and the Moulin du Radet, which along with the Moulin de la Galette (below) are the only two still standing today.

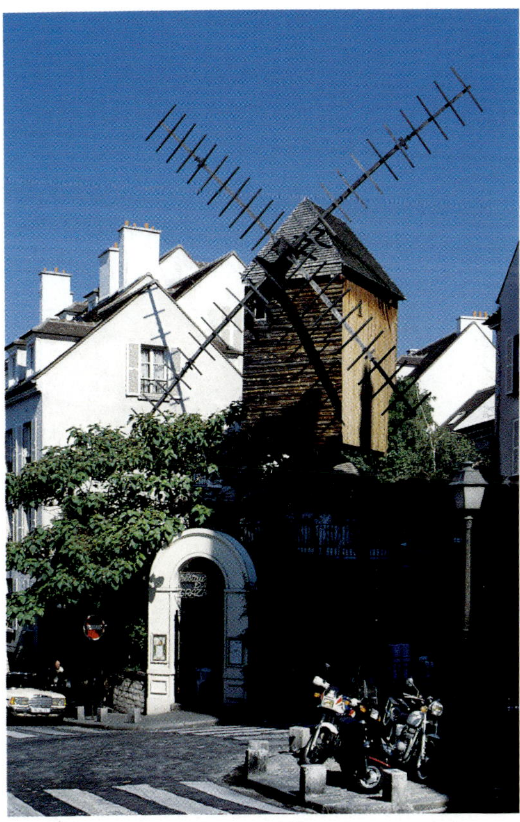

which produced the famous cabaret singer, Aristide Bruant. For a long time, Montmartre was symbolised by the familiar "petit poulbot" character - the cartoon of a street kid from Montmartre similar to another famous figure, Gavroche - who was named after his creator, Francisque Poulbot.

After the defeat of France following the 1870 war, traditionalist Catholics, supported by Guibert, the Archbishop of Paris, decided to erect a Basilica in the capital dedicated to the worship of the Sacred Heart. This was to expiate the "sins" of the century that had lost religion and which had seen the loss of Alsace and Lorraine and the Pontifical States in Rome and the insurrection of the Paris Commune. And it was in Montmartre, the birthplace of the Commune, that they wished to build their new Basilica. Recognised as a public utility by the ultra conservative Chamber of 1873, the construction of the church from 1876 to 1910 came up against both political controversy and technical difficulties. In effect, the foundations were laid on ground weakened by the galleries of former gypsum mines, exploited during the preceding centuries.

The church was designed by Paul Abadie, the architect responsible for restoring the Saint-Front Roman-Byzantine cathedral in Périgueux, which greatly influenced the design of the new Basilica. Sacre-Cœur, whose walls Huysmans described as "stones of vanity, sealed with the cement of pride", is characterised by a mass of cupolas, domes and bell towers - the tallest measures 80 m and houses La Savoyarde, a bell weighing over 19 tons. Highly controversial for both its design and the reasons behind its construction, Sacre-Cœur, is now a familiar feature of the Parisian landscape.

Some prefer the venerable Saint-Pierre church, a vestige of the ancient Benedictine convent. Over the centuries the edifice has undergone many transformations. The chancel, ending in an apse and two absidal chapels, the transept and the first three bays of the nave, all date from the 12th century, while their vaults are from the 15th century. The original Gothic façade was replaced with the present façade in the 18th century.

Monument

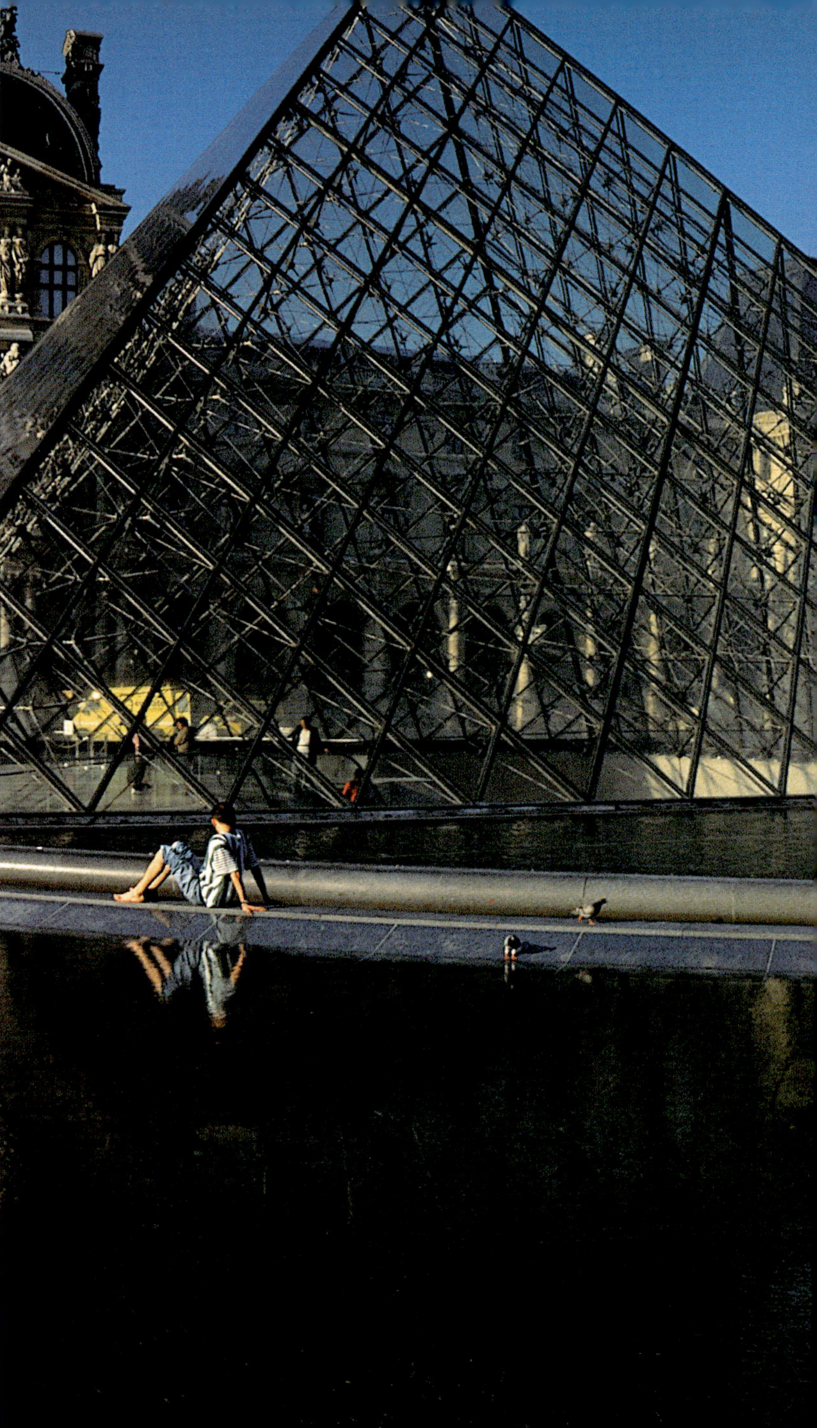

1st arrondissement

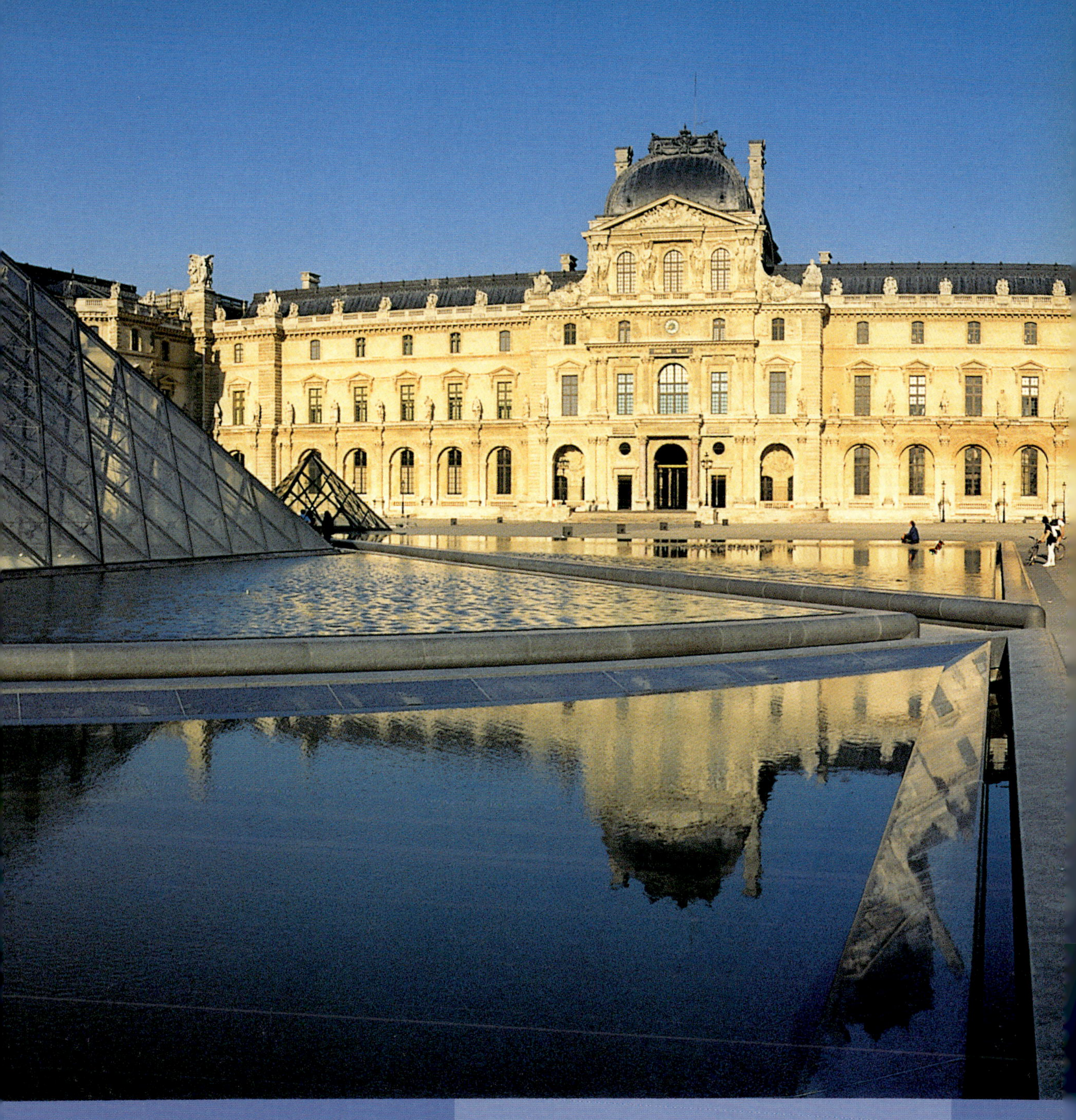

Louvre – Palais Royal

Louvre
Arc de triomphe
du Carrousel
Tuileries Gardens
Palais-Royal

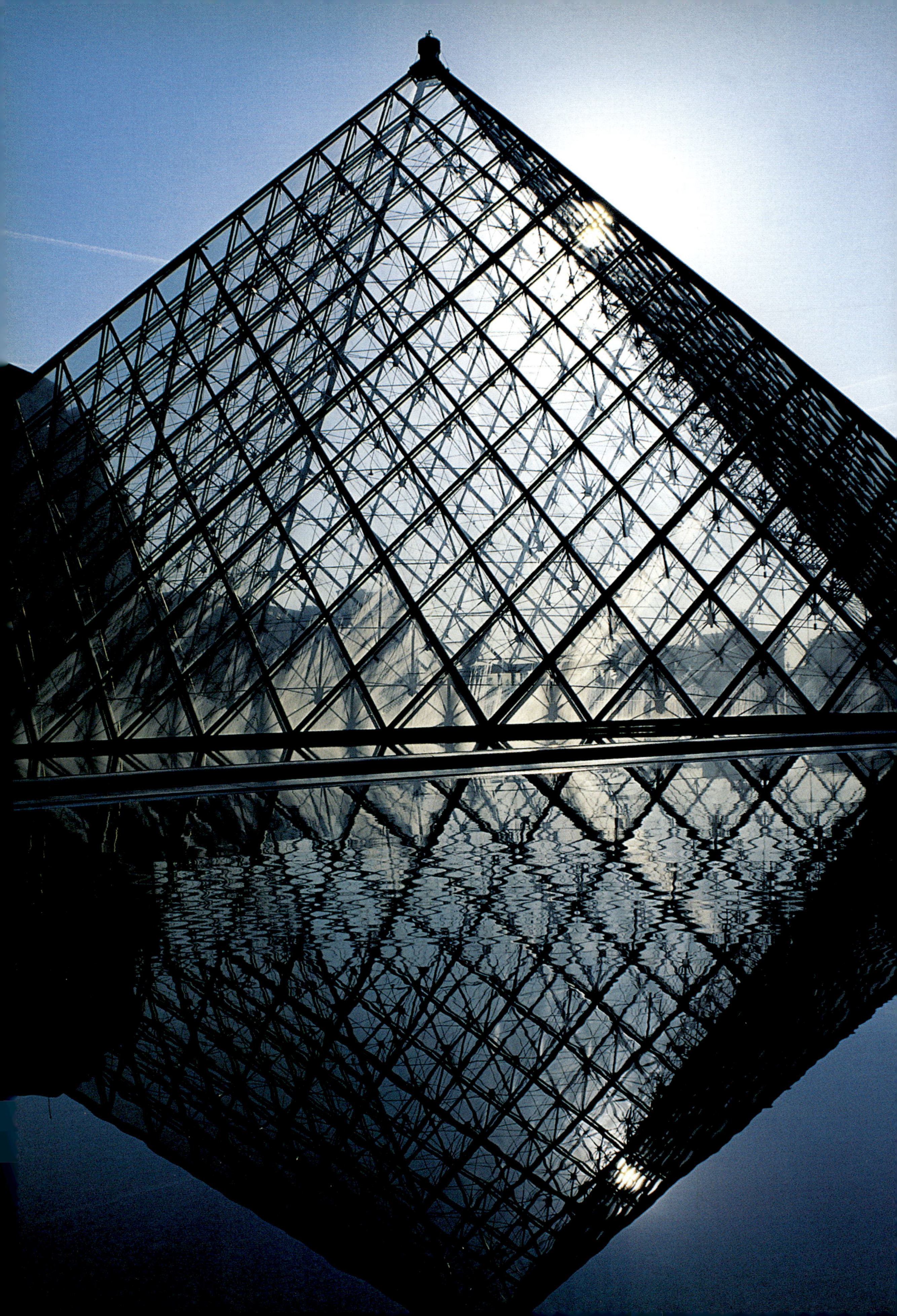

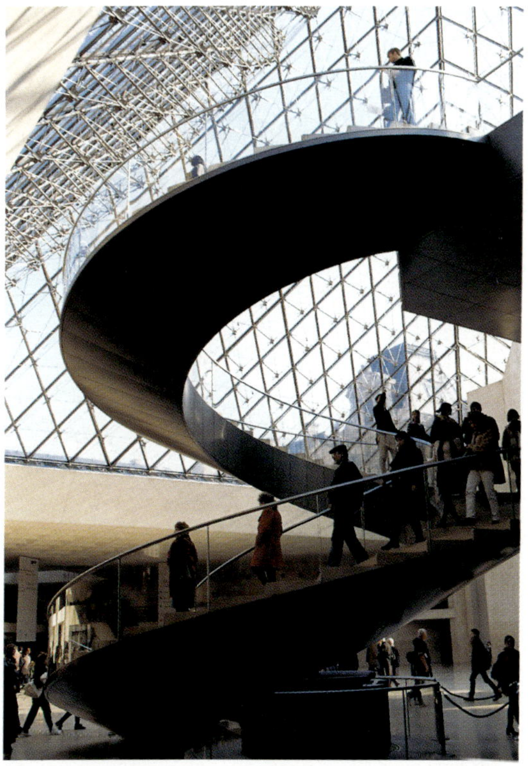

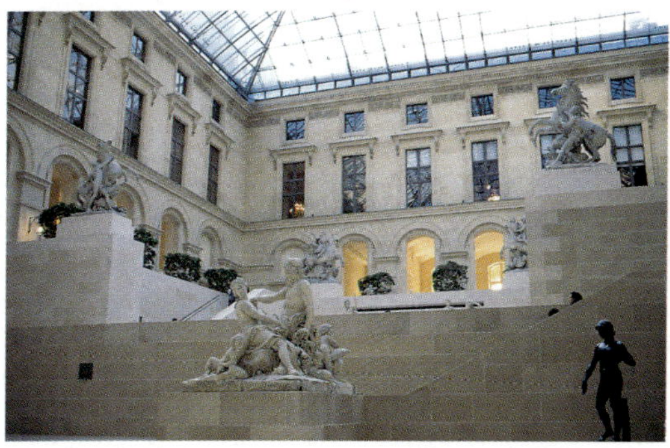

The glass pyramid by the architect Ieoh Ming Pei comprises
793 diamond-shaped glass panels (left).
Located in the Cour Napoléon, it gives easy access to
the museum's various departments (top).
Vast glass roofs light up the new halls devoted to sculpture
(below).

Louvre

The palace

The Louvre is not just the largest and richest museum
in the world… it has also been the residence of Kings and
Emperors for the past eight hundred years and is nothing less
than a sumptuous, beautifully illustrated history book. The
Louvre began life as a fortress constructed by Philippe Auguste
in 1204 and was later extended and improved under Saint
Louis, Philippe le Bel and Charles V. It underwent consider-
able change during the Renaissance under Francis I and then
Henry II, who appointed the architect Pierre Lescot and sculptor Jean Goujon to carry out renovation and decoration work.
Catherine de' Medici later commissioned the construction of
the Tuileries Palace which she planned to join to the Louvre
by a gallery. Her project, interrupted by the Wars of Religion,
was then continued by Henry IV in 1594 when peace was
restored. Louis XIII quadrupled the surface area of the buildings and his successor, Louis XIV, continued with extension
work. After the departure of the court for Versailles in 1682,
the royal residence was occupied by various Academies, artists
and royal favourites. Later, the building work abandoned
after the fall of the Empire was finally completed by Napoleon
III. Following a fire during the Commune of 1871, the
Château des Tuileries was eventually demolished in 1882.

A century later, in 1981, François Mitterrand launched
the Grand Louvre project. This included the development
of the land under the Cour Napoleon, the discovery of vestiges of the ancient fortress built by Philippe Auguste and
the construction of the pyramid designed by the architect
Ieoh Ming Peï.

The museum

In creating the royal collection, it was Francis I who began
the Louvre's history as a museum. But it was not until the
arrival of Louis XIV and the efforts of Colbert, that the museum
significantly grew in size and status - by 1710, the museum

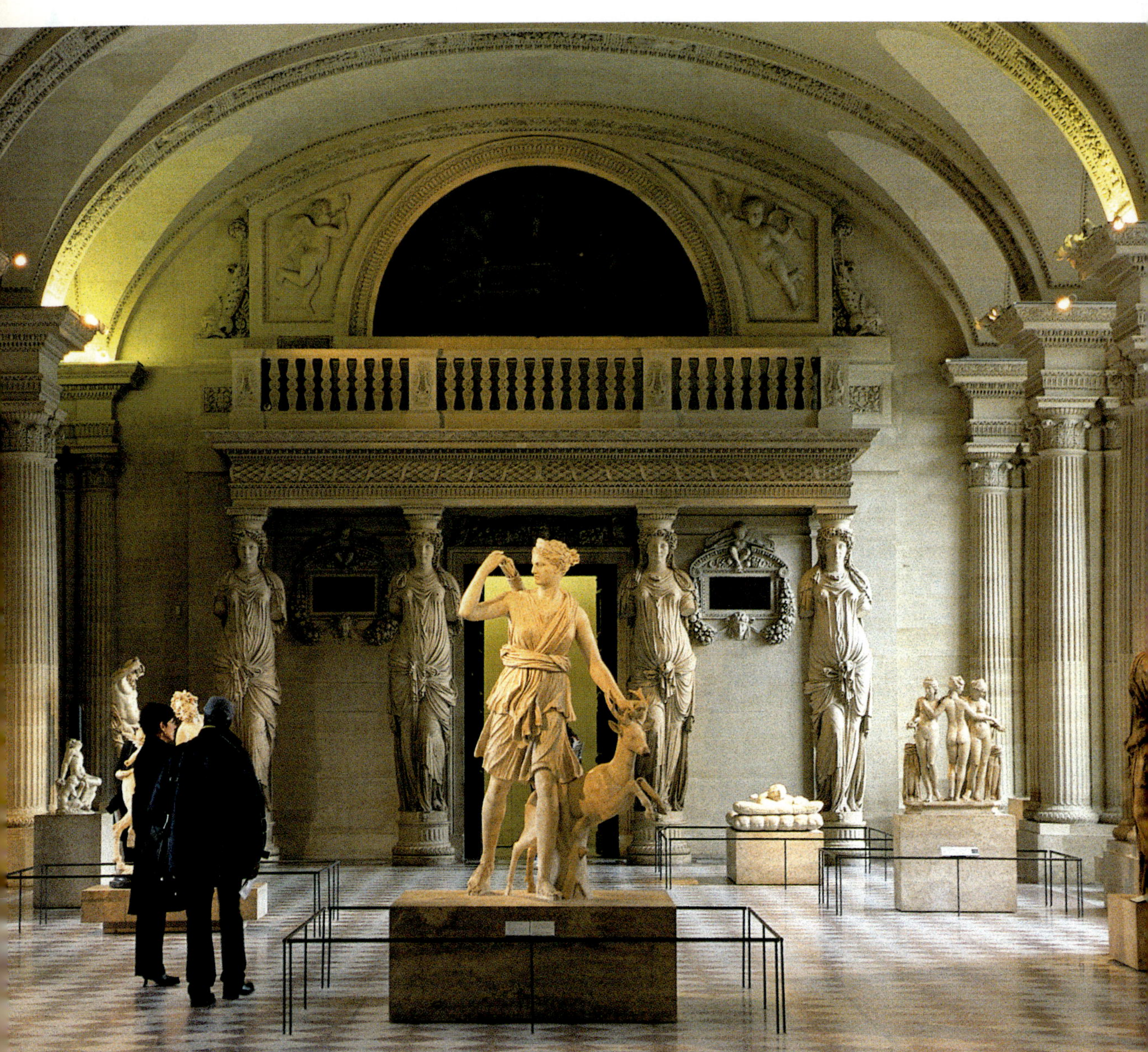

held 1,500 paintings, compared to just 200 when the King came to the throne. The museum grew further under Louis XVI, with new purchases and works commissioned from some of the great French masters. Louis XVII continued to increase the collection, acquiring various Dutch and Flemish paintings. During the Revolution, the Louvre was officially made France's national museum, the "Museum du Palais du Louvre", by a decree of 27 July 1793 and received paintings from the Château de Versailles. It then became the Napoleon Museum, and under the management of Vivant Denon grew

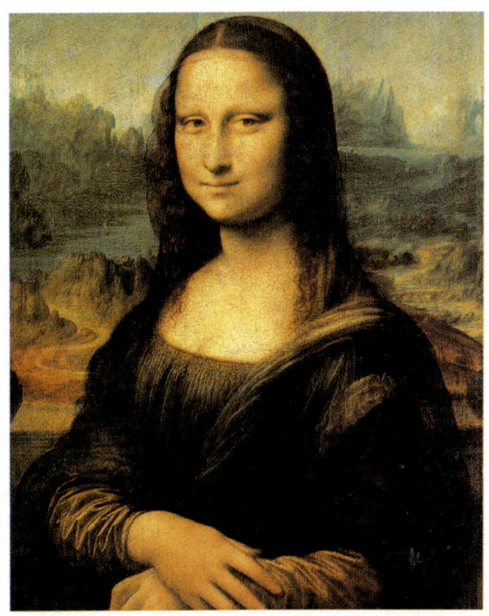

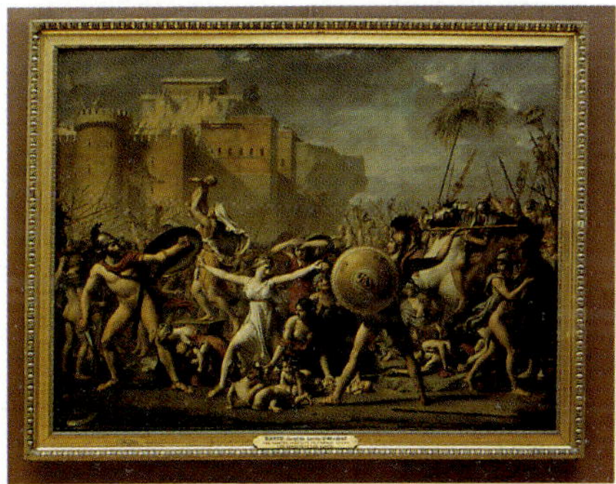

The Salle des Caryatides houses an exhibition of Greek sculptures from the 4th century BC (left). *The Mona Lisa*, **painted by Leonardo da Vinci around 1505 and acquired by Francis I, is the Louvre Museum's most famous work,** (above). **The painter J.-L. David (1748-1825) was often inspired by Antiquity. Here is his painting** *'Les Sabines arrêtant le combat'* (above).

dramatically with the addition of thousands of pieces taken from various European cities after the Empire's victories. Some were later returned in 1815. Under Louis XVIII and Charles X, new collections were acquired and rooms devoted to modern sculpture and Greek, Egyptian and Assyrian antiquities

were opened. The museum became state property in 1848 and continued to grow thanks to numerous purchases and various large donations. Today, the Louvre Museum is divided into seven Departments.

Following work on the Grand Louvre, the sculptures now benefit from a much improved display. Italian sculpture is on show in the Donatello gallery and Michelangelo gallery and French sculpture exhibited under the glass roofs of the Cour Marly and Cour Puget. The latter include works representative of Roman art, Gothic art (mainly religious), the Renaissance and the Classical period, which is characterised by the exaltation of royal power. Small works, often made of terracotta, illustrate sculpture of the 18th century.

The collection of art objects comprises some 10,000 pieces: the Louvre's Medieval treasures include a set of ivory objects from Byzantium and statuettes from the period of Charlemagne. From the Renaissance period, there are marquetry panels from a church in Padua, medals from Pisanello, painted enamels from Limoges, Italian majolica, series of tapestries made by the Gobelins. The gold and silver pieces, such as the helmet and shield of Charles IX, come from the collection of relics belonging to the Order of the Holy Spirit. Rooms are also dedicated to French furniture from the 16th and 17th centuries, with ceramics by Bernard Palissy and furniture by Boulle.

Since 2000, the Ethnic Art of Africa, Asia, Oceania and America is housed in the Louvre and includes around 120 pieces mainly consisting of statues and objects in terracotta or stone.

No visit to the Louvre would be complete without passing through the Apollo Gallery, a room decorated by Le Brun which houses the *Régent*, a magnificent 140 carat diamond, the *Côte de Bretagne*, a 107 carat ruby.

The Napoleon III apartments are also a must - a magnificent universe of gold and velvet, illuminated by sparkling crystal chandeliers.

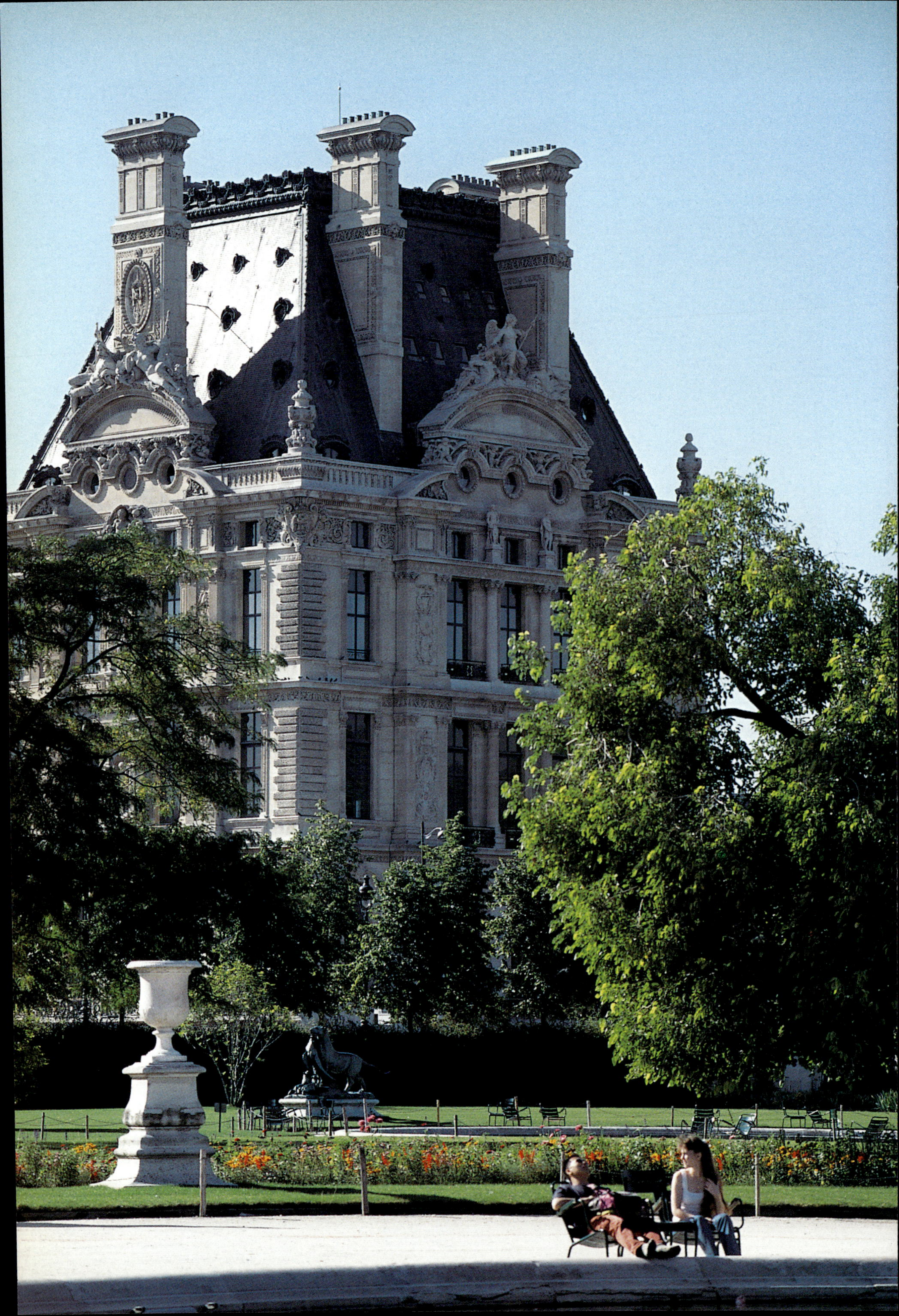

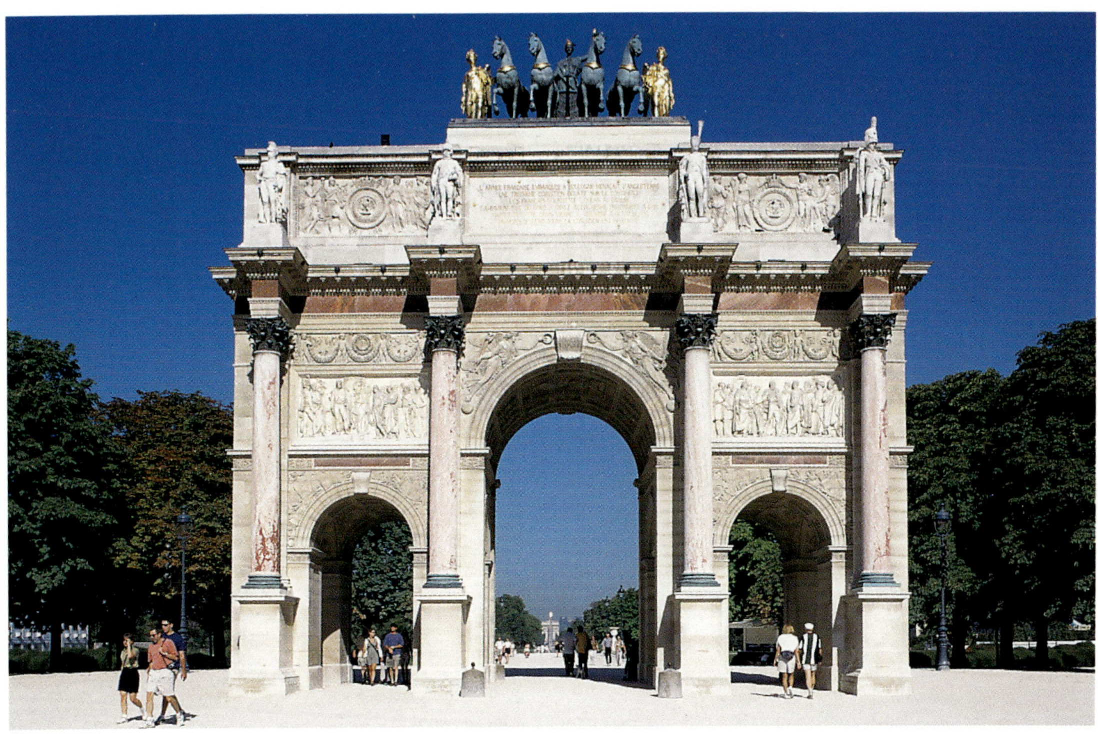

Arc de Triomphe du Carrousel

Between the Carrousel Gardens and Tuileries Gardens stands the Arc de Triomphe du Carrousel, built in 1806 along the lines of the Septimus Severus in Rome to celebrate the Napoleonic victories. The monument was originally topped by the group of horses from Saint-Mark's Square in Venice but these were returned to the city in 1815. Today, the statue crowning the monument is a copy by Bosio.

Tuileries Gardens

The Tuileries Gardens are named after a former tile works which once stood on the land where Catherine de' Medici built the new château, adjacent to the Louvre, in 1564. She also commissioned the design of an Italian garden, with pavilions, mazes and fountains. Henry IV installed an orangery and greenhouse for the breeding of silkworms and Louis XIII later set up a menagery in the park. In 1664, Louis XIV commissioned Le Nôtre to transform the Tuileries into a French garden, which involved the creation of a large central path surrounded by ornamental lakes, along with two terraces, quincunxes and flower beds.

At the far end of the Terrasse des Feuillants which borders the Rue de Rivoli, stands the Jeu de Paume Museum which hosts temporary exhibitions of contemporary art.

The Orangerie Museum, located at the far end of the terrace bordering the Seine which runs along the Quai des Tuileries, houses the celebrated *Waterlilies* by Monet and works by contemporary painters.

The Pavillon de Flore, at the far end of the Grande Galerie, once belonged to the Tuileries Palace and was renovated under the Second Empire (left).
The Arc de Triomphe du Carrousel was erected in praise of Napoleon I (top).

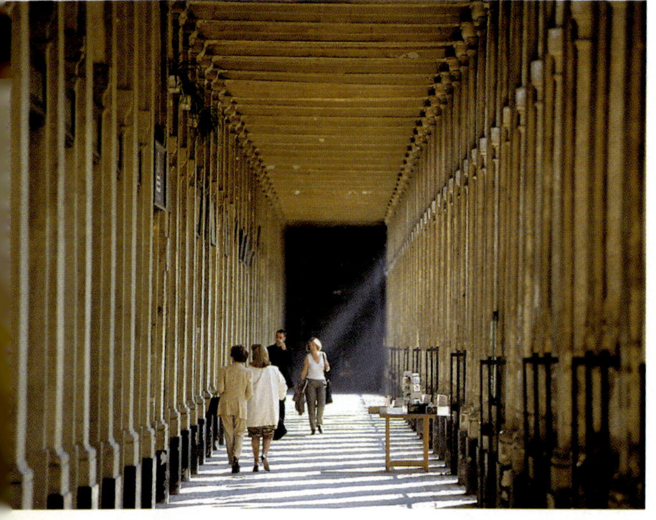

The Palais-Royal gardens are surrounded on three sides by
passages with colonnades leading to a host of boutiques
and private residences (top).
Hidden away behind its walls, the Palais-Royal gardens
are an oasis of calm in the heart of Paris (right).

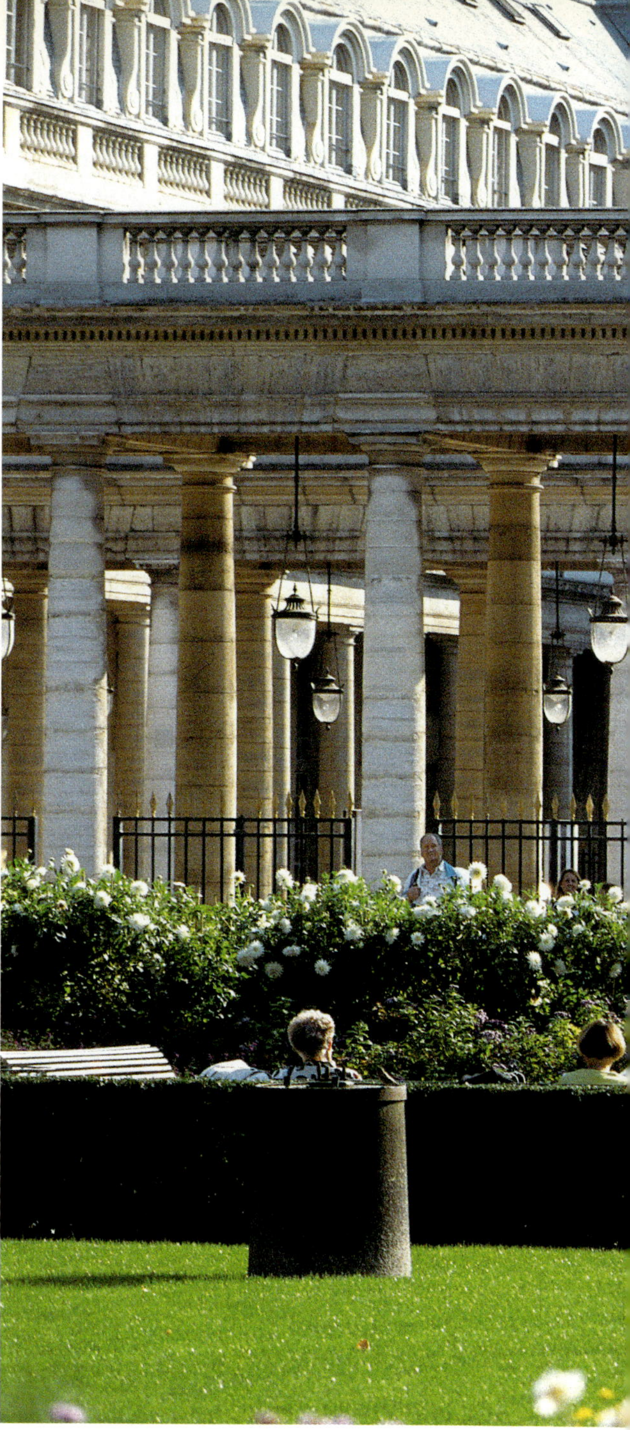

Palais-Royal

When Richelieu died in 1642, he bequeathed his residence, the Palais-Cardinal, to the King. The building, which
the Cardinal commissioned from the architect Lemercier, was
built between 1629 and 1636. It later became the Palais-
Royal and in 1692, Louis XIV gave it to his brother, Philippe
d'Orleans. The latter carried out large scale extension work
on the edifice which was continued by his son, the Regent.
The grand staircase was built in 1765 and the façade's colonnade in 1774. In 1780, the Duc de Chartres, the future
Philippe Egalité, needed to pay some debts and decided to
build some rented buildings in the garden, with the 180
arcades on the ground floor to house various boutiques. The
palace and gardens, now a privately owned area where the
security forces had no right of entry, soon became a den of
vice and illegal trafficking. Political clubs moved in, which
soon transformed into revolutionary hotbeds. After the exe-
cution of Philippe Egalité in 1793, the property was turned
over to the State. With its restaurants, cafés, gambling clubs,
bookshops and jeweller's boutiques, the Palais-Royal was one
of the most fashionable areas of Paris under the Consulate
and the Empire. In 1815, the Orléans family recovered its
property and built the gallery which bears its family name,

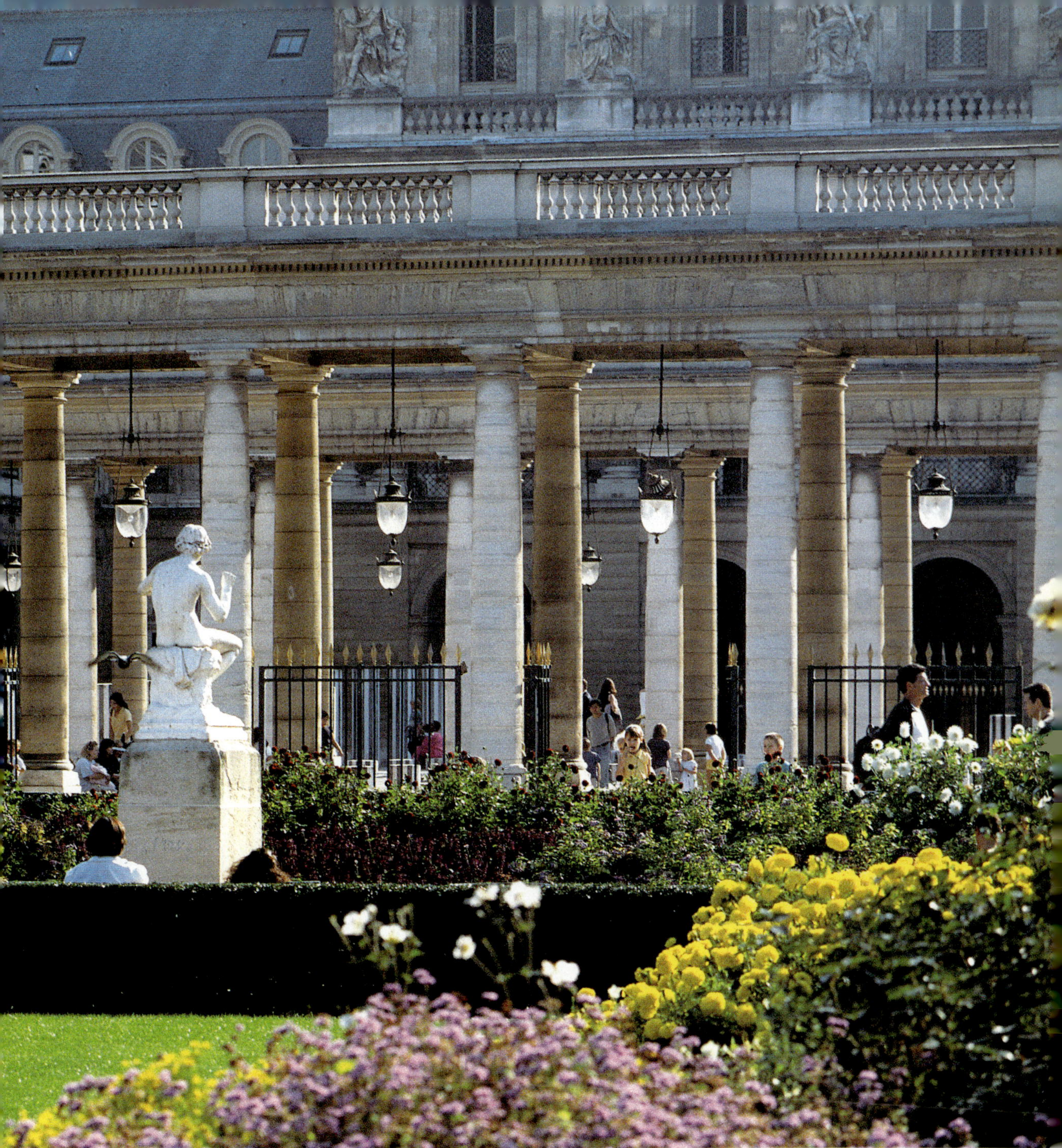

between the garden and main courtyard. Its cafés and gambling houses were closed in 1836, by King Louis-Philippe.

Today, the Palais-Royal is home to the Council of State, the Constitutional Council and a part of the Ministry of Culture. Opened in 1784, the Comédie-Française was the venue for most of Labiche's plays. Past writers and artists who resided in the apartments built by the Duc de Chartres include Cocteau and Colette. The installation of the columns by Buren and steel sculptures by Pol Bury in the main courtyard, until then used as a car park, created a great deal of controversy.

The gardens, created in 1629 and redesigned by Desgots in the 18th century cover around two hectares and are shaded by four double lines of lime trees.

Monument

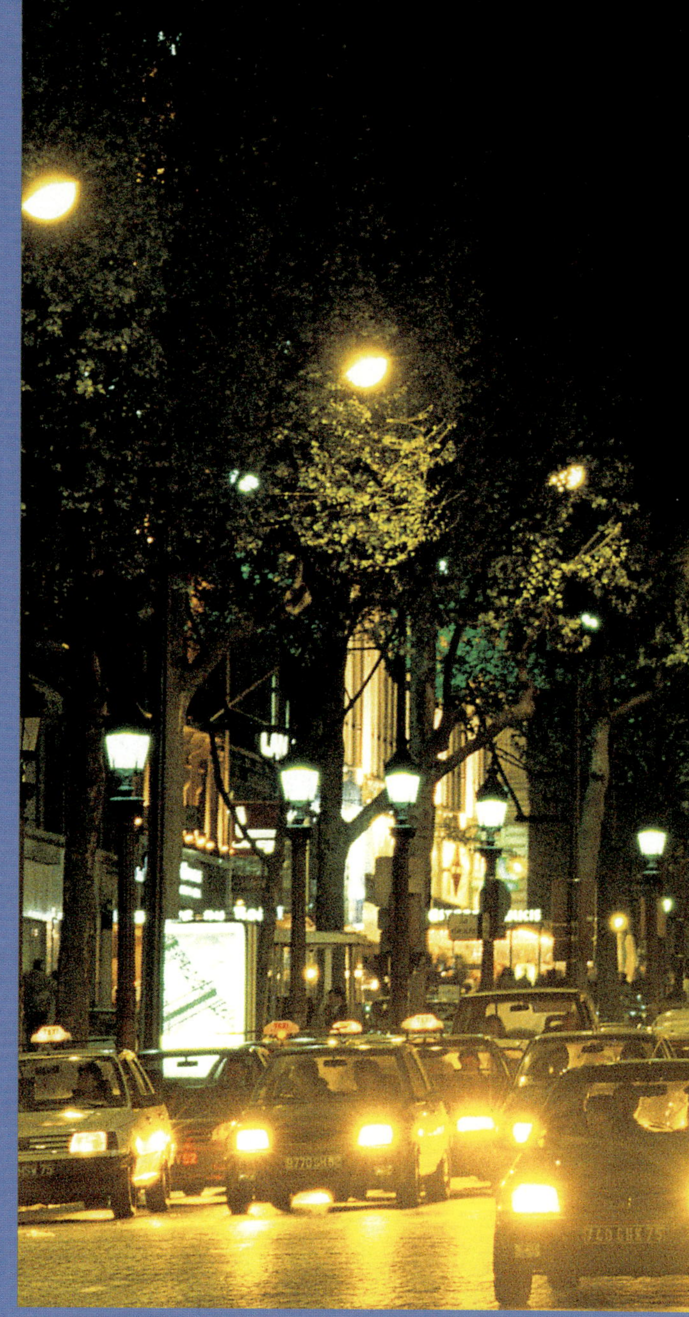

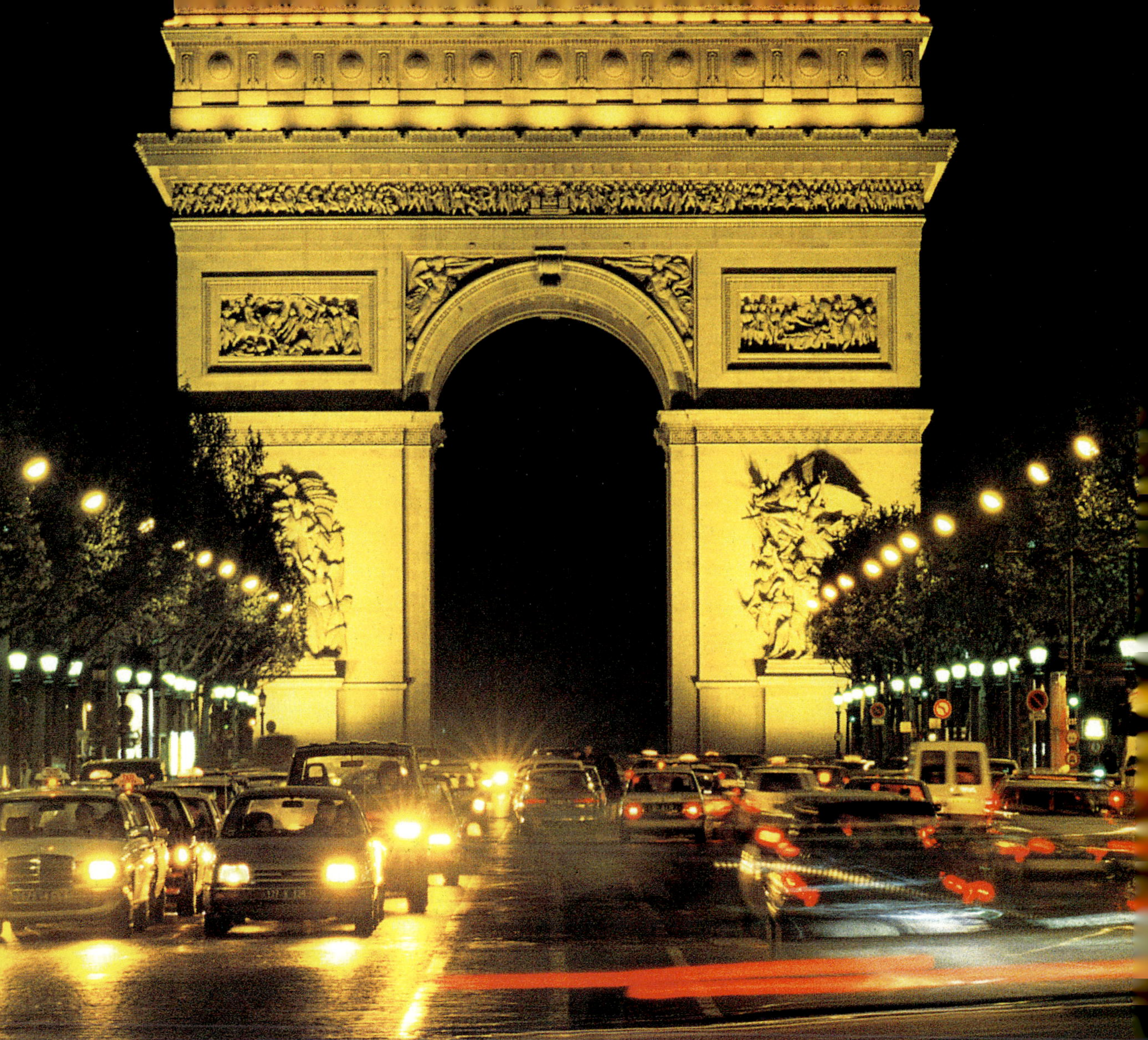

Champs-Élysées

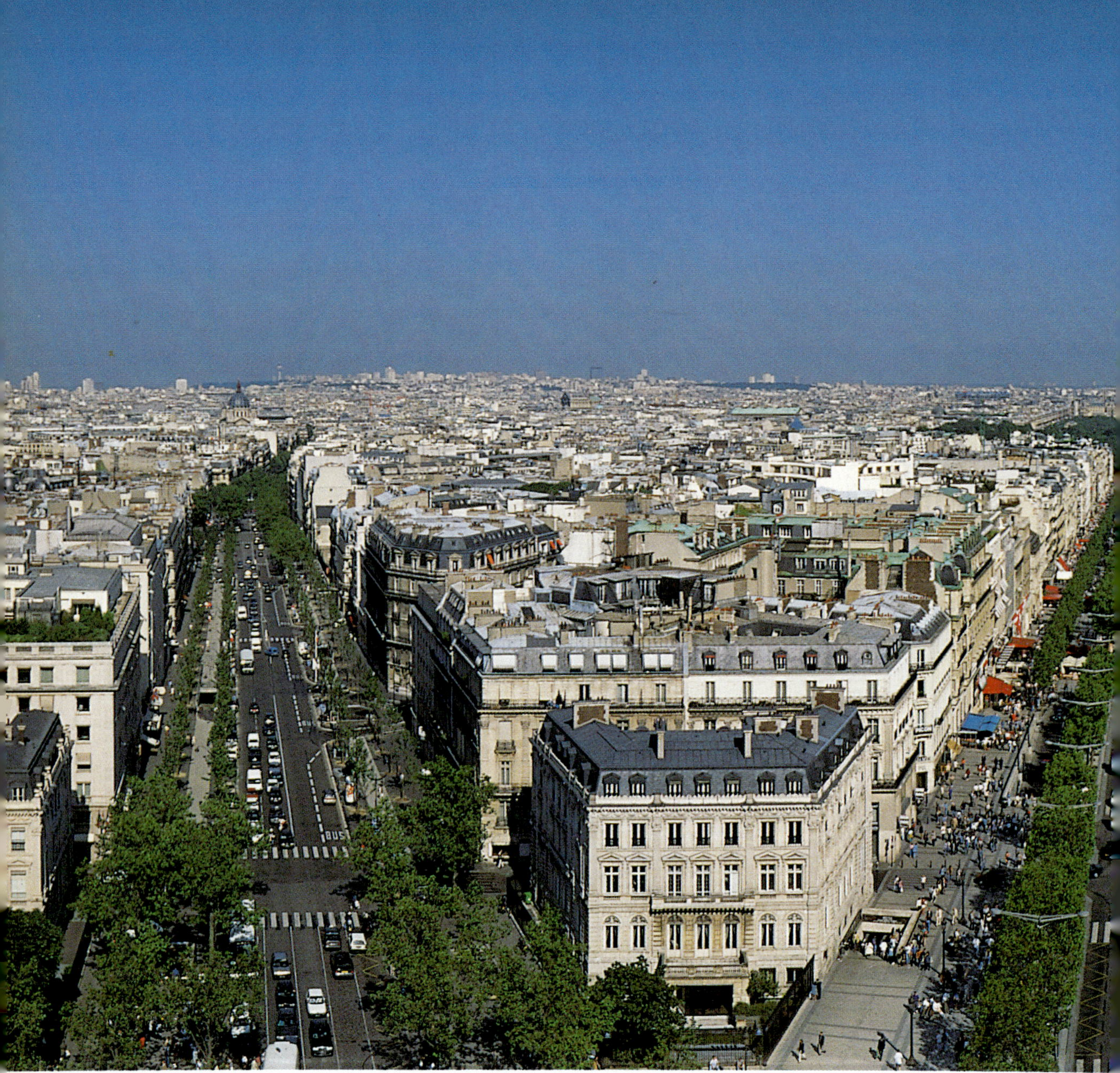

Champs-Élysées

On the site of what many have called the most beautiful avenue in the world, which measures an impressive 2 km long and 70 m wide, there was once just waterlogged fields. Inspired by the Corso she had left behind in Florence, Marie de Medici developed the area in 1616, planting trees to create what came to be known as the Cours-la-Reine. In 1628, a road was built in the direction of the Château des Tuileries, which in 1709 was named the Champs-Élysées (Elysian Fields), an allusion to the home of the gods from Greek Antiquity. In 1664, Louis XIV appointed Le Nôtre to create gardens bordering the new avenue, which was also extended up to the roundabout. However, the surrounding district was not developed until much later, and in 1777, cows still grazed just a stone's throw from the leisurely strollers. The Champs-Élysées really became a popular place for walking and entertainment at the end of the 18th century, after the construction of cafés, country cottages and open-air lotteries and ballrooms. Under the Directory, "Muscadins" and "Incroyables" started the fash-

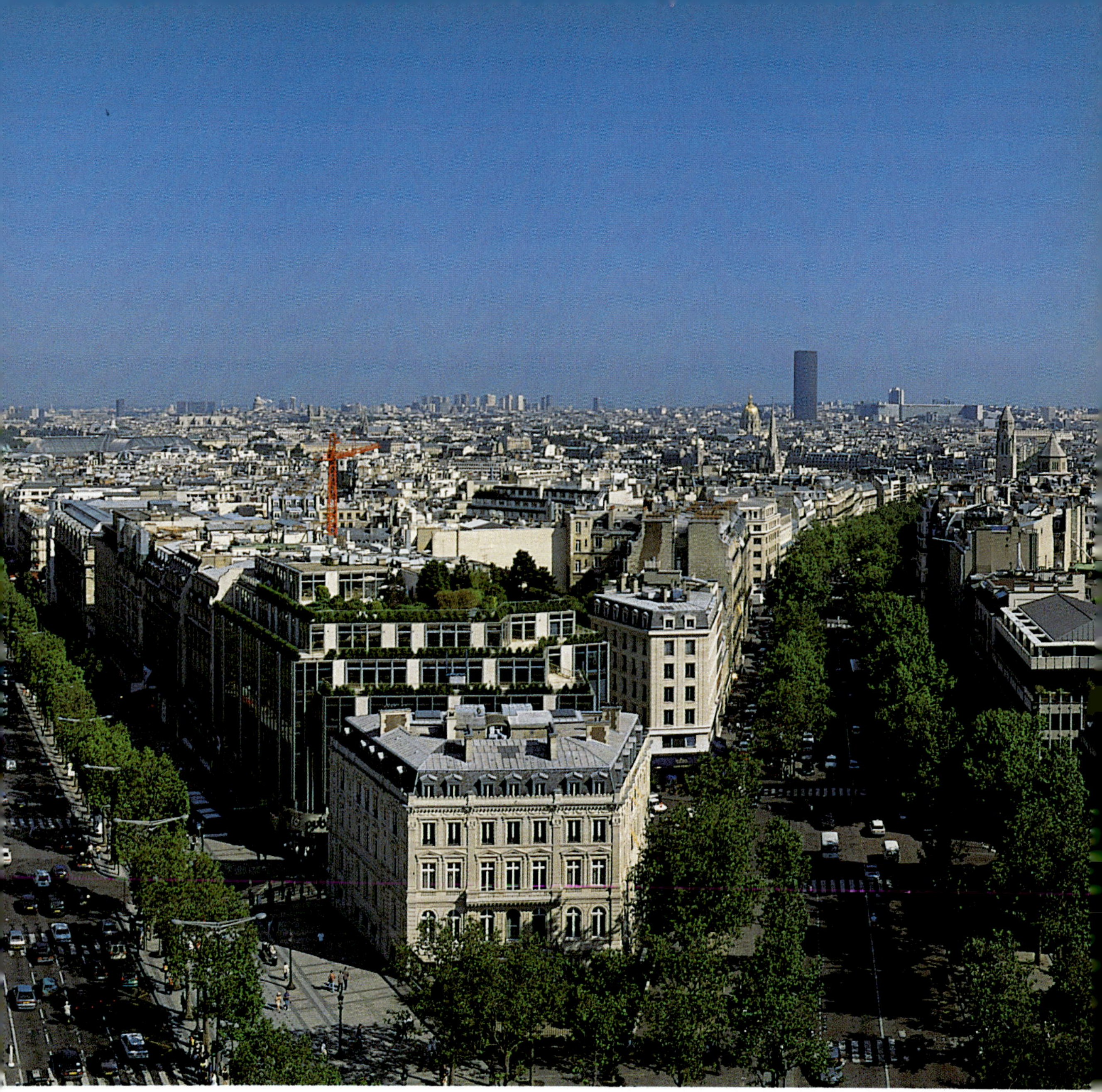

From the top of the Arc de Triomphe there is a spectacular
view of Paris (above).

ion of "going to the Champs" to show off one's extrava-
gant dress. Under the First Empire, it was the venue for military parades. In 1828, the Cossacks, Prussians and English
were billeted here and the Champs-Élysées was made the
property of the City of Paris. By the Second Empire it had
become a magnificent avenue, illuminated by 1,200 street
lamps which buzzed with carriages belonging to aristocrats
and bankers visiting the local café-concerts, such as the
Alcazar d'Eté or *Les Ambassadeurs* From the middle of the
19th century, businessmen and the wealthy bourgeoisie
built private mansions here, such as the Hôtel de la Païva
at No.25, one of the few still standing today. Other establishments also appeared, including numerous hotels, cafés
and theatres, such as *Le Lido*, and restaurants like *Ledoyen*,
Claridge, the *Elysée Palace* and *Fouquet's*. Between the

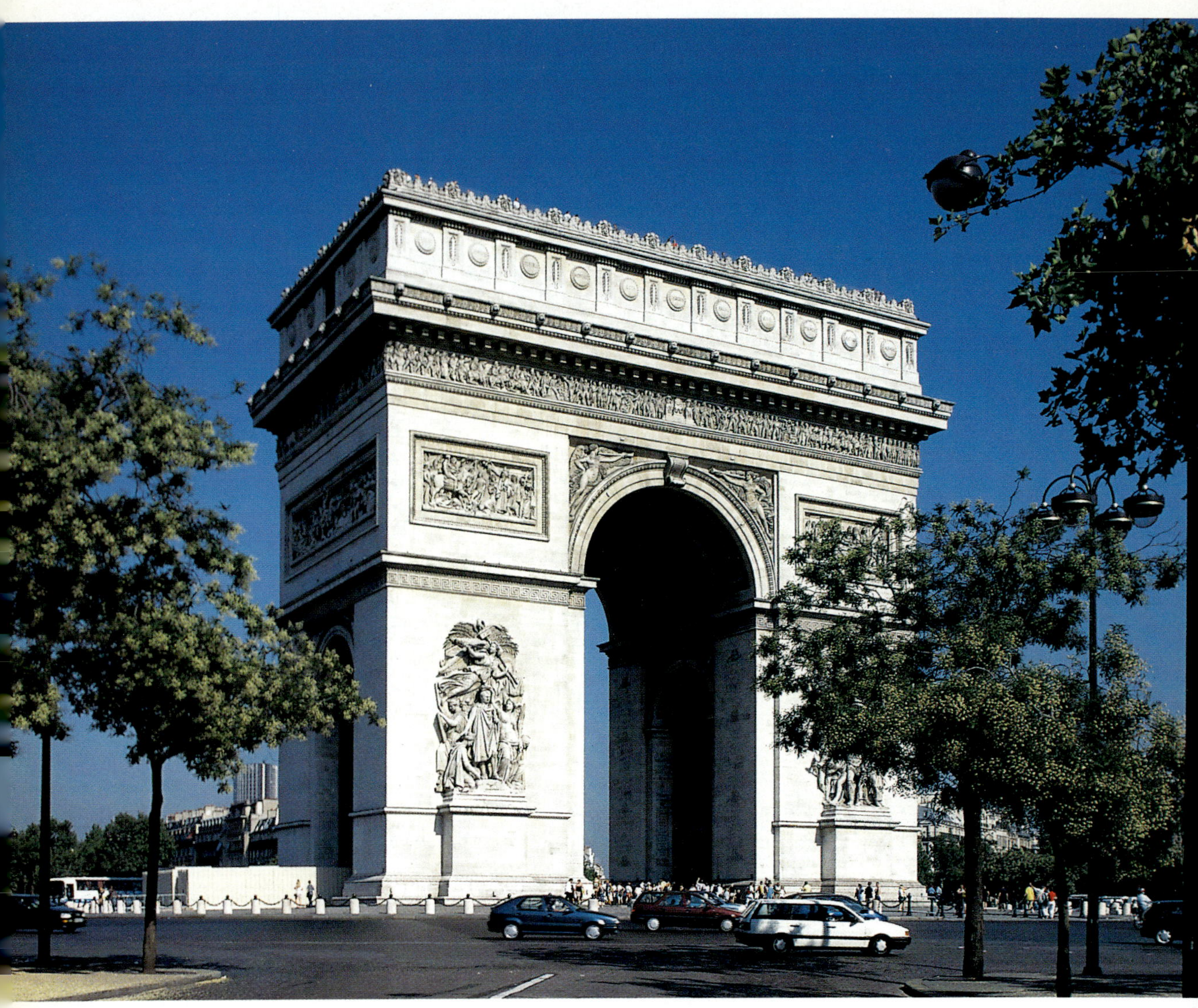

wars, the Champs-Élysées became the avenue we know today, a showcase of consumerism and luxury, with its many boutiques, shopping arcades, designer showrooms, banks, brasseries and cinemas. Today, the avenue has been extended into the Avenue de la Grande-Armée and Avenue Charles-de-Gaulle and is part of the impressive view which begins at the Arc du Carrousel and stretches 7 km to the Arche de la Défense. In 1994, the local council gave the avenue new street furniture and prohibited on-road park-ing, to restore some of its former glory and make walking along its pavements a pleasure again.

The military parade for the 14 July bank holiday is tra-ditionally held here. For the past few years, the Champs-Élysées has been used by cyclists for the last stage of the Tour de France. The avenue has also been used for some more unusual events, such as in 1990 when it was trans-formed in just a few hours, into a vast field of ripe wheat harvested by farmers

Arc de Triomphe

The Place Charles-de-Gaulle was formerly known as the Place de l'Etoile (Star Square) because of the thirteen avenues which radiate out from its centre. Situated at the top of the Roule hill which was lowered five metres by the architect Gabriel in 1774, it was transformed into the Place we see today by Haussmann in the 19th century. As early

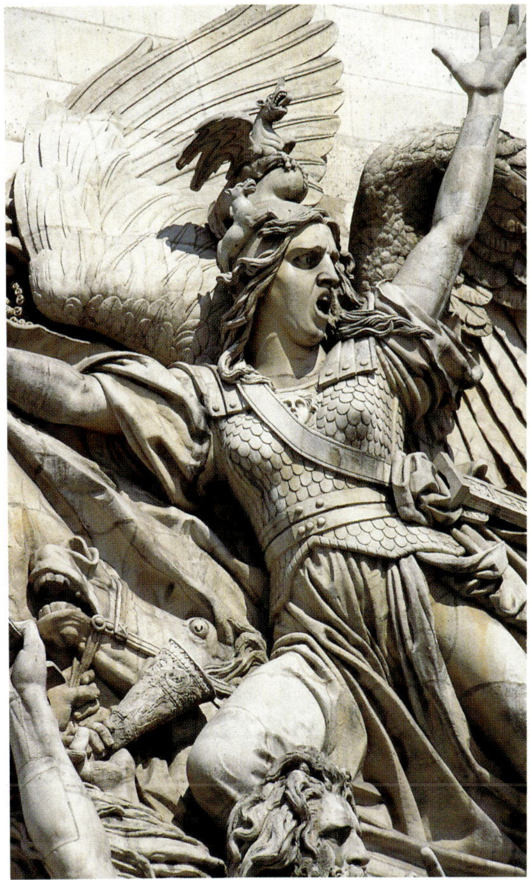

Along with the Eiffel Tower, the Arc de Triomphe is the most famous monument in Paris and a national symbol (far left). **The most famous of the bas reliefs on the façade of the Arc de Triomphe, sculpted by Rude, represents the Marseillaise** (opposite). **The Champs-Élysées gardens are home to various fountains, theatres and celebrated restaurants** (bottom).

as the reign of Louis XV, there were plans to erect a monument on the site - firstly a fountain in the shape of an elephant and then an obelisk, two projects which were never carried out. Finally in 1806 after the victory of Austerlitz, Napoleon decided to erect a monumental arch under which the victorious French army would march. Chalgrin was chosen for the project. The construction of this magnificent edifice - measuring an impressive 45 m wide, 50 m high and 29 m beneath its central arch - was interrupted during the Restoration but completed under the reign of Louis-Philippe. The groups of statues and high reliefs which decorate the arch commemorate the great feats of the Revolution and Empire. Among the most famous are *The Departure of the Volunteers in 1792*, still called *The Marseillaise,* sculpted by Rude and the *Triumph of 1810* by Cortot. In addition, the names of 128 of the most glorious feats of arms of the Republic and Empire are engraved on its walls, along with the names of 660 Generals, the heros of these victorious battles.

In 1921, the remains of an unknown soldier - chosen from among the unidentified remains of soldiers killed during the 1914-1918 War - were laid to rest under its arches and are now watched over by an eternal flame (the flame of Memory).

The Arc de Triomphe is one of the most visited monuments in France and its terrace offers one of the most spectacular views of Paris. It has also been the scene of some unusual exploits. In the 1980s, the Black Baron hit the headlines by flying through the arch in a small tourist plane, in defiance of danger… and the law!

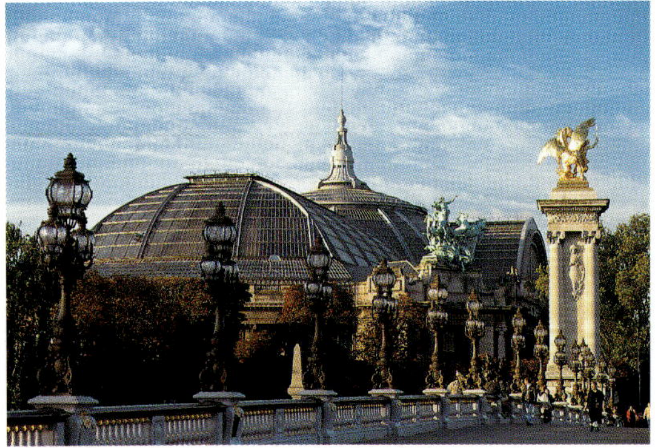

The bronze lamp posts which light up the Pont Alexandre III
are decorated with cupids and sea creatures.
At the top of the pillar is a statue representing Fame
of the Sciences. In the background is the glass roof
of the Grand Palais (above).
The many houseboats moored along the quays
of the Seine are privately owned and rarely leave
their mooring sites (right).

Grand Palais and Petit Palais

Like the nearby Pont Alexandre-III, the Grand Palais
and Petit Palais were built for the Universal Exhibition of
1900, on the site of the Palais de l'Industrie constructed for
the Exhibition of 1855. The colonnades, friezes, sculptures,
monumental porch and dome of the Grand Palais are all
illustrations of Art Nouveau, which appeared at the beginning of the century. The architect responsible for the two
buildings, Girault, combined a variety of new techniques
- metallic frames and structures supporting glass windows
- with a theatrical decoration composed of curves and arches
and façades made of stone. The buildings are a reflec-
tion of the spirit of the Belle Epoque, a confidence in the
future born of the many advances of the new industrial age.
The Grand Palais hosted the 1906 Autumn Salon dedicated
to Gaugin and the Salon of 1907, devoted to Cézanne.

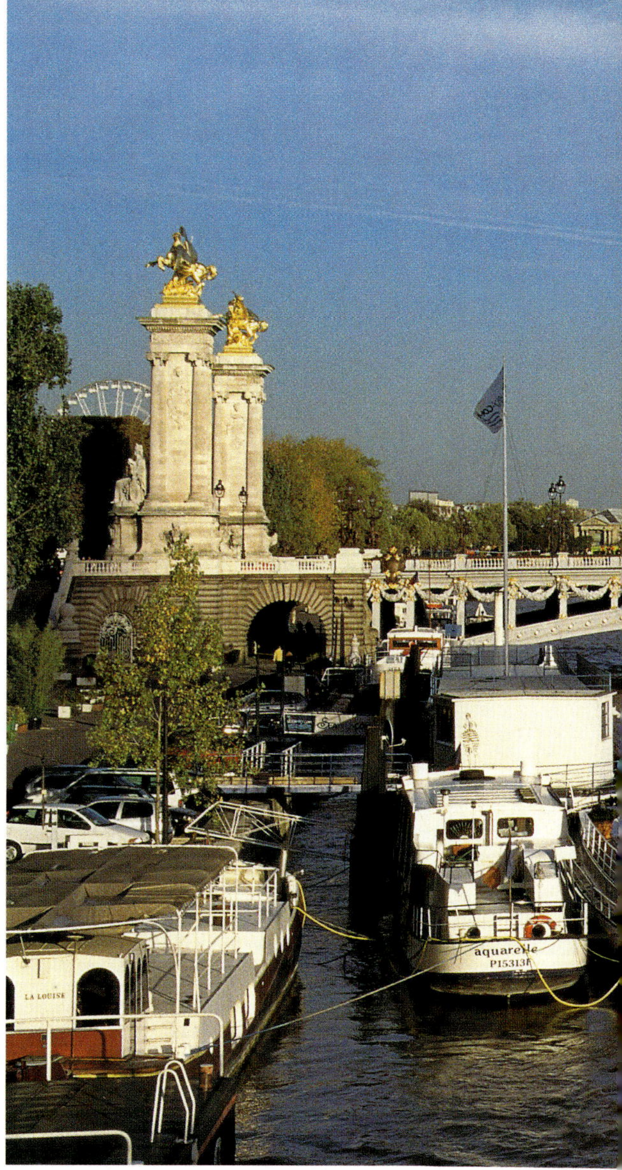

Restored in 1998, the Grand Palais is now a venue for
major exhibitions. The Petit Palais houses the impressive
art collection of the city of Paris, comprising French art from
the 19th century and an important collection of Egyptian,
Greek and Roman antiquities, bequeathed in 1902 by
the Dutuit brothers, two passionate art collectors. Since
1937, the wing opening onto the Avenue Franklin-Roosevelt
has been occupied by the Palais de la Découverte. Here,
visitors can take an interactive tour involving live experiments, to learn about astronomy, chemistry, physics, biol-
ogy and earth sciences.

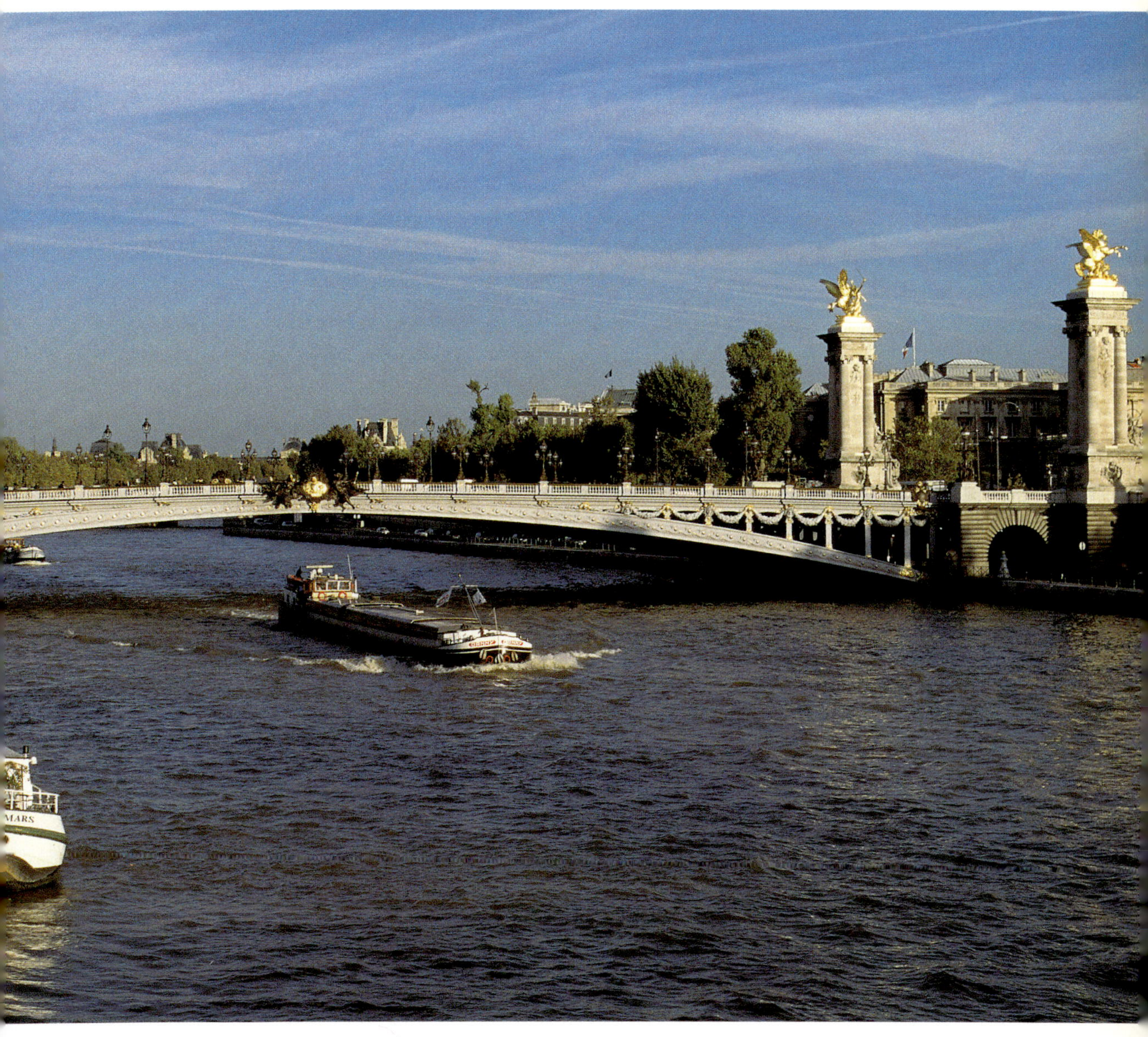

Pont Alexandre III

Between the Champs-Élysées and Esplanade des Invalides a single metallic arch measuring 107 m crosses the Seine - the Pont Alexandre-III. It was designed by the architects Résal and Alby and engineers from the establishment Schneider du Creusot. Instead of stone - the material traditionally used for artistic works - they used metal, reflecting the period's enthusiasm for modern techniques and materials, the symbols of the industrial age. Like the Grand Palais and Petit Palais, the Pont Alexandre-III was also built for the 1900 Universal Exhibition and stands out for its decoration: the statues were created by the sculptors Lenoir, Dalou and Frémiet and the street lamps are decorated with charming cupids, garlands and winged horses. On the right bank, two statues representing Medieval France and Contemporary France mark the entry to the bridge and on the left, Renaissance France and France of the Classical period.

To seal the Franco-Russian alliance signed in 1892, it was decided to name the bridge after the Russian Emperor. His son, Nicolas II laid the first stone on an official visit on 17 October, 1896.

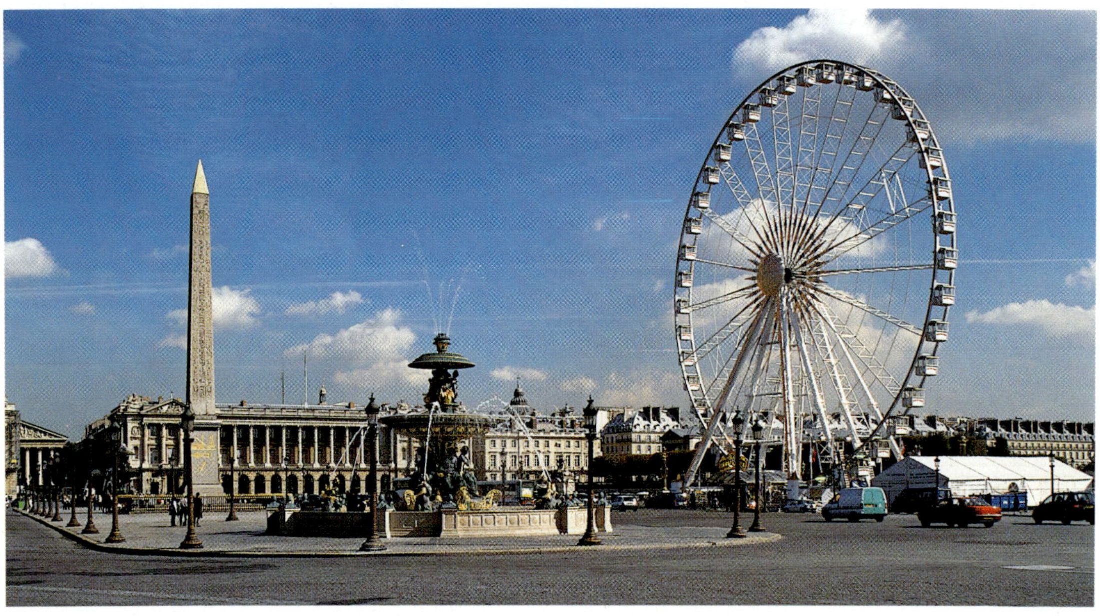

Erected for the year 2000 celebrations, the Big Wheel on the
Place de la Concorde now seems part of the landscape (top).
The two fountains which frame the obelisk are dedicated
to river navigation and sea navigation (right).

Place de la Concorde

A project to create a new royal square dedicated to
Louis XV was launched in 1748, after the city of Paris had
commissioned an equestrian statue of the King from the
sculptor Bouchardon. The architect Jacques Ange Gabriel
was charged with designing a vast square covering over
80,000 m² between the Champs-Élysées, the Seine and the
Tuileries Gardens, with buildings on only one side. In addition to the royal statue placed in the centre, the square has
statues by Pigalle representing the Virtues at each of its four
corners. The work took twenty years to complete, from
1755 to 1775. During this time, the King's popularity
declined and on the unveiling of the statue, a placard was
hung round the horse's neck with the slogan, "The Virtues
are on their knees and Vice on horseback". In 1792, the
statues were overturned by a crowd of rioters, then melted
down and replaced by a representation of Liberty. In October

the same year, the guillotine was erected on the square,
now renamed the Place de la Revolution. In two years,
1,343 people were executed here, including Louis XVI,
Marie-Antoinette, Danton, Madame Roland and Robespierre.
To erase the memory of this bloody episode in France's history, the Directory renamed the square the Place de la
Concorde. The square was redeveloped under Louis-Philippe
in 1836 by the architect Hittorff, who remained faithful
to Gabriel's original design. The obelisk from the Temple
of Ramses II at Luxor was erected at its centre, a gift from
the Sultan of Egypt, Mehemet-Ali in 1831. Two fountains
were built on each side, inspired by those on Saint Peter's
Square in Rome. Standing on the eight pedestals at the
corners of the square are statues respresenting the major
towns of France - Lyons, Marseilles, Bordeaux, Nantes, Brest,
Rouen, Lille and Strasbourg.

From the Place de la Concorde looking towards the
Champs-Élysées, one can see the Horses of Marly by Coustou
(in 1984, copies replaced the originals which are now housed
in the Louvre) while towards the Tuileries and Louvre, one
can see the Winged Horses by Coysevox. On the north side
of the square are the two pavilions fronted by Corinthian
columns designed by Gabriel, which are now occupied by
the Ministry of the Navy and the Hôtel Crillon.

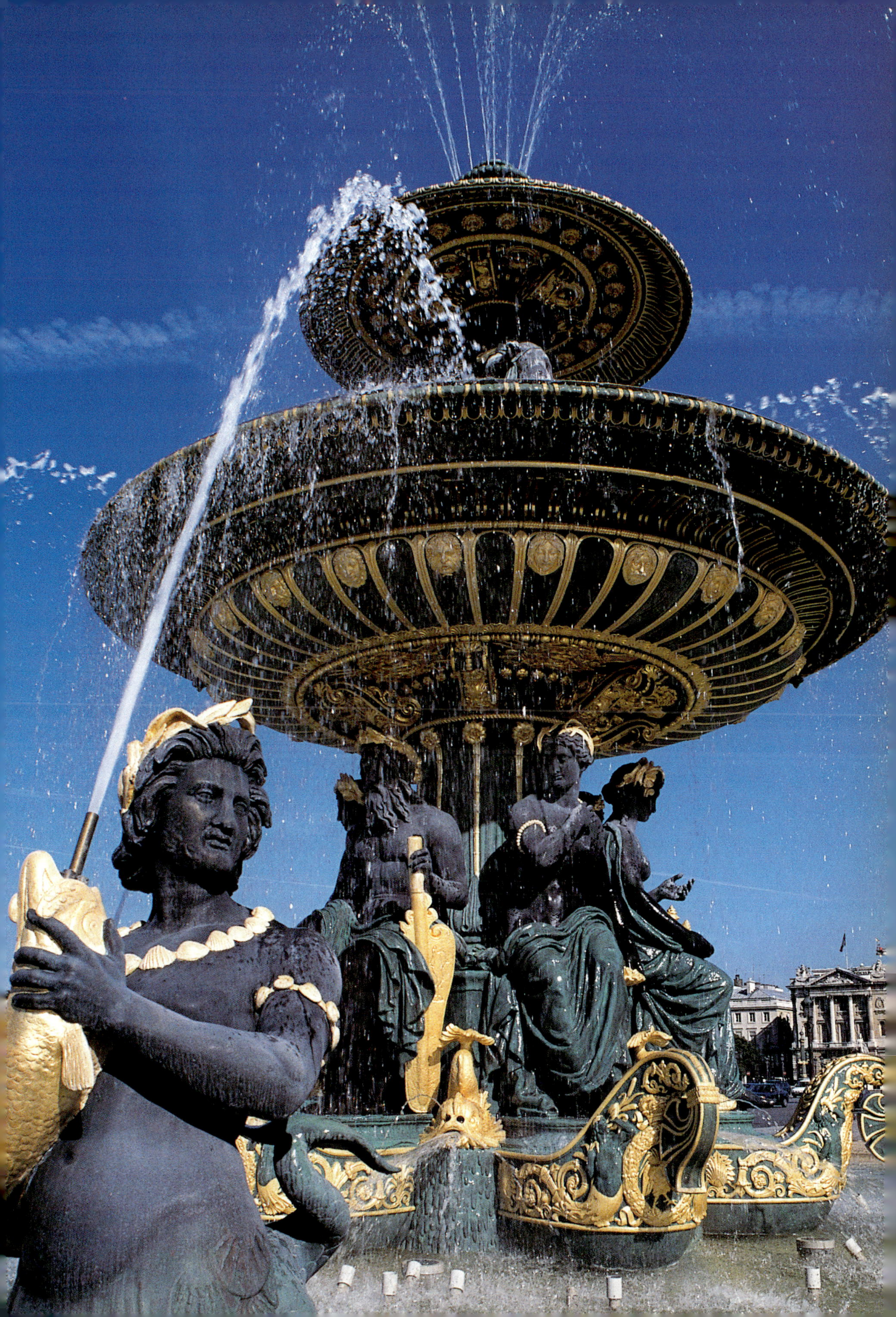

Monument

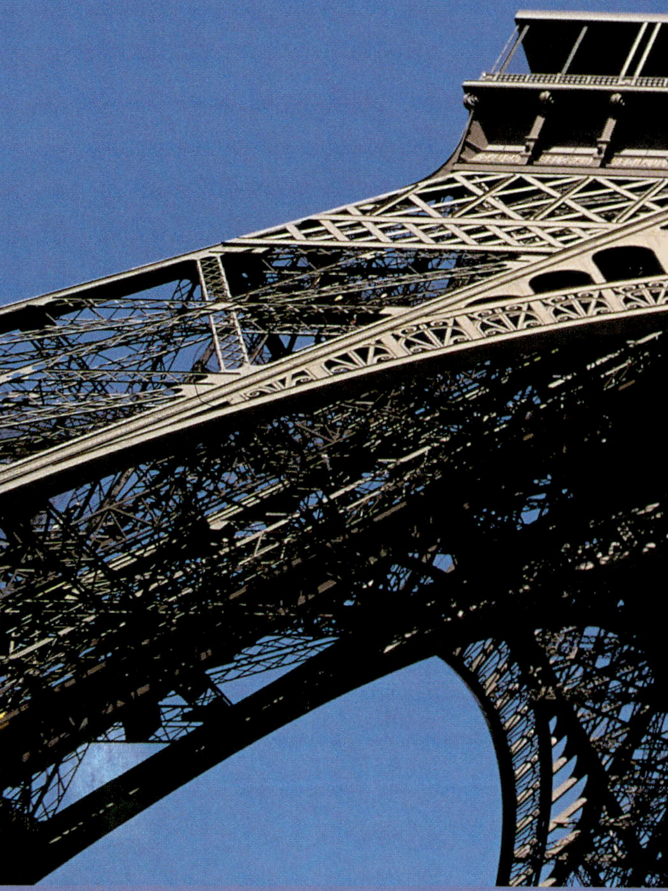

7th and 16th arrondissements

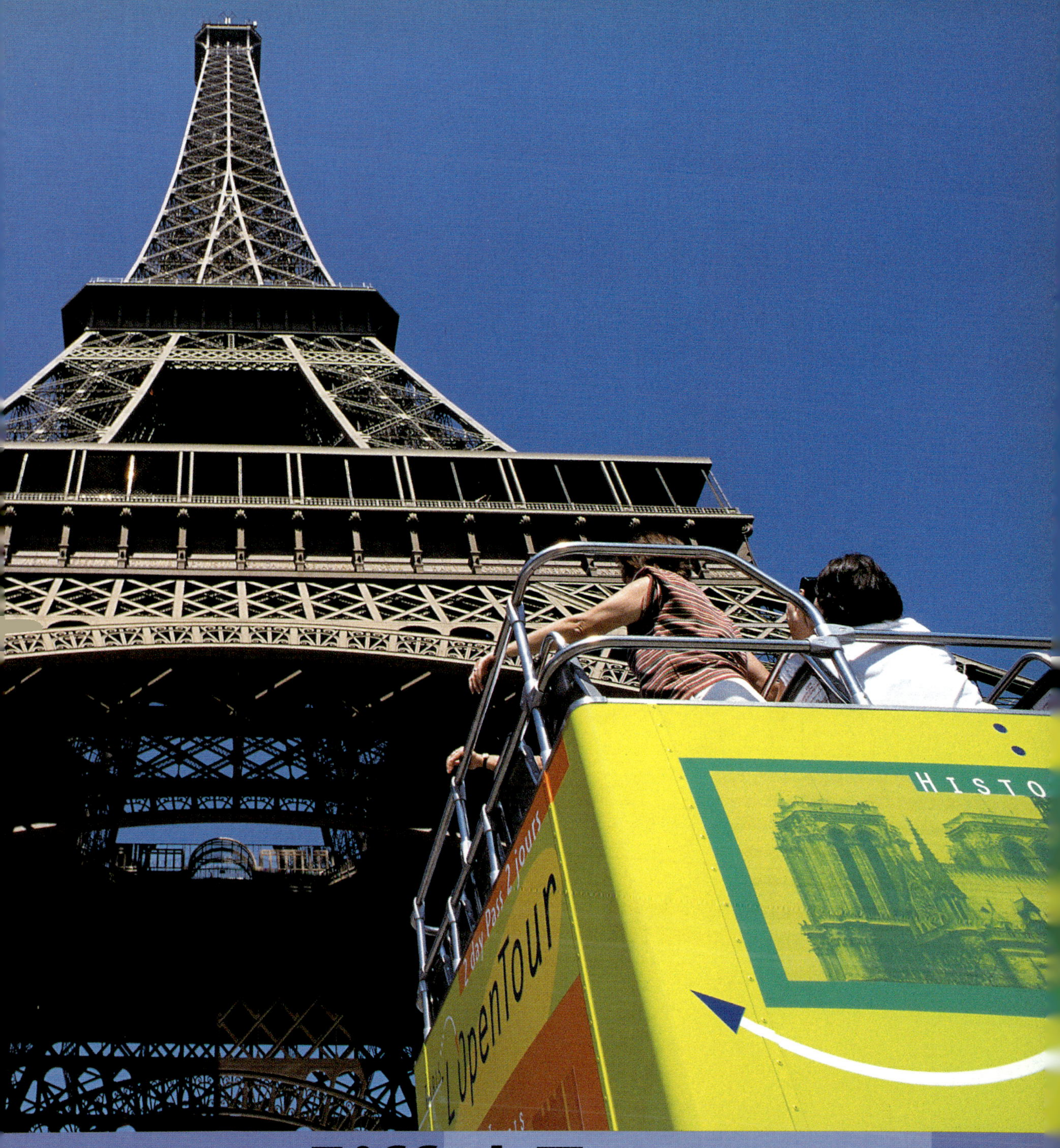

Eiffel Tower

Eiffel Tower
Palais de Chaillot
Palais de Tokyo
Champ-de-Mars
École militaire

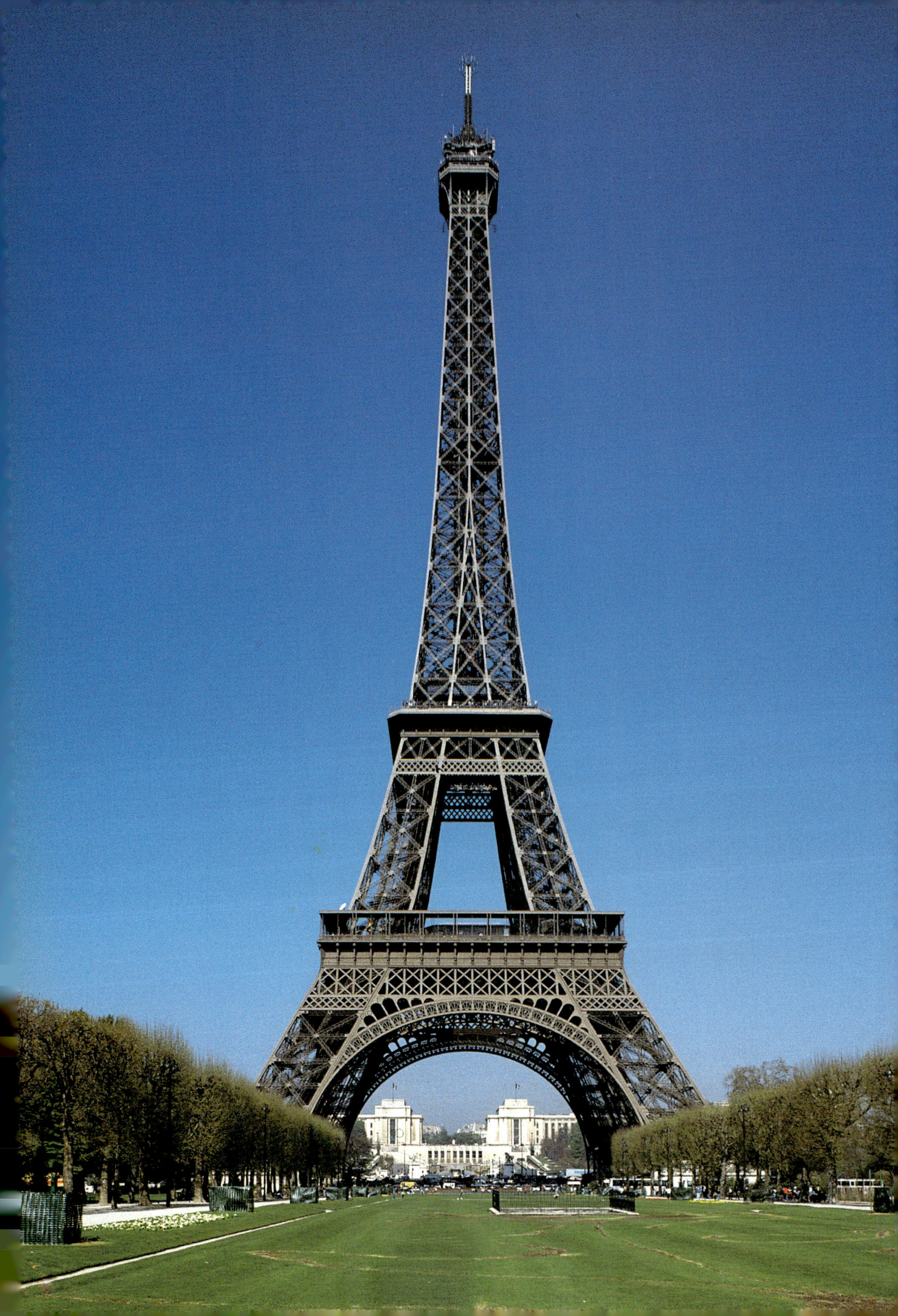

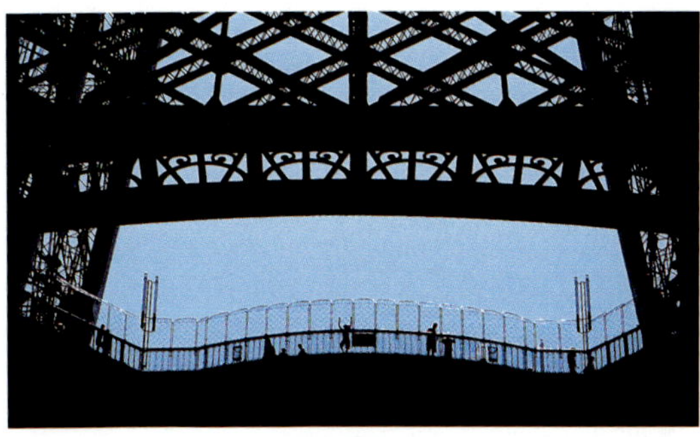

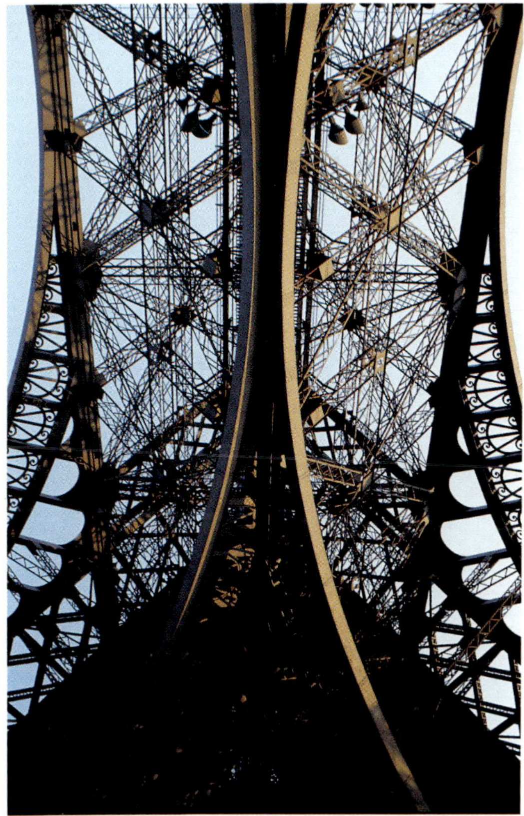

Certainly one of the most photographed monuments in the world, the Eiffel Tower is here seen from the Champ-de-Mars, with the Trocadéro behind (left).
The tower's three floors are open to the public: the first stands at 57 m, the second at 115 m and the third at 274 m. From the top floor and in good weather, you can see up to 90 km in all directions (above).

Eiffel Tower

The tower built by Gustave Eiffel for the 1889 Universal Exhibition has become the world famous emblem of the capital of France. At the time however, it was the subject of great controversy. Many artists, including Maupassant, Gounod and Leconte de Lisle signed a petition against its construction while the writer Huysmans called it the "hollow candlestick." Later however, it became the inspiration of painters like Dufy, Pisarro, Utrillo and Delaunay and other writers such as Apollinaire and Jean Cocteau, who based a play on it, entitled *"Les Mariés de la tour Eiffel"*. In 1964, Roland Barthes wrote "It adds to the urban myth, so often sombre, a romantic dimension, a harmony and relief". But more recently, Julien Green declared in 1983, "I have wished the Eiffel Tower at the bottom of the sea a thousand times".

Its construction began in 1887 and involved 300 labourers, who in under two years were able to assemble its 18,000 metallic pieces with the help of no less than 2,500,000 rivets. Gustave Eiffel was the first to climb its 1,710 steps on 31 March, 1889, followed by the future King of England Edward VII on 5 November of the same year. The Tower, which should have been demolished after twenty years was preserved for reasons which have nothing to do with its aesthetic qualities. From its summit on 5 November, Ducretet carried out the first radioelectric link and in 1918, it was here that the first wireless transoceanic communication was established. More recently in 1957, a television antenna was installed on the top. Its three floors and summit, at a height of 320 m, offer visitors a spectacular panoramic view of Paris and its surrounding area.

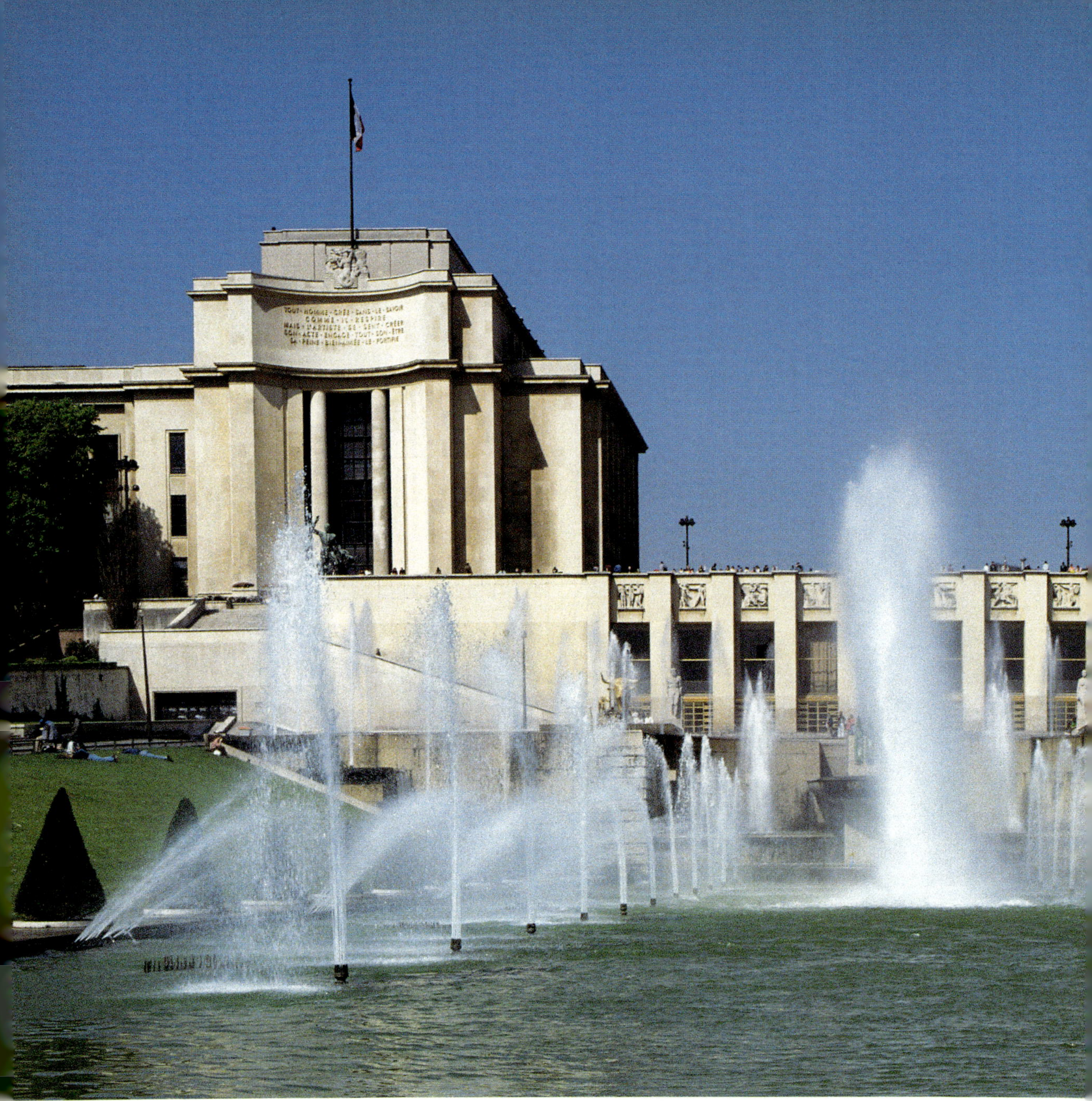

Palais de Chaillot

Overlooking gardens covering 10 hectares is the Palais de Chaillot which was built for the International Exhibition of Arts and Techniques in 1937. This was to replace the Palais du Trocadéro constructed by Davioud and Bourdais for the Exhibition in 1878. The Palais is the work of the architects Boileau, Azéma and Carlu, whose project was chosen over that of Auguste Perret and Le Corbusier. It comprises two curved wings, each flanked by a pavilion, which frame a terrace. Lower down is a spectacular stretch of water containing a number of fountains. The intentionally restrained style of the buildings emphasises the statuary of the front square and terrace. The square, a traditional spot for Human Rights demonstrations and other major humanitarian causes is also a meeting place for skateboarders and rollerbladers. The statues along the sweeping, elegant square, contrast with the statue groups of *Apollo* by Bouchard and *Hercules* by Pommier located

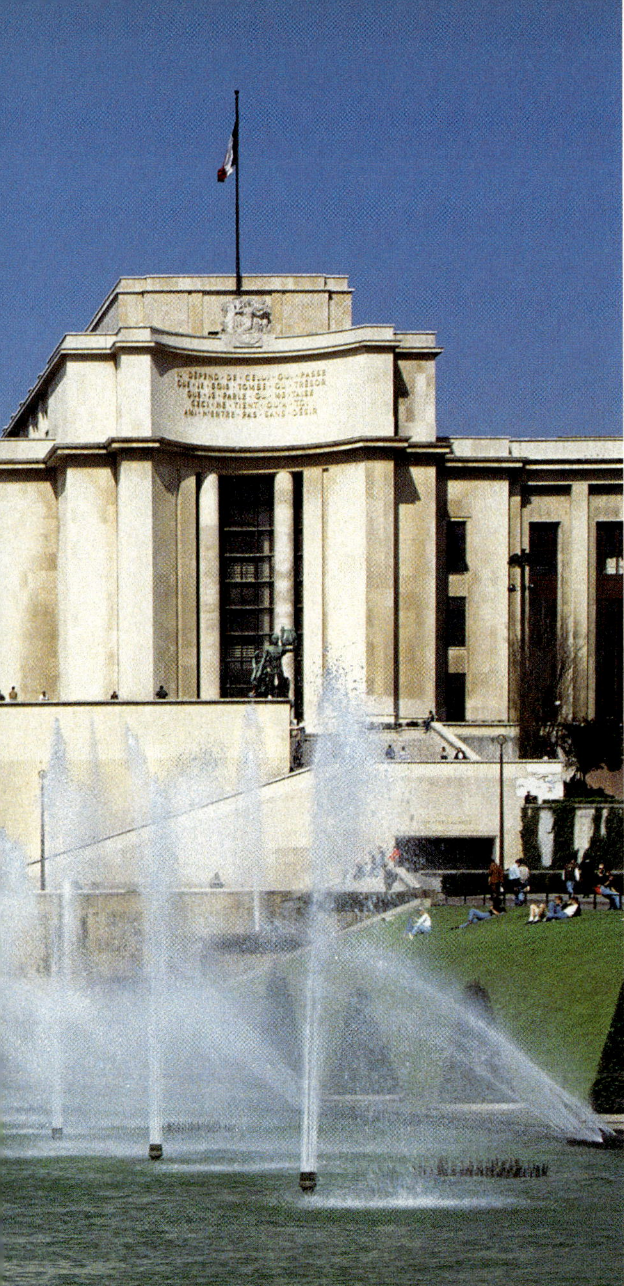

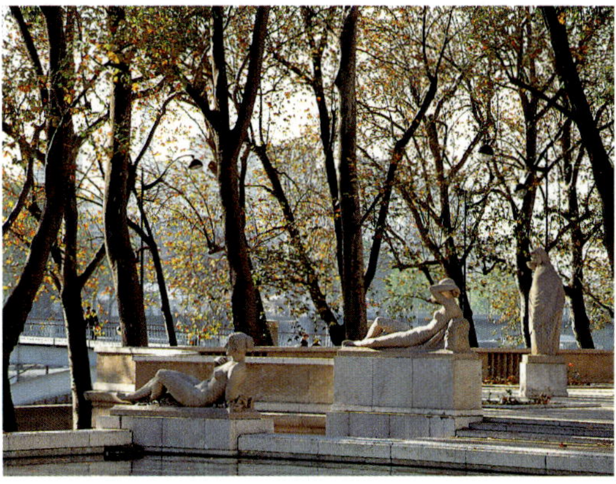

The large basin stretching out below the Palais de Chaillot comes alive with fountains in fine weather. It provides a soft contrast to the colossal, monumental feel of the palace (left). The courtyard of the Palais de Tokyo is also an exhibition area. Lying sculptures by Drivier, Dejean and Guénot surround the central water feature (above).

Palais de Tokyo

The Palais de Tokyo was constructed for the International Exhibition of 1937 by the architects Dondel, Aubert, Viard and Dastugue, whose project was adopted in preference to that proposed by Le Corbusier and Mallet-Stephens. The entire architectural design is based on the quest for light, with the majority of the rooms benefiting from zenithal lighting. Around a central patio, a portico composed of a colonnade links the two wings of the building which is home to the Musée d'Art Moderne de la Ville de Paris, the Musée National d'Art Moderne, the Centre National de la Photographie and the Fondation Européenne des Métiers de l'image et du son.

The Musée d'Art Moderne de la Ville de Paris, located in the east section of the Palais, presents an impressive, regularly updated panorama of the major art movements of the 20th century and contemporary art.

on the terrace. The Palais de Chaillot houses the Musée des Monuments Français, the Musée de l'Homme, Musée de la Marine, the Cinémathèque and the Musée du Cinéma. It is also occupied by the Théâtre National de Chaillot, formerly known as the Théâtre National Populaire created by Firmin Gémier in 1920. The latter, under the direction of Jean Vilar and with stars such as Gérard Philipe and Jeanne Moreau, became one of the top theatres in France, from 1951 to 1963.

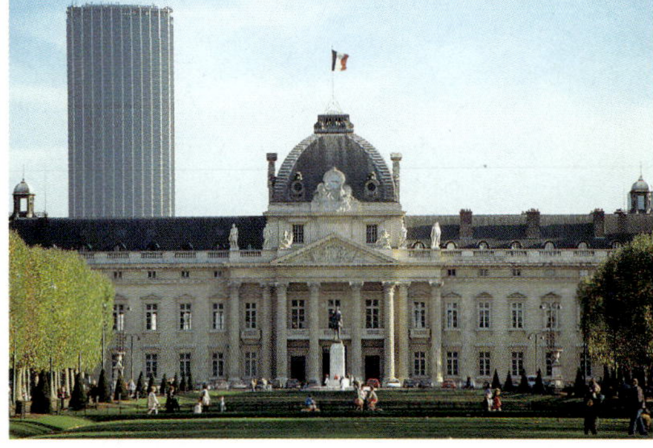

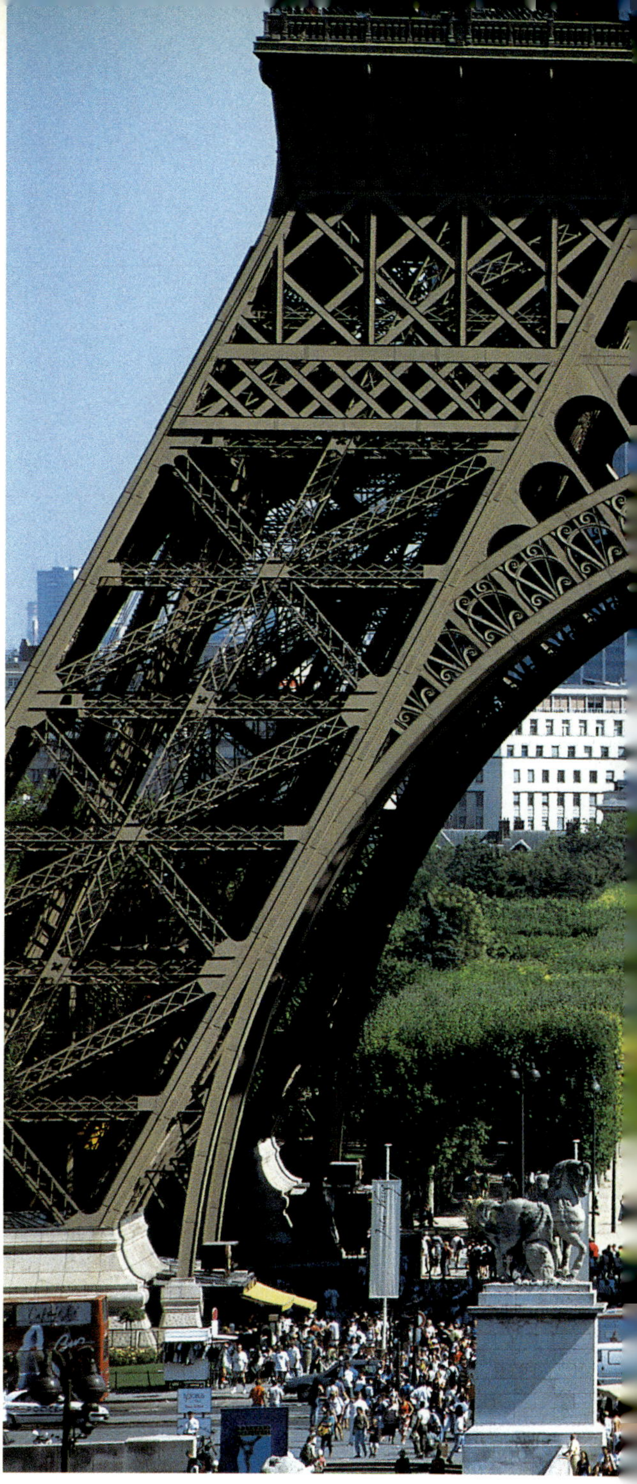

Champs-de-Mars

The Champ-de-Mars was originally designed as a parade ground for students at the Ecole Militaire. It hosted the first horse race in 1780 and was later the scene of major events during the Revolutionary period, including Federation Day on 14 July 1790 and the Day of The Supreme Being on 8 June 1794. The monument to Human Rights by Teimer, built in 1989, recalls these events.

At the end of the 19th century, the Champ-de-Mars hosted the Universal Exhibitions of 1867, 1878, 1889 and 1900. A big wheel also stood here until 1937. Today, it is a vast park and one of the most popular in the capital. Here, you can admire one of the most exceptional trees in Paris, a "February" from America.

École Militaire

This institution was created by Louis XV in 1751, on the request of Madame de Pompadour, to receive five hundred young nobles with no fortune, wishing to pursue a military career. Construction of the Ecole Militaire then began, following the plans of the architect Jacques Ange Gabriel but had to be stopped during the Seven Years War due to lack of funds. Building work restarted in 1768 and continued until 1773, following the architect's revised plans. Bonaparte, who had spent a year at the school as a cadet, set up his headquarters here in 1795. This vast building stands at the southern end of the Champ-de-Mars. It comprises two wings framing a pavilion topped by a quadrangular dome and a pediment supported by Corinthian columns. The Neo-classical façade is identical on the side of the main courtyard. The two lower wings, designed

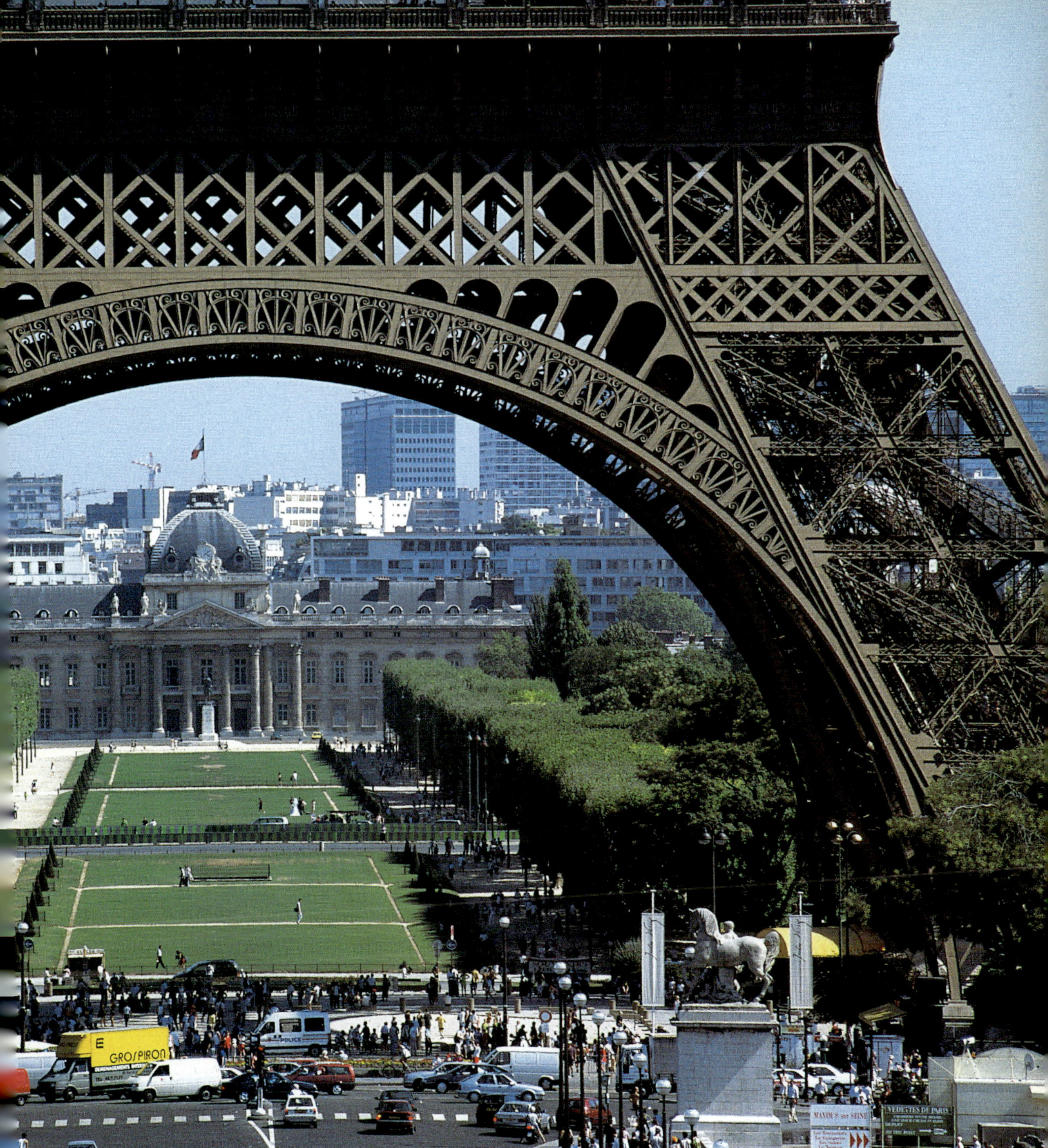

by Brongniart and situated on either side of the central building were added later under the Second Empire. Today, the Ecole Militaire houses various military establishments - the Institut des Hautes Etudes de Défense Nationale et d'Economie de Guerre, the École supérieure de guerre and the École Supérieure de l'Intendance.

Behind the beautiful façade of the Ecole Militaire stands the imposing 200 m high Tour Montparnasse (top left). Covering 21 hectares, the Champ-de-Mars offers a beautiful green space between the Eiffel Tower and Ecole Militaire (above).

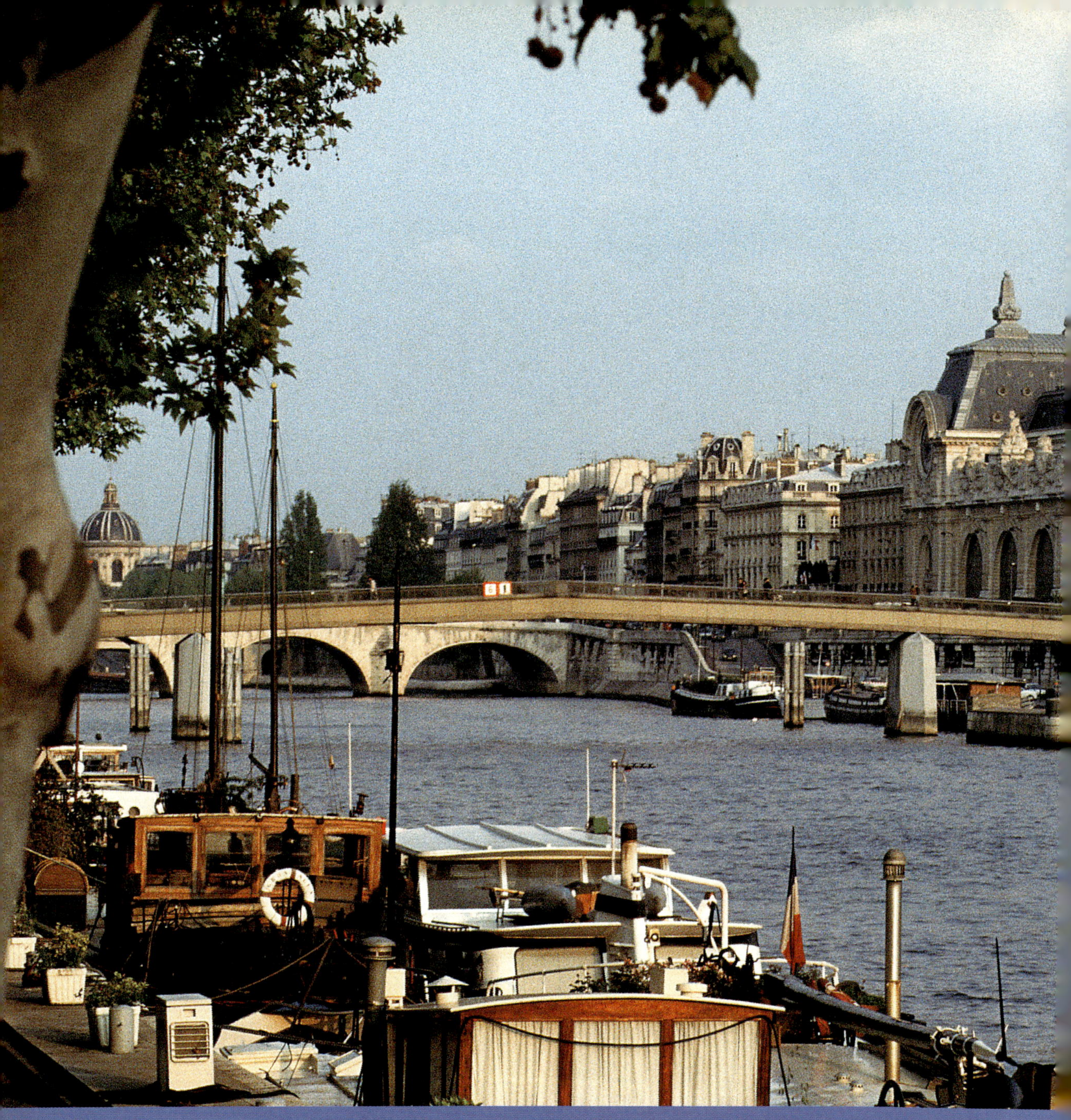

City life

7TH arrondissement

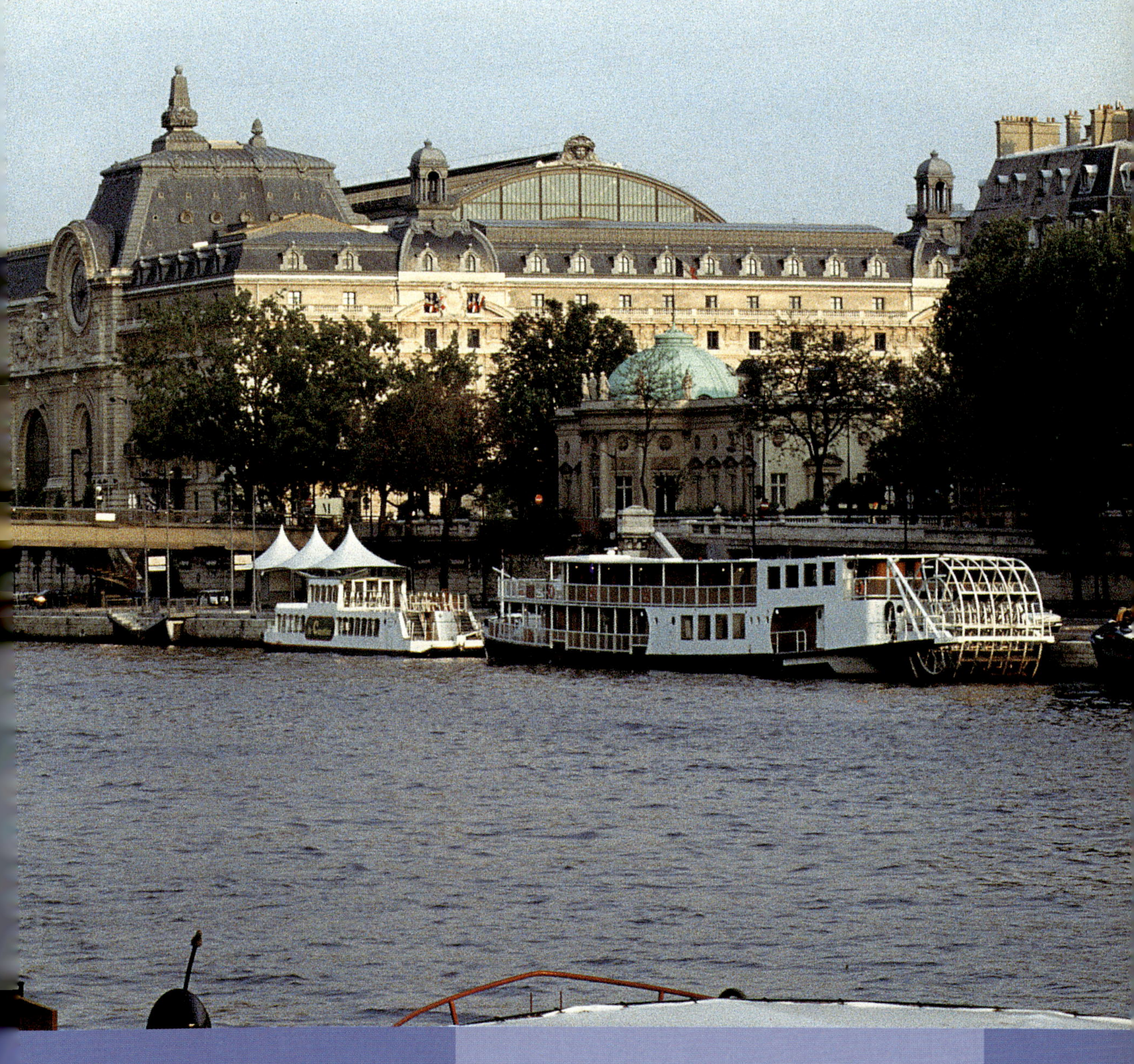

Invalides – Orsay

Les Invalides
The Rodin Museum
The Musée d'Orsay

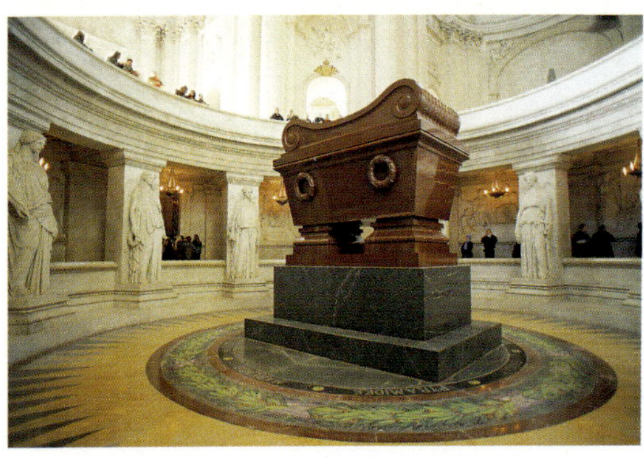

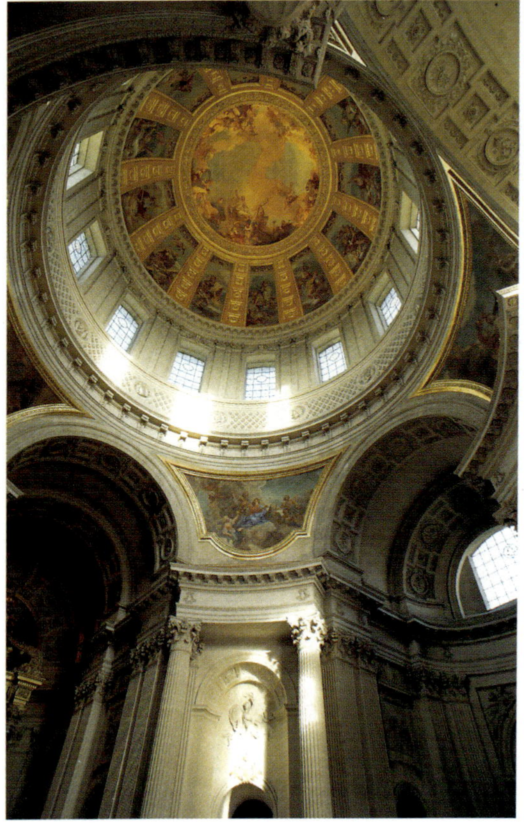

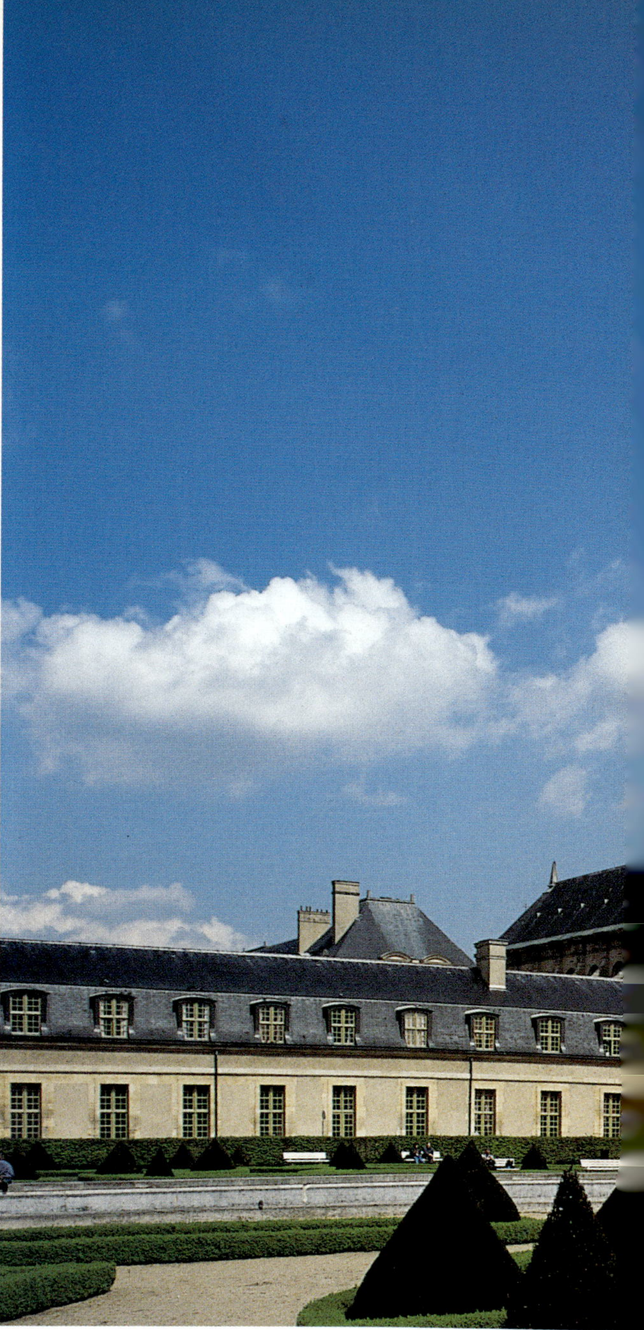

Through a circular opening under the Invalides dome, the crypt containing the tomb of Napoleon I is visible (top left). At the centre of the cupola is a composition representing Saint Louis handing his sword to Jesus Christ. Above the windows are the Apostles (above left).

Since its completion in 1706, the Invalides dome has been re-gilded no less than 4 times: in 1807 under the reign of Napoleon I, in 1869 under Napoleon III, in 1937 for the Universal Exhibition and recently in 1989 for the Bicentenary of the French Revolution (right).

Les Invalides

In 1671, Louis XIV decided to erect a public building to house crippled war veterans who until then had been reduced to living on the streets and begging. Located on the Pré-aux-Clercs, it would be home to around 6,000 invalids. Under the authority of Louvois, Secretary of State for War, the architect responsible for the Hôpital de la Salpêtrière, Libéral Bruant, was put in charge of the project. Jules Hardouin-Mansart then completed the edifice and its two churches:

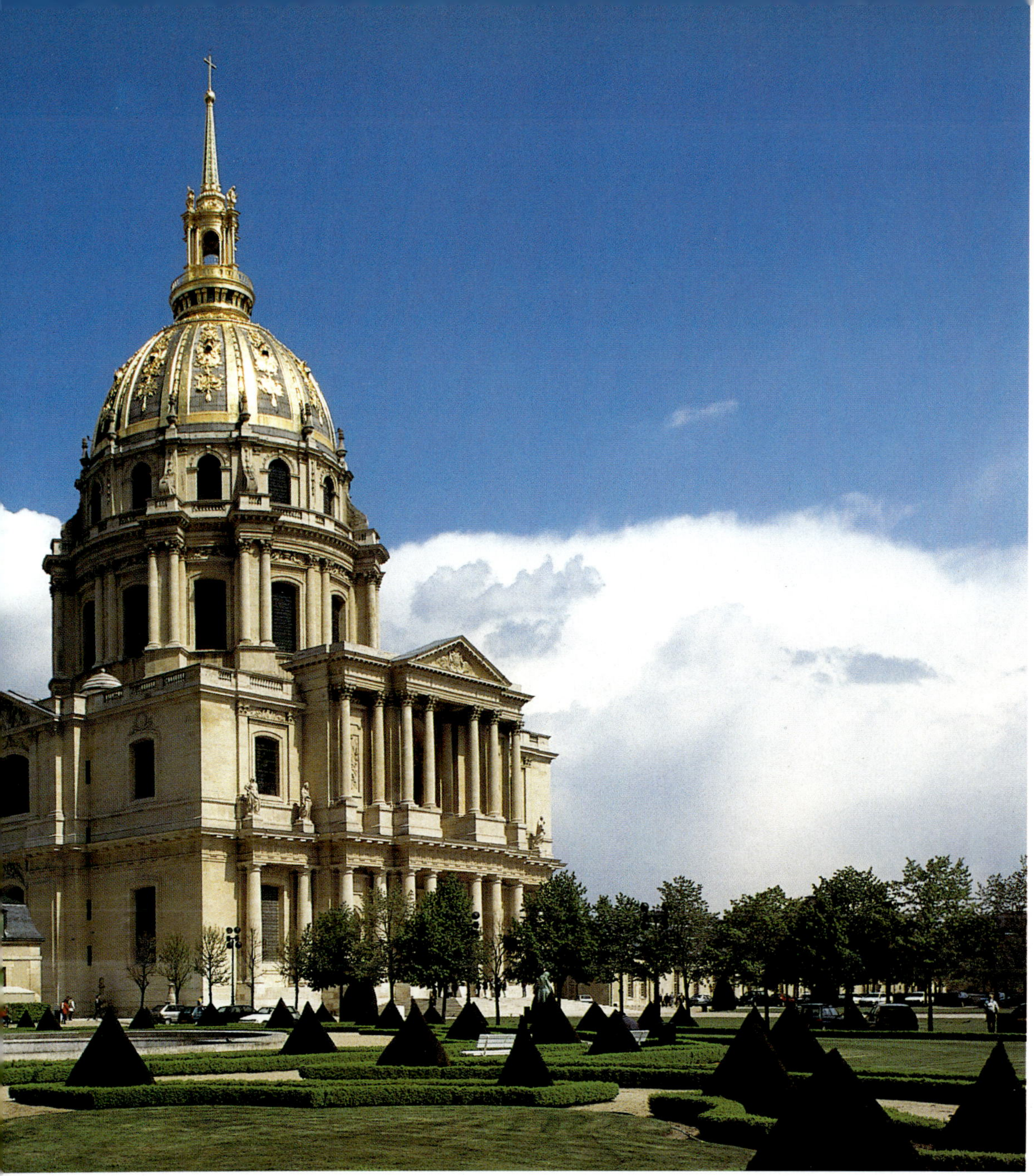

the elongated Saint-Louis church finished in 1677 and open to soldiers and the Dome church inaugurated in 1706 which was exclusively for the King and Court and designed to serve as the Mausoleum of the Bourbons

The façade of the edifice is separated from the esplanade by a trench lined with old cannons and the main building itself comprises three floors of windows, surmounted by a mezzanine and a row of decorated dormer windows. The entrance is a semicircular gateway, surmounted by an eques-trian statue of Louis XIV, surrounded by allegories of Justice and Prudence. This leads to the main courtyard, bordered by buildings which are striking for their pure, simple lines.

The dining halls were located in the left and right wings and the central pavilion was used for administrative pur-poses. The veteran soldiers were housed in five or six bed dormitories and had access to an infirmary and workshops where they could weave, make pottery or work on the illu-mination of manuscripts. It was not long before the sur-

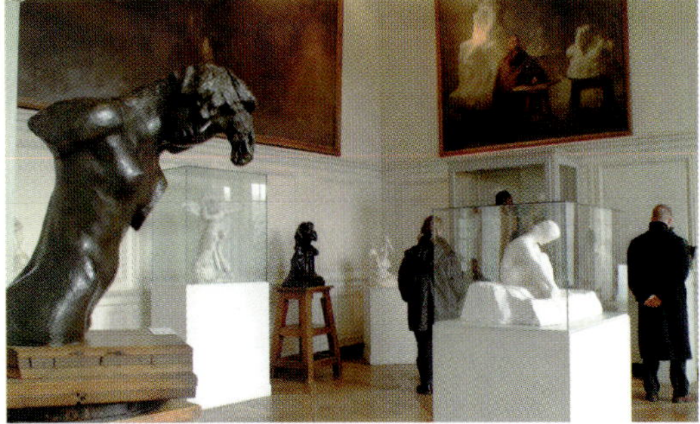

The different rooms in the Rodin Museum exhibit numerous works by the artist along with all his studies and sketches for his monumental sculptures (above).
Located on the corner of Rue Varenne and Boulevard des Invalides, the gardens of the Rodin Museum are the largest in the Saint-Germain district after those of the Hôtel Matignon (right).

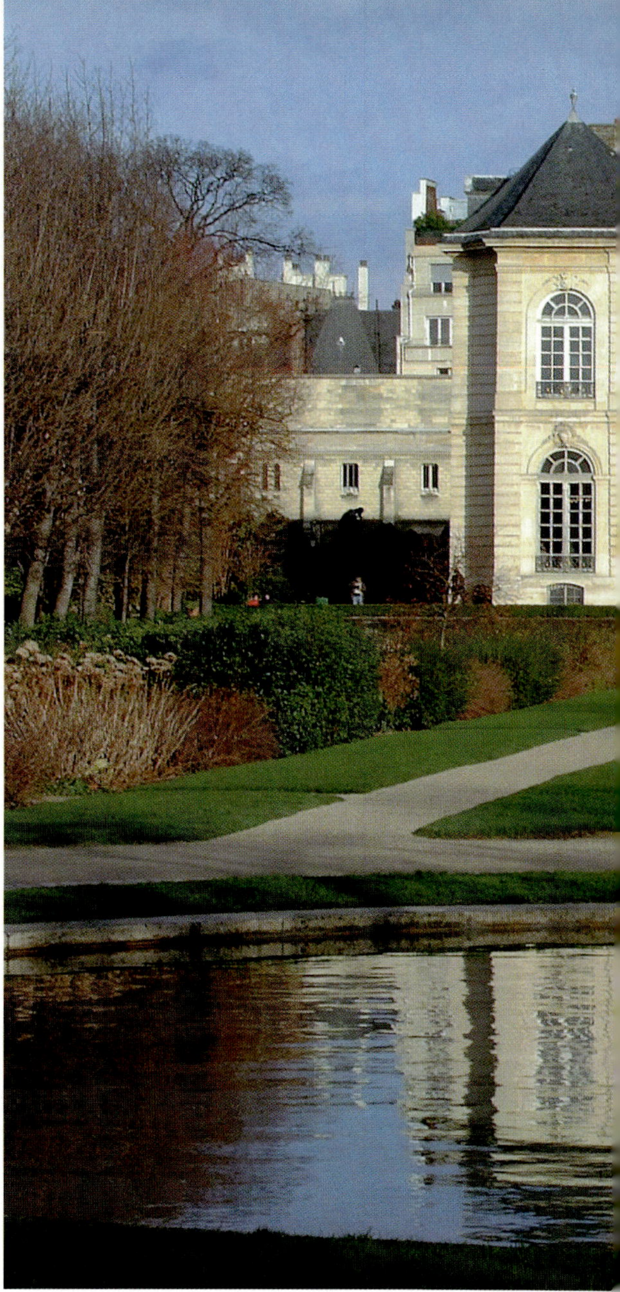

geons at Les Invalides acquired a high reputation. Other scholars, including Parmentier in the 18th century, worked here in their laboratories.

At the back of the courtyard is the façade of the Saint-Louis church, located on the axis of the gateway. Inside, the white stones of the nave highlight the flags seized from enemy troops which now hang from the vaults. This is where the rebels came on 14 July 1789, to get hold of some 20,000 guns and 24 cannon parts which were used for the storming of the Bastille.

The Dome church, built in line with the extension of the Saint-Louis church, follows the classical design of a Greek cross placed inside a square. It is surmounted by a cupola - the famous Invalides dome - which in reality is two cupolas overlapped in such a way as to achieve maximum illumination. The interior decoration was carried out by the painters Charles de La Fosse and Jouvenet and the sculptors Coysevox and Coustou. The six circular chapels house the tombs of some great French military leaders including Turenne, Maréchal Lyautey and Maréchal Foch, two of Napoleon's brothers, Joseph and Jérôme Bonaparte and a cenotaph dedicated to Vauban. Since 2 April 1861, the crypt also houses Napoleon's tomb. Created by Visconti from Finnish red porphyry, it contains the ashes of the Emperor which were brought back from Saint Helena in 1840. In 1989, the Dome was restored and covered in 550,000 gold leaves and today is one of the city's most famous monuments.

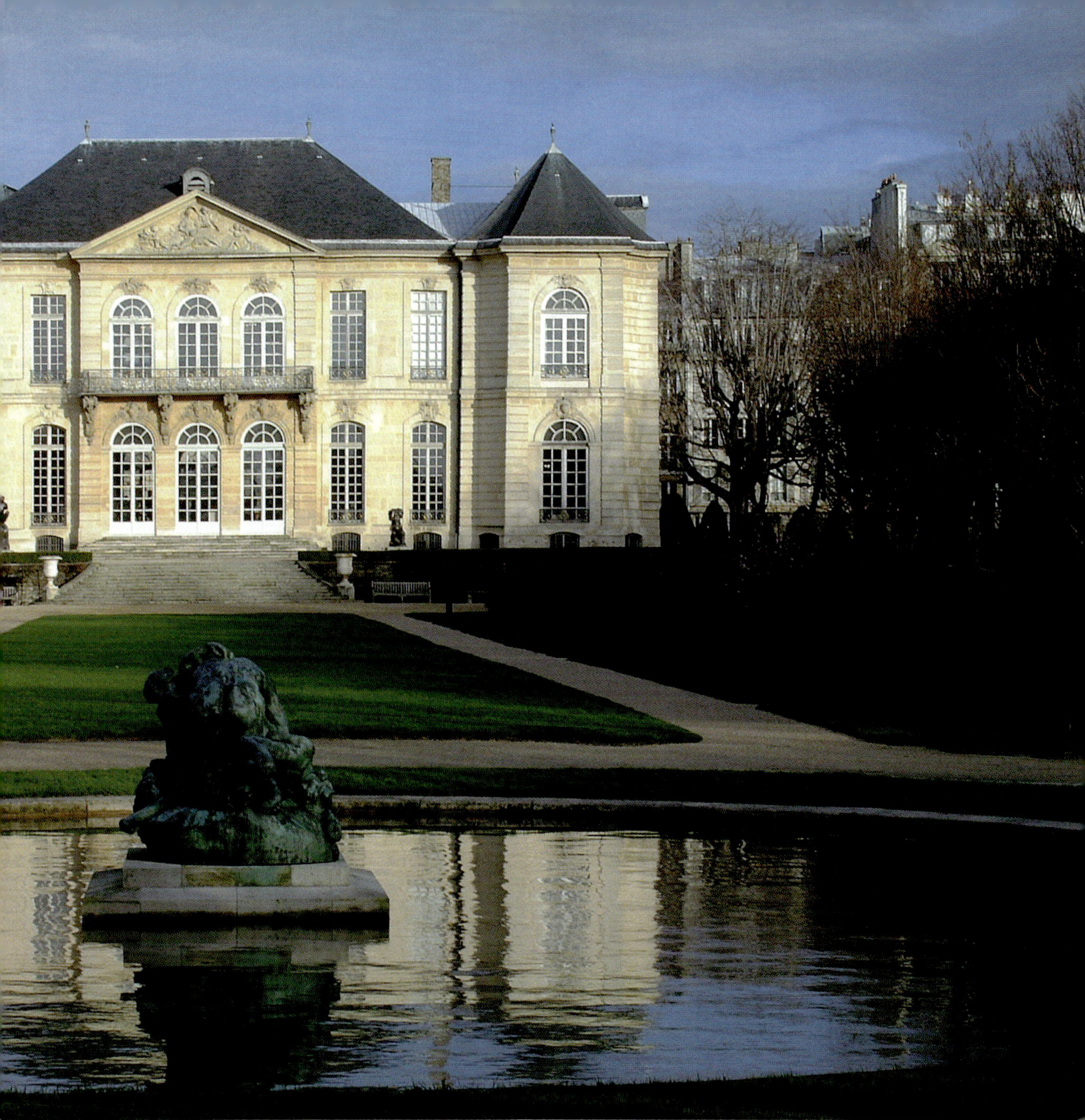

Although only a few dozen people now live in the building, it also houses a famous surgical hospital and various military museums - the Musée de L'Armée, Musée de l'Ordre de la Libération and the Musée des Plans-Reliefs.

Rodin Museum

The Rodin Museum occupies the former Hôtel Biron built between 1728 and 1730 by the architect Aubert for the financier Abraham Peyrenc de Moras. With its refined, elegant style, it is a perfect example of an 18th century private mansion and various architectural elements from châteaux of the same period can be found in its vast grounds. In 1820 it was sold to the religious community of the Dames du Sacré-Cœur who lived there until 1904, when it became State property. Its most famous resident is most certainly Auguste Rodin who, on the advice of his friend Rainer Maria Rilke, set up his studios here in 1908. A year before his death in 1917, the sculptor

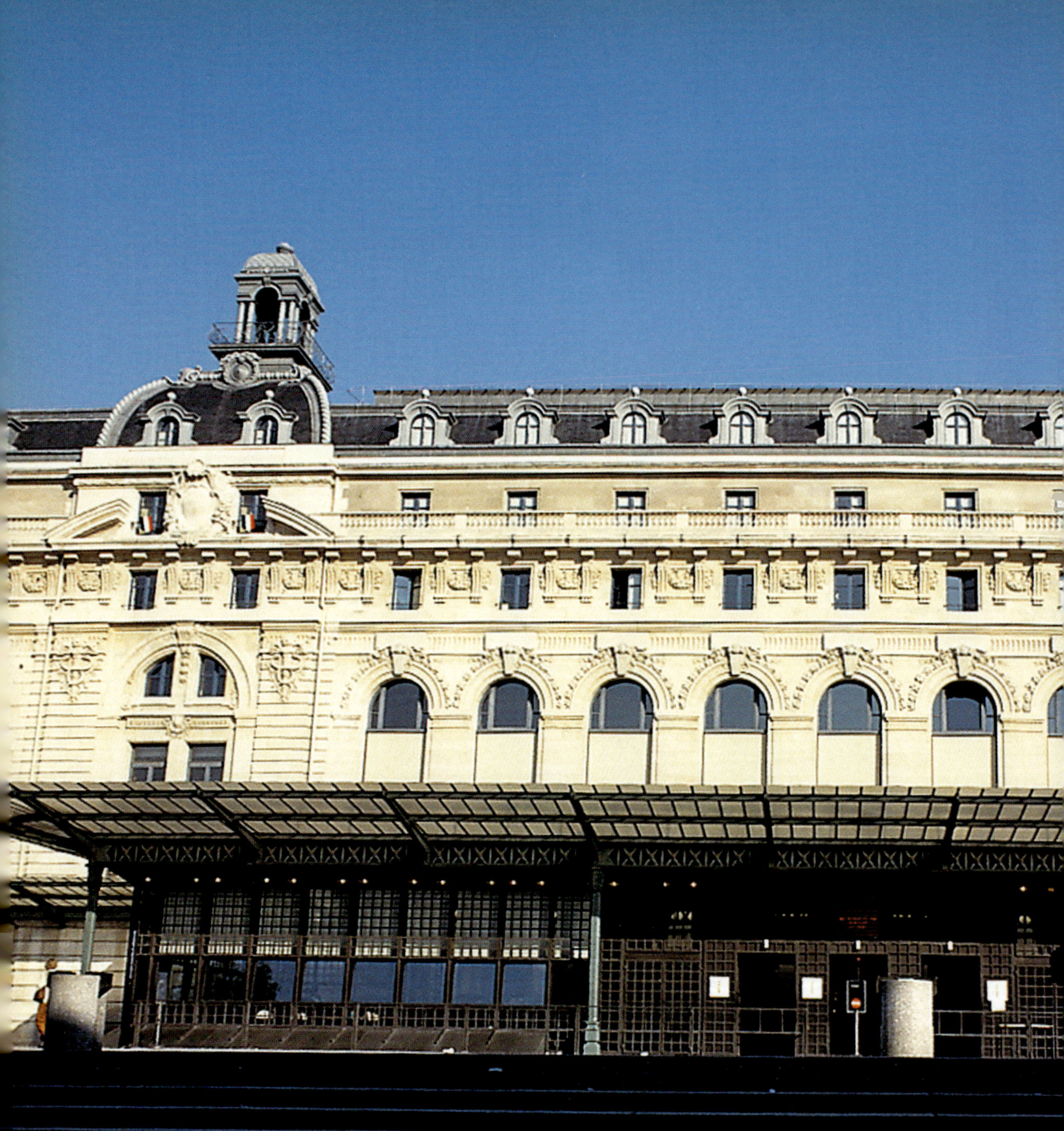

donated his entire works and collections to the State. In the main courtyard is a display of his monumental works including The Burgers of Calais, The Gates of Hell and The Thinker. The museum's seventeen rooms house an imposing collection of the artist's sculptures, with one room entirely devoted to Camille Claudel, his model, student and troubled companion.

Musée d'Orsay

In 1897, the Compagnie des Chemins de fer d'Orléans (Orleans Railway Company) bought some State land formerly occupied by a cavalry barracks and the Palais d'Orsay. The latter had once housed the Council of State and Audit Office which were burnt to the ground during the Commune (1870-1871). The architect Victor Laloux built

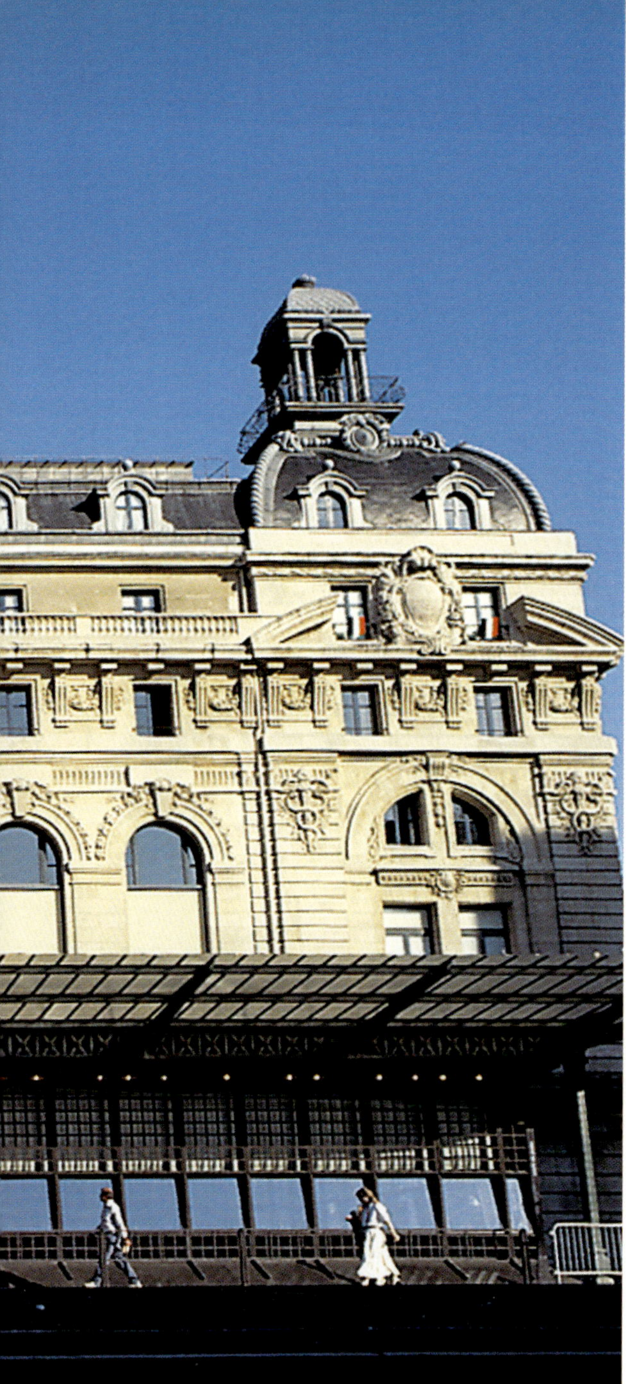

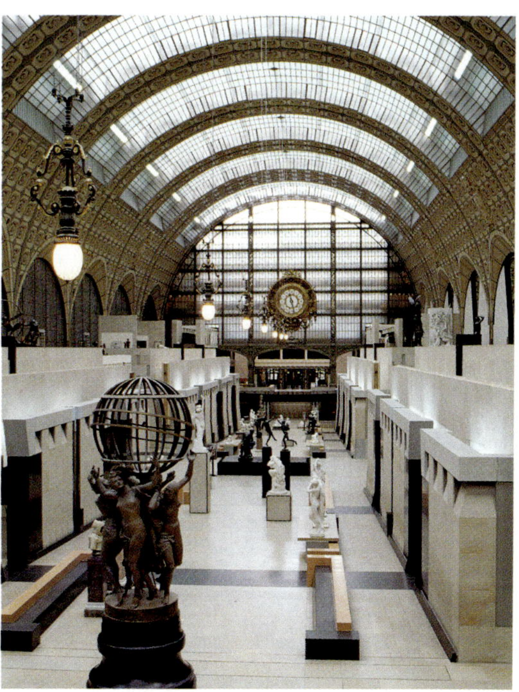

Standing on the banks of the Seine, the old Orsay station
was preserved during the creation of the museum.
The rail link (RER C) to Versailles left bank is located
in the basement (left).
Along the central aisle on the museum's ground floor
is a display of sculptures dating from 1850 to 1870.
In the foreground: the "Quatre Parties du Monde"
by Carpeaux (above).

a railway station on the site, a vast steel and glass hall with a façade inspired by the Louvre, providing rail links to Nantes, Bordeaux and Toulouse. Despite being closed down in 1939 and destined for demolition, the building was the venue for sales from the Hôtel Drouot and theatre plays by the Renaud-Barrault Company. In 1971, the building was in an extremely poor state of repair and in 1978 the deci-sion was made to transform it into a museum. The main hall was to be preserved and the Italian architect, Gae Aulenti was put in charge of its interior design.

Since 1986, the three floors of the Musée d'Orsay offer visitors a chronological discovery of the painting, sculpture, graphic and decorative arts, visual arts, architecture, town planning, cinema, photographs, posters, press and illus-trated books from the period 1848-1914. The majority of the collections come from the Louvre and Musée du Jeu de Paume which was previously devoted to Impressionism.

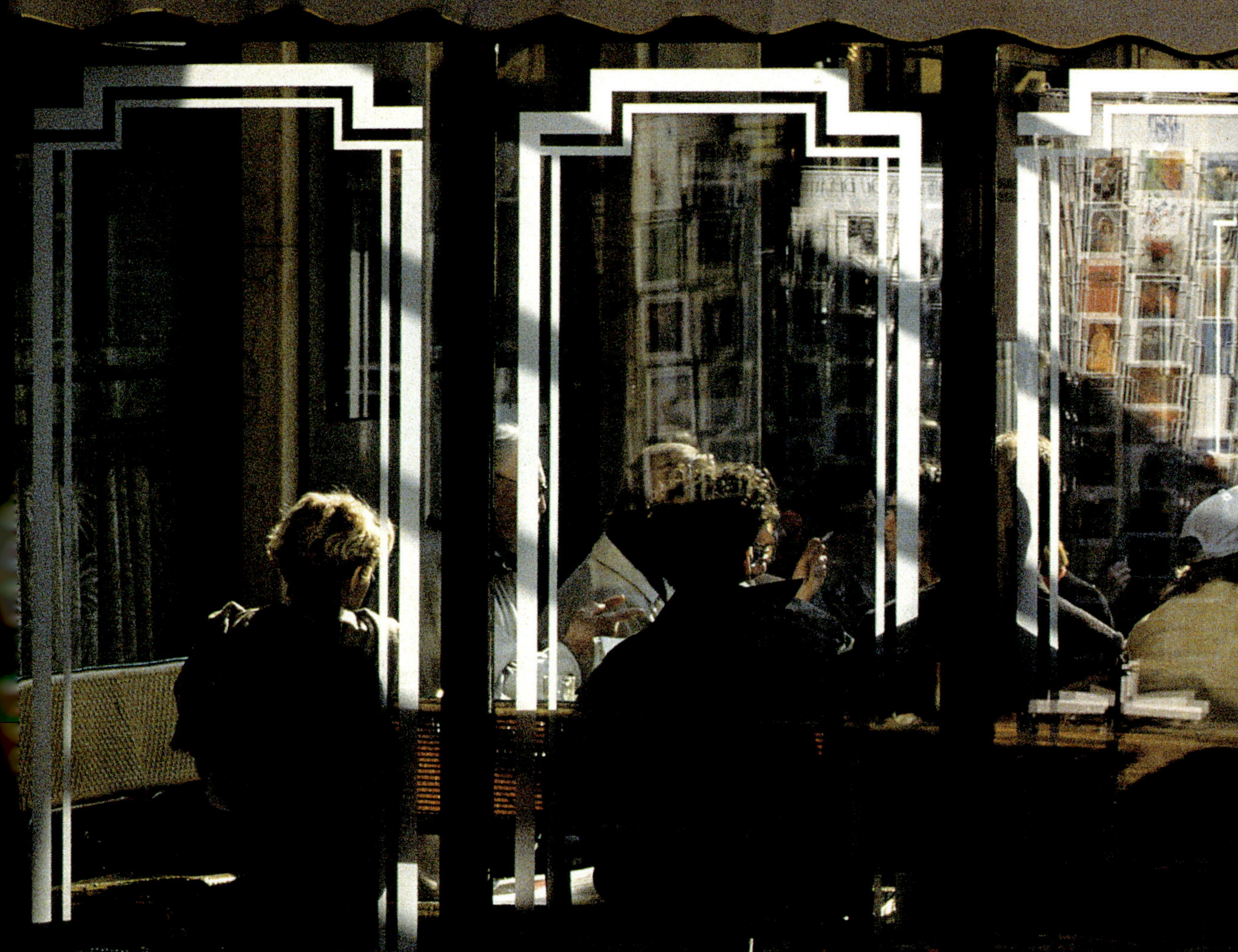

City life

6th arrondissement

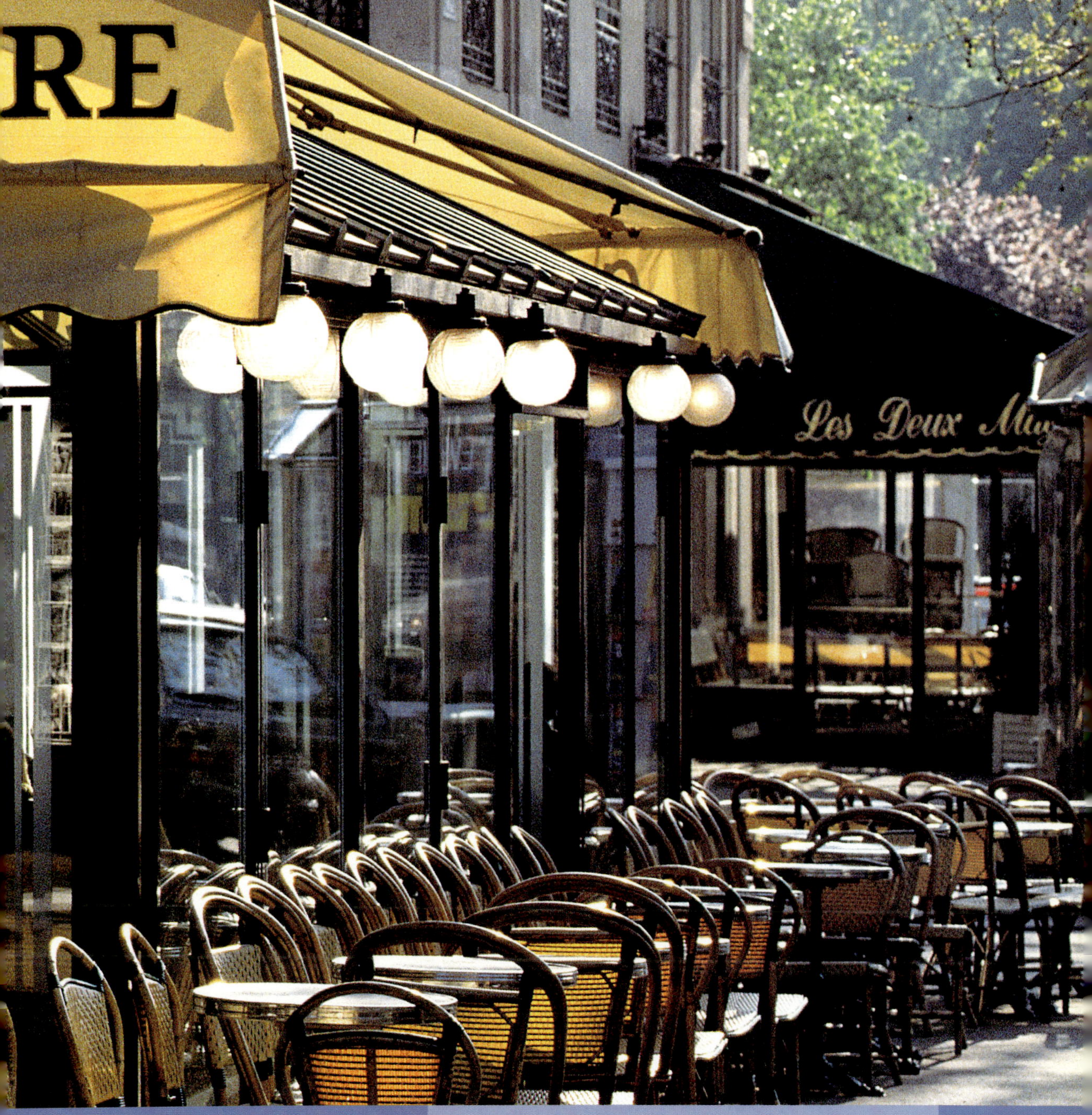

Saint-Germain-des-Prés

Saint-Germain-des-Prés church

The Literary cafés of Saint-Germain-des-Prés

Saint-Sulpice church

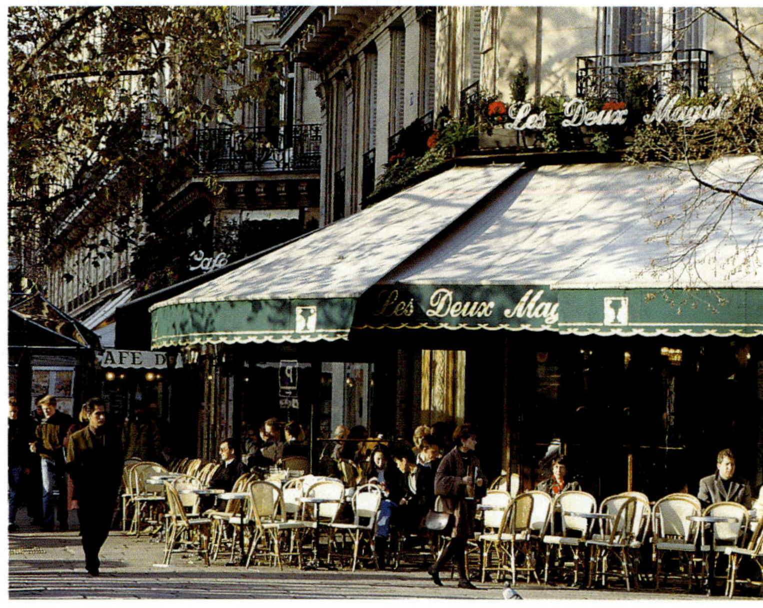

In the 1950s, cafés such as
Les Deux-Magots and Café Flore
were popular with intellectuals
and artists (left).
Until the French Revolution,
the Saint-Germain-des-Prés abbey
was one of the most important
Benedictine abbeys in France
(right).

Saint-Germain-des-Prés church

In 542, the Bishop of Paris, Germain, decided to construct a basilica around which an Abbey was later founded. It was built to house the tunic of Saint Vincent and a magnificent gold cross which, according to legend, had been brought back from Sarragossa by the son of Clovis, Childebert I. Following damage to the church and monastery in the 9th century during the Norman invasions, a new church and monastery were built around 1000 and extended from 1227 to 1273. The Abbey grew in importance in the 17th and 18th centuries, then experienced a decline with the start of the Revolution. The buildings were sold off and the church transformed into a saltpetre storage warehouse. On 19 August 1794, an explosion destroyed the dining-hall and part of the library which contained some 50,000 books and 7,000 manuscripts. Of the 9th century Roman church, only the side aisles, transept and bell tower remain - located outside the city walls built in the 14th century, the tower is said to have been used by Henry IV as a look-out post during the siege of Paris. Of the two other bell towers, demolished in the 19th century, only their foundations remain. The church interior has been completely transformed and only the chancel and its ambulatory have kept their original appearance. The church was reopened as a place of worship in 1821. The second chapel on the right houses the tomb of Descartes.

The Literary cafés of Saint-Germain-des-Prés

The Abbey at Saint-Germain-des-Prés became a spiritual focus, influencing the surrounding district and transforming it over the centuries into one of the most important centres of Parisian intellectual and artistic life. At the end of the 18th century, *Le Procope* - the oldest café in Paris, founded in 1686 by a Sicilian called Francesco Procopio and where a new drink known as "coffee" was first served - became popular with writers such as Voltaire, D'Alembert and Rousseau, and later, George Sand, Musset and Balzac. Under the Occupation (1940-1944), artists and writers such as André Breton, Jean-Paul Sartre, Simone de Beauvoir, Albert

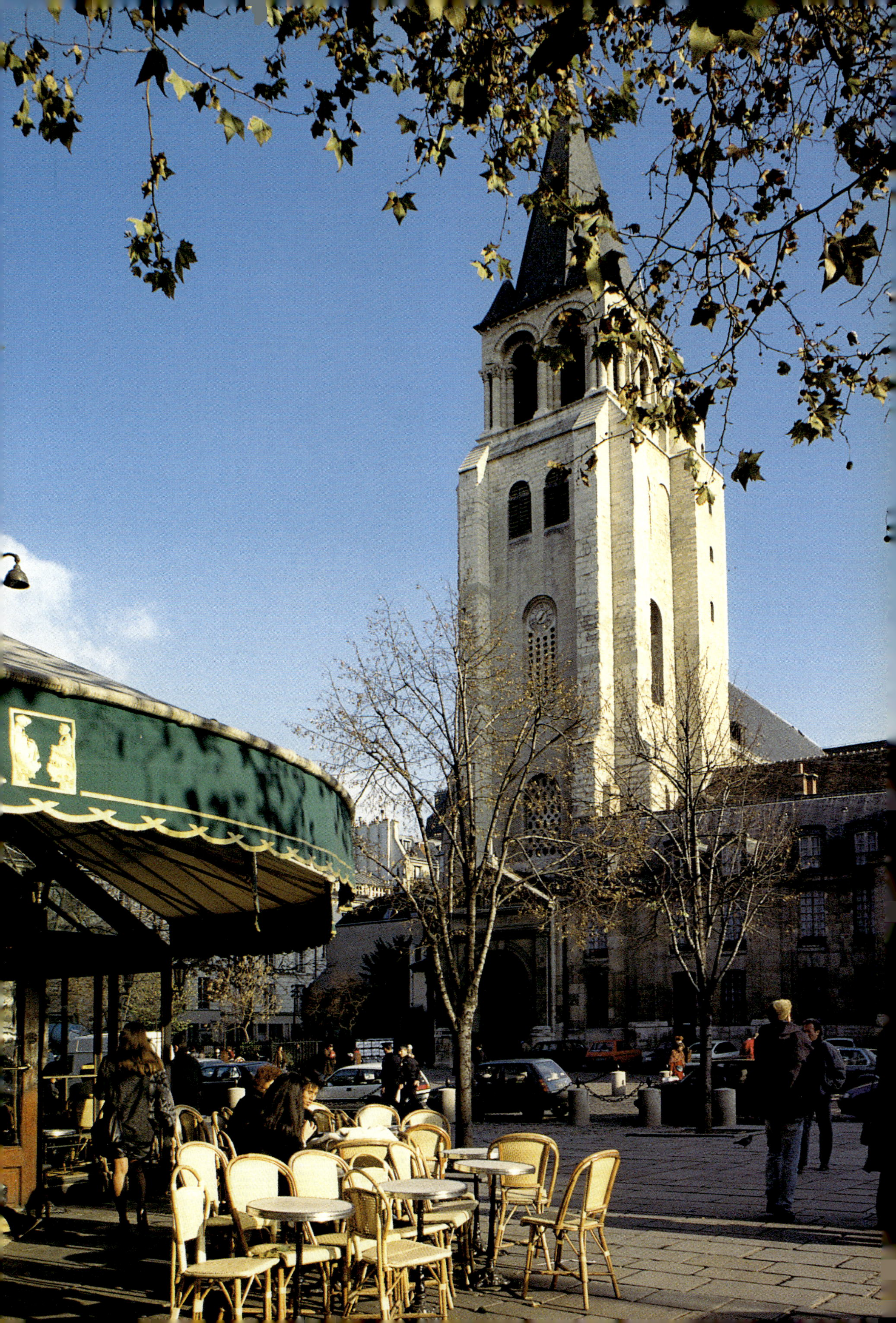

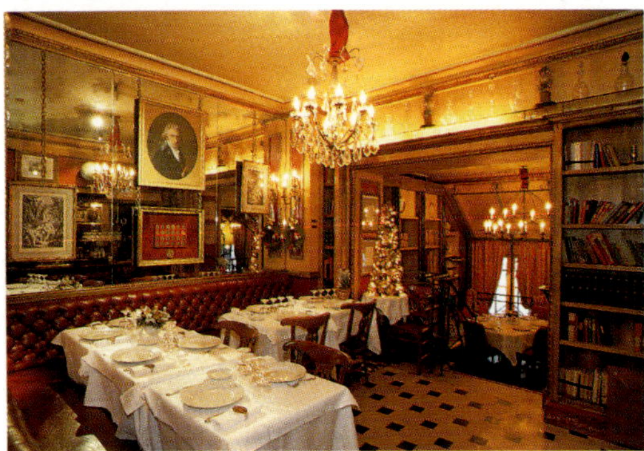

Camus and Jacques Prévert used to meet at the *Café Flore*, *Deux-Magots*, *La Rhumerie* or the *Brasserie Lipp*. After the Liberation, the district's popularity soared. A host of cafés, nightclubs and jazz clubs - some of which were set up in cellars - attracted a cosmopolitan crowd of writers, painters, actors, musicians and singers who were soon described by the press as "existentialist", in reference to the philosophical movement initiated by Sartre. Hangouts such as *Le Tabou*, *La Rose Rouge*, *Le Club Saint-Germain*, *Le Quod-Libet*, *Le Caveau de la Huchette* and *Le Vieux-Colombier* were to produce many great artists including Sydney Bechet, Claude Luter, Boris Vian, Mouloudji and Juliette Gréco who left their mark on the theatre, literature, songs, music and cinema of the time. Although Saint-Germain-des-Prés and its surrounding area are still home to a number of publishers, it has now been invaded by an army of luxury and designer boutiques and visitors are hard put to find the bohemian post-war Saint-Germain once considered the "Artistic Capital of the Republic". However, you can still take a pleasant stroll along the Rue de Seine and Rue De Buci, stopping at the Place Furstenberg - once the home of Delacroix. Then admire the 18th century private mansions on the Rue Jacob, visit the Cour de Rohan and wander along the Rue Saint-André-des-Arts, Rue des Grands-Augustins and Rue Séguier... before coming out on the Place Saint-Michel to admire the fountain by Davioud,

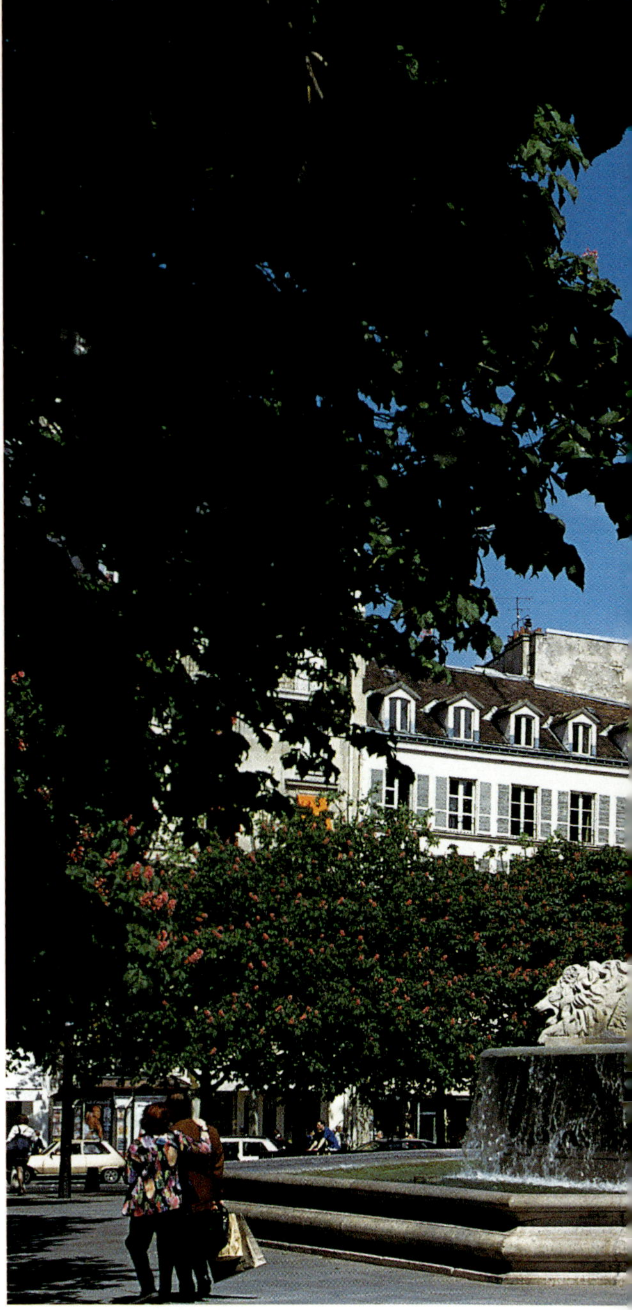

Saint Michael Slaying the Dragon, which was commissioned by Haussman in the 19th century. And why not idly wander around the district and try to recapture its lost past, before the shops and boutiques arrived...

Saint-Sulpice church

The construction of the Saint-Sulpice church, one of the biggest in Paris, began in 1646. It was 129 years until the edifice would be (almost) completed. The final

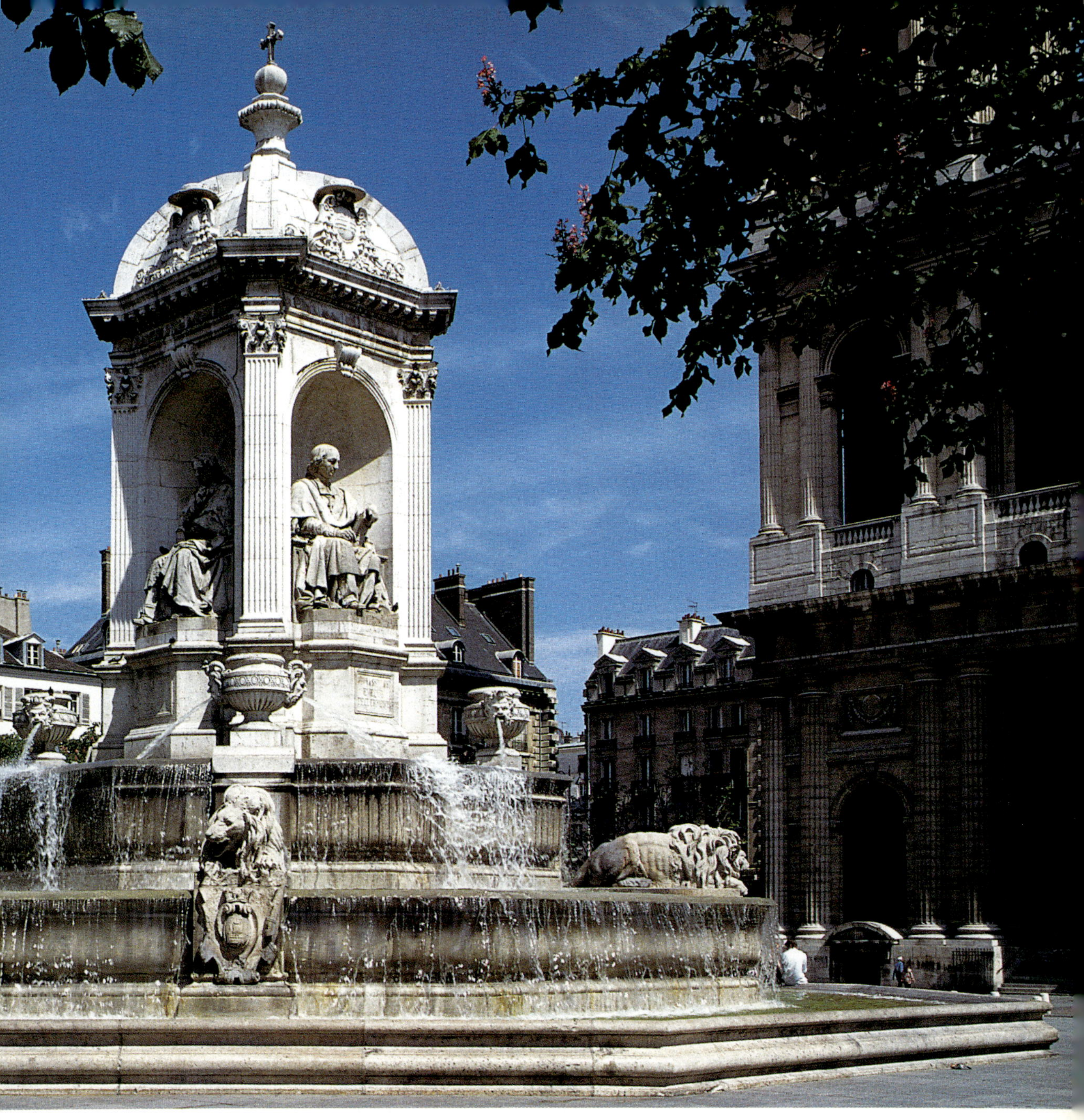

works for the façade, designed by the architect Servandoni in 1732, were interrupted in 1775 and never seen through to completion. Of the two towers, only the northern was finished by Chalgrin in 1788. The interior of the church itself, based on the design of a Latin cross, consists of high archways which separate the nave from the side aisles.

The Saint-Sulpice church houses an important collection of art works, paintings and sculptures by 18th and 19th century artists.

The café known as Le Procope, on Rue de l'Ancienne-Comédie, is believed to be the oldest in Paris.
Today it is a restaurant (left).
On the Place Saint-Sulpice is the Fountain of the Four Bishops (Bossuet, Fènelon, Massillon and Fléchier) which was built by Visconti in 1844 (above).

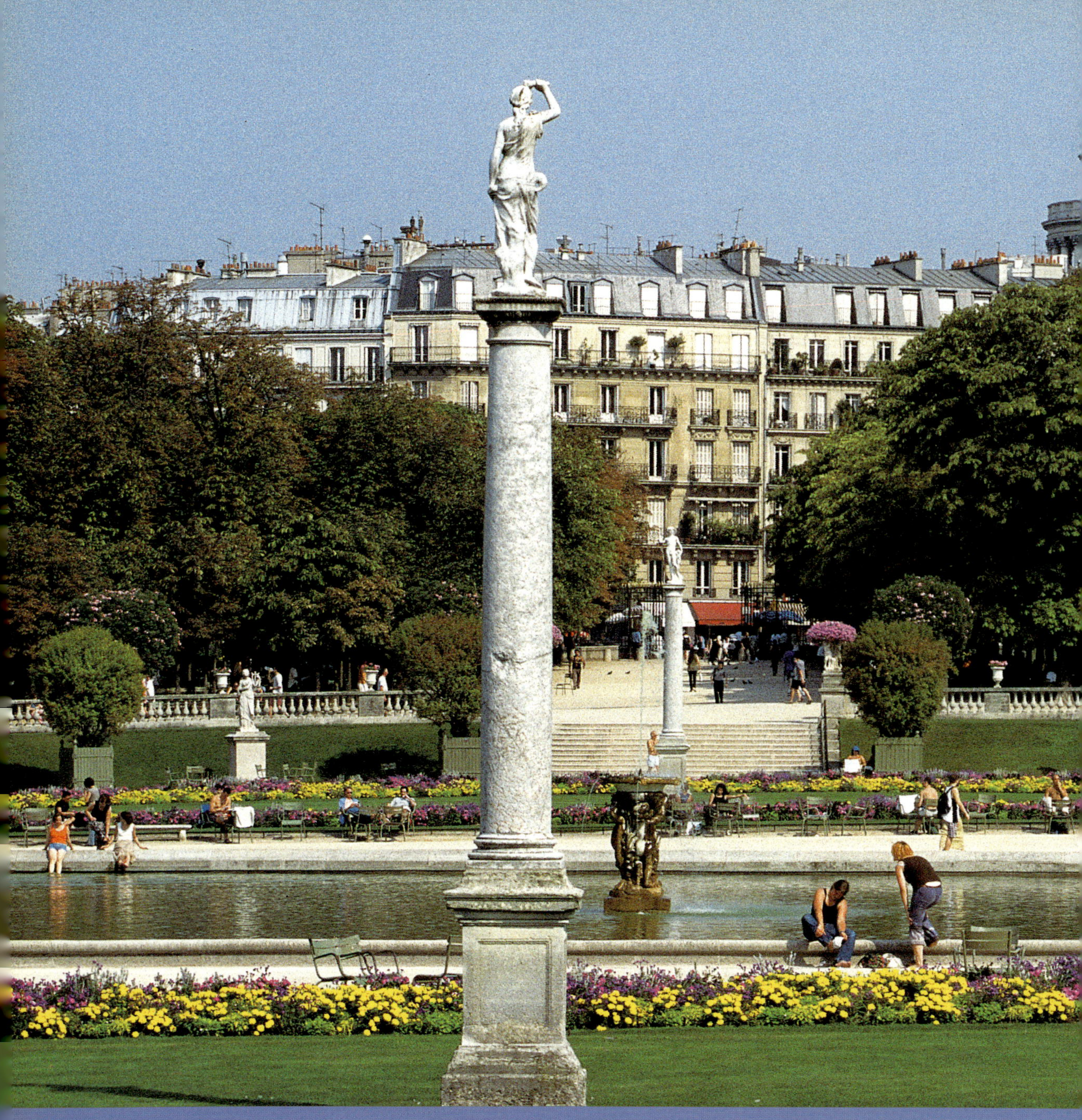

City life

5th and 6th arrondissements

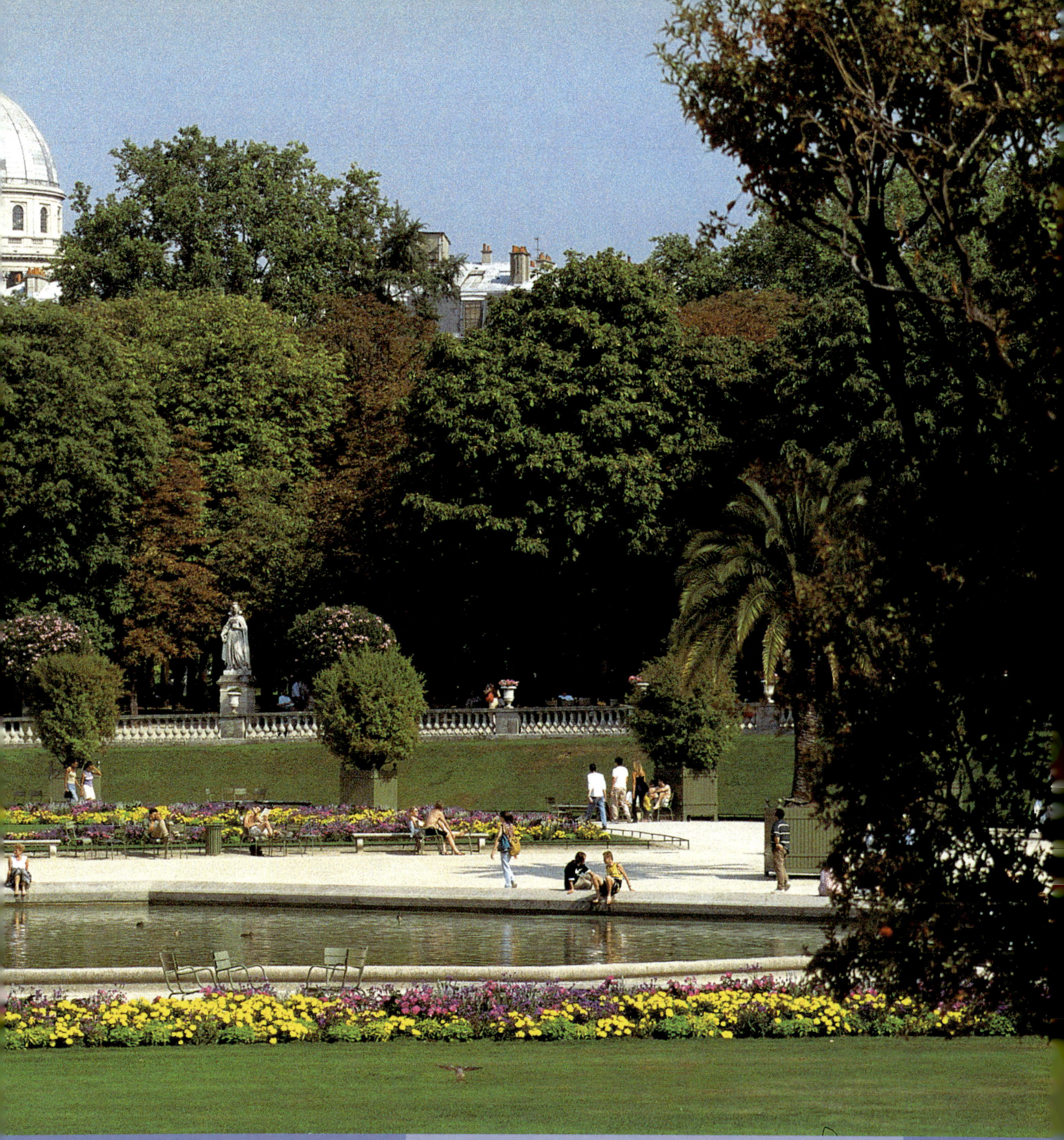

Luxembourg Gardens

Luxembourg palace
and gardens

The Panthéon

Cluny Museum
and Roman Baths

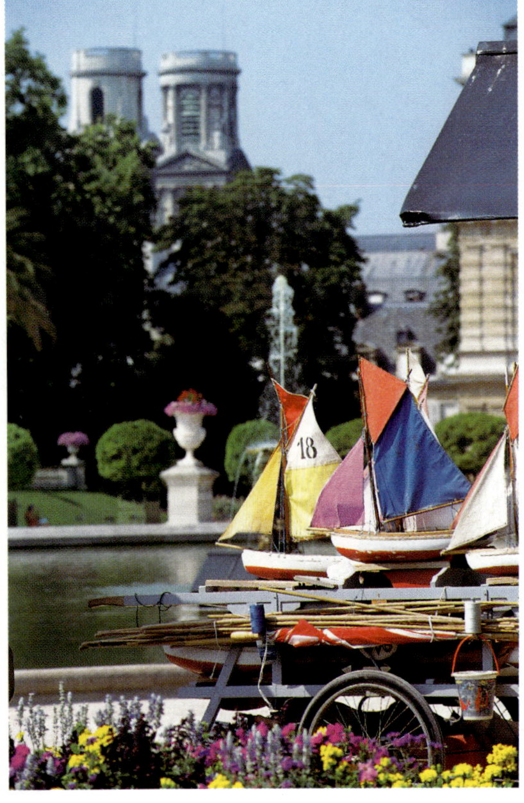

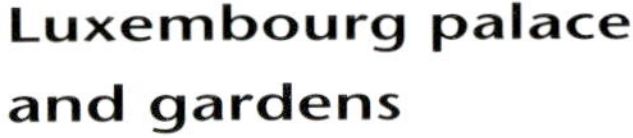

Familiarly known as the "Luco", the Luxembourg Gardens are a haven for young Parisians who can sail model boats on the lake and also find ponies, puppet shows and sweet stands (above). Despite being redesigned in the 19th century, the façade on the garden side is an exact reproduction of the original (right).

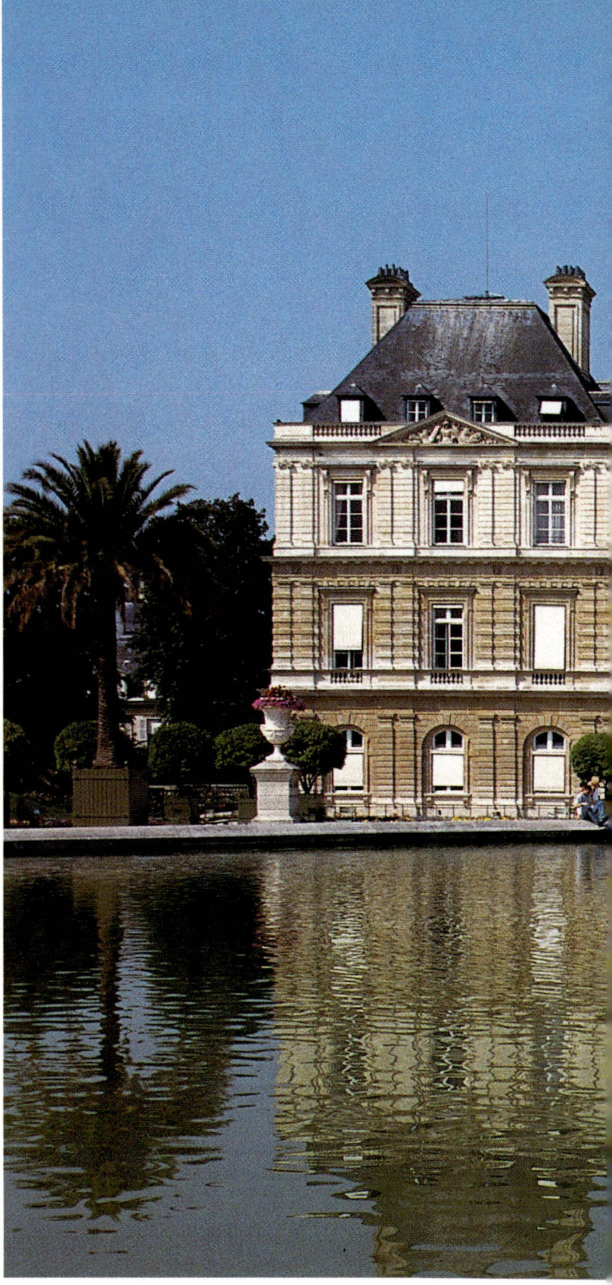

Luxembourg palace and gardens

The palace

The site of the Luxembourg palace and gardens was formerly occupied by the Château de Vauvert, built by Robert le Pieux in the 10th century. Later on, it became a popular place for brigands, before being taken over by a Carthusian Monastery under the reign of Saint Louis. In 1613, Marie de'

Medici, the widow of Henry IV, bought the private hotel belonging to Duc François de Luxembourg located near the monastery walls. She then commissioned the architect Salomon de Brosse to build a château which resembled the Pitti Palace in Florence where she had spent her childhood. The château was sumptously decorated, with work carried out by celebrated artists such as Rubens, who executed a series of canvases recounting the life of the Queen and which are now housed in the

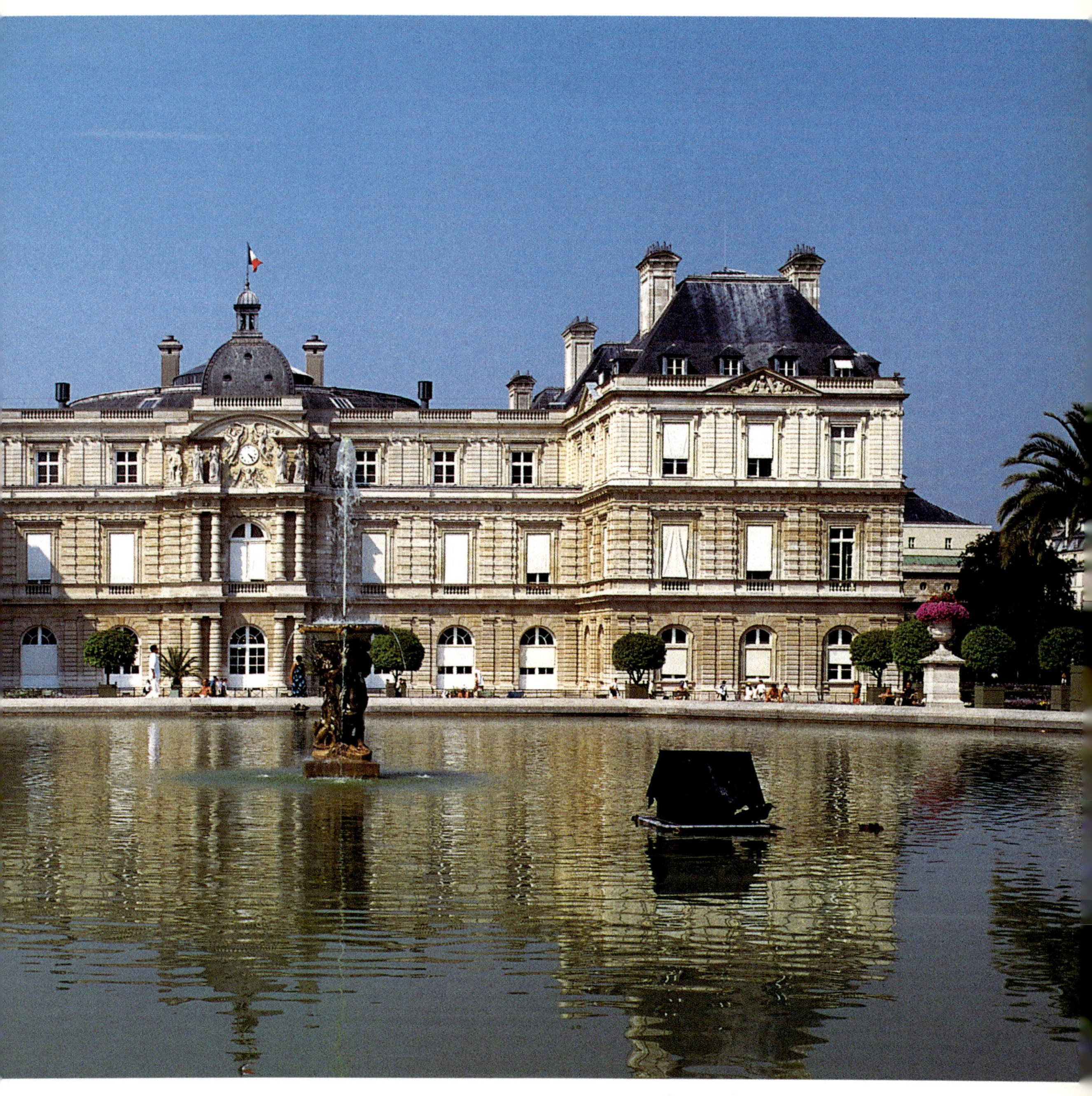

Louvre Museum. In 1631, Marie de' Medici was forced into exile. The palace then passed through the hands of King Louis XIII, his brother Gaston d'Orléans, Mademoiselle Montpensier, Louis XIV, the Count of Provence, the brother of Louis XVI and finally the future King Louis XVIII, before being transformed into a prison during the Revolution. Danton, Camille Desmoulins and the painter David were all imprisoned here. It became the Government's headquarters under the Directory, then the Palais du Sénat during the Empire and finally the House of Lords under the Restoration. In 1834, it was extended to become the national palace which stands today.

Under the First Empire, the palace's interior was considerably changed by Chalgrin and later extended by Gisors from 1836-1841. The Palais du Luxembourg consists of a central building on two floors, topped by a cupola and flanked by two side pavilions and is a beautiful example

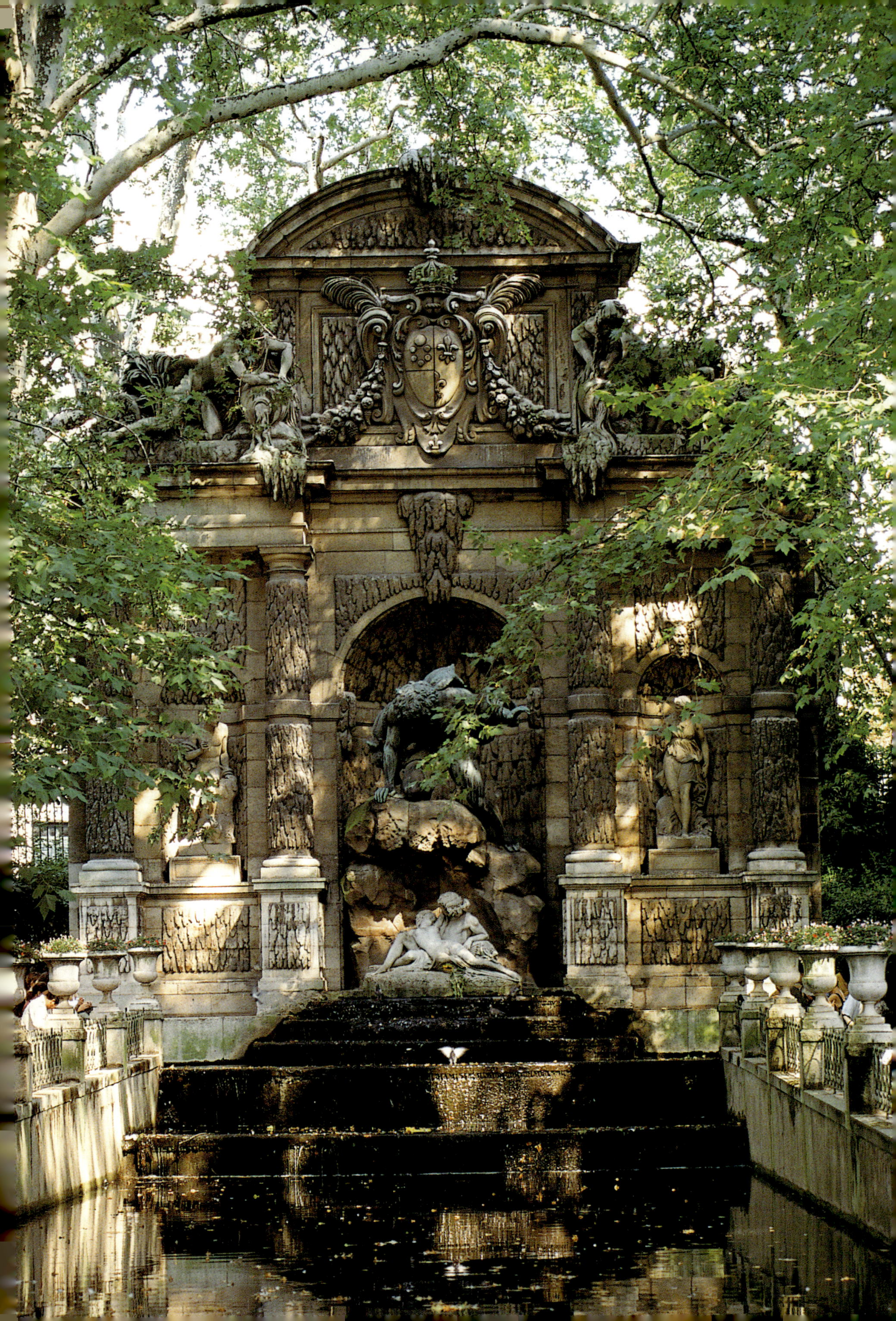

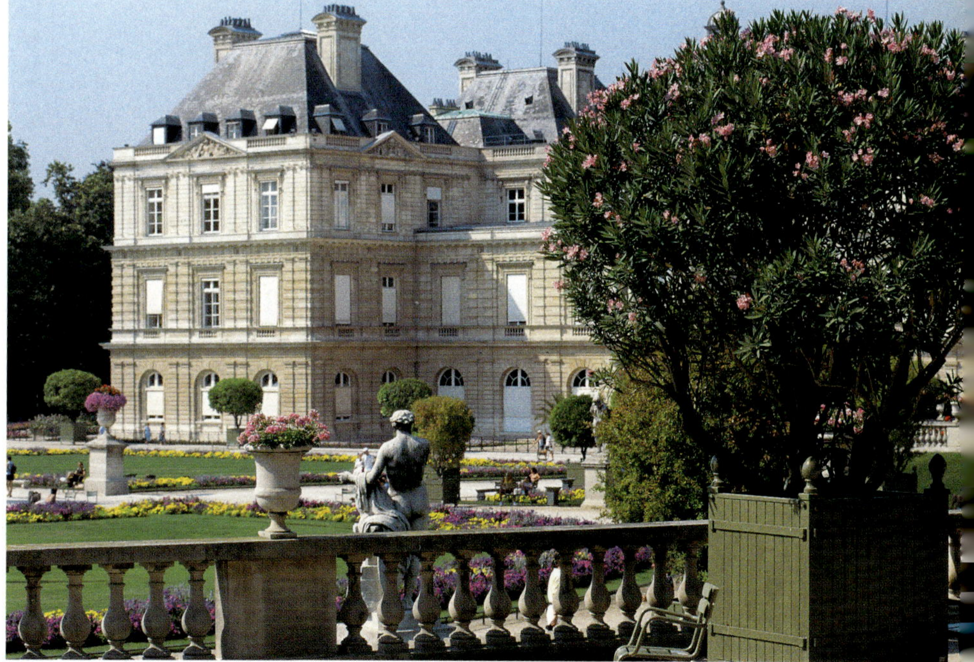

The Medici fountain which displays the Queen's coat of arms, was designed by Salomon de Brosse in 1630 in the Italian Renaissance style. The allegories represent the Rhône and the Seine while the group of Acis and Galatée in the foreground was added in the 19th century (left). The terrace overlooks the French garden (right).

of a synthesis between Florentine art and the French classical tradition. The façade, decorated with the three overlapping Tuscan, Doric and Ionic orders, displays a clear Italian influence with its boss and ringed columns.

It has housed the Senate since 1558 and is open to the public. Inside, visitors can admire the gallery of busts, the lecture and meeting rooms, the Salon Victor Hugo, the library decorated with works by Delacroix, the gallery containing the twelve paintings by Jordaens illustrating the signs of the zodiac, Marie de' Medici's bedroom and the chapel built under Louis-Philippe. The grand staircase designed by Chalgrin, is decorated with Gobelins tapestries.

The gardens

The surrounding gardens were created at the same time as the palace, by Boyeau de la Béraudière upon the request of Marie de' Medici. The Luxembourg Gardens soon became a popular place for walking - it is said that Watteau and Diderot were fond of strolling along its paths.

After being extended by Chalgrin, architect to the Count of Provence, the garden was later reduced in size during the development of adjacent avenues by Haussmann. The gardens contain some 80 sculptures representing Queens, famous women from history, writers and works by various artists such as Frémiet and Bourdelle.

Around the main ornamental lake framed by two terraces, stretch the French gardens whose flower beds, borders and copses offer visitors an infinite variety of flowers, trees and species of shrubs.

The English garden, created in 1867 and formerly known as the Jardin de l'Observatoire, was recently renamed the Jardin Cavelier-de-La-Salle et Marco-Polo. A section has been transformed into an orchard and houses the Quatre-Parties-du-Monde fountain, a work executed by various different sculptors including Carpeaux and Frémiet, following a design by Davioud.

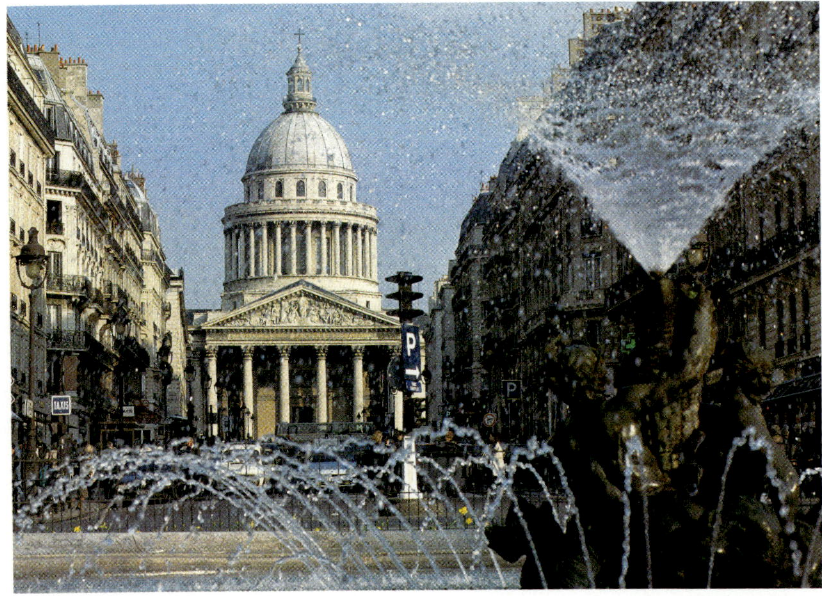

Rue Soufflot, opened in 1760, leads to the Panthéon (left). The interior of the Panthéon is supported by one hundred Corinthian columns. The windows have been walled up and the light comes from the dome at the centre of the edifice (right).

Panthéon

In 1744, King Louis XV, suffering from a serious illness during the siege of Metz, vowed that if he recovered, he would restore the Saint-Geneviève Abbey church. The reconstruction work was given over to Jean-Germain Soufflot and completed in 1790 by his successor, Rondelet. It was the first edifice built in the Neo-Classical style and follows the design of a Greek cross surmounted by an oval dome. The latter is supported by four pillars and preceded by a monumental peristyle inspired by the Pantheon in Rome which can be entered by climbing a series of wide steps. The pediment, supported by 22 Corinthian columns, was decorated by David d'Angers in 1830. The interior, measuring 110 m across and 83 m high, with naves flanked by side aisles demarcated by one hundred columns, is striking for its solemn, cold, almost sepulchral appearance. On its blind walls - the windows have been blocked out - is a fresco to the glory of France including the *Vie de Sainte Geneviève* by Puvis de Chavannes. The cupola is decorated with a work by Antoine-Jean Gros, the *Apothéose de Sainte Geneviève*.

In 1791, the constituent Assembly decided to transform the church into a necropolis where the remains of the country's illustrious figures would be laid - as the words engraved on the pediment declare, "Aux grands hommes, la Patrie reconnaissante" (To our great men, your devoted country). The edifice was reopened as a church by Napoleon, turned back into a necropolis under Louis-Philippe, then made a church again under Napoleon III and was finally returned to its original function with the state funeral of Victor Hugo in 1885.

Some of the great figures laid to rest in the Panthéon include Rousseau, Diderot, Voltaire, Zola, Lazare, Sadi Carnot, Berthelot and his wife (the only woman buried here) and Louis Braille. In the 20th century, there has been Jean Moulin, Abbé Grégoire, Monge and Condorcet to mark the bicentenary of the Revolution, Jean Jaurès, Jean Monnet and André Malraux. In 1981, François Mitterrand inaugurated his first seven-year term here with a grand ceremony, during which he entered the building alone and laid a rose on the tombs of Jean Jaurès, Victor Schoelcher and Jean Moulin.

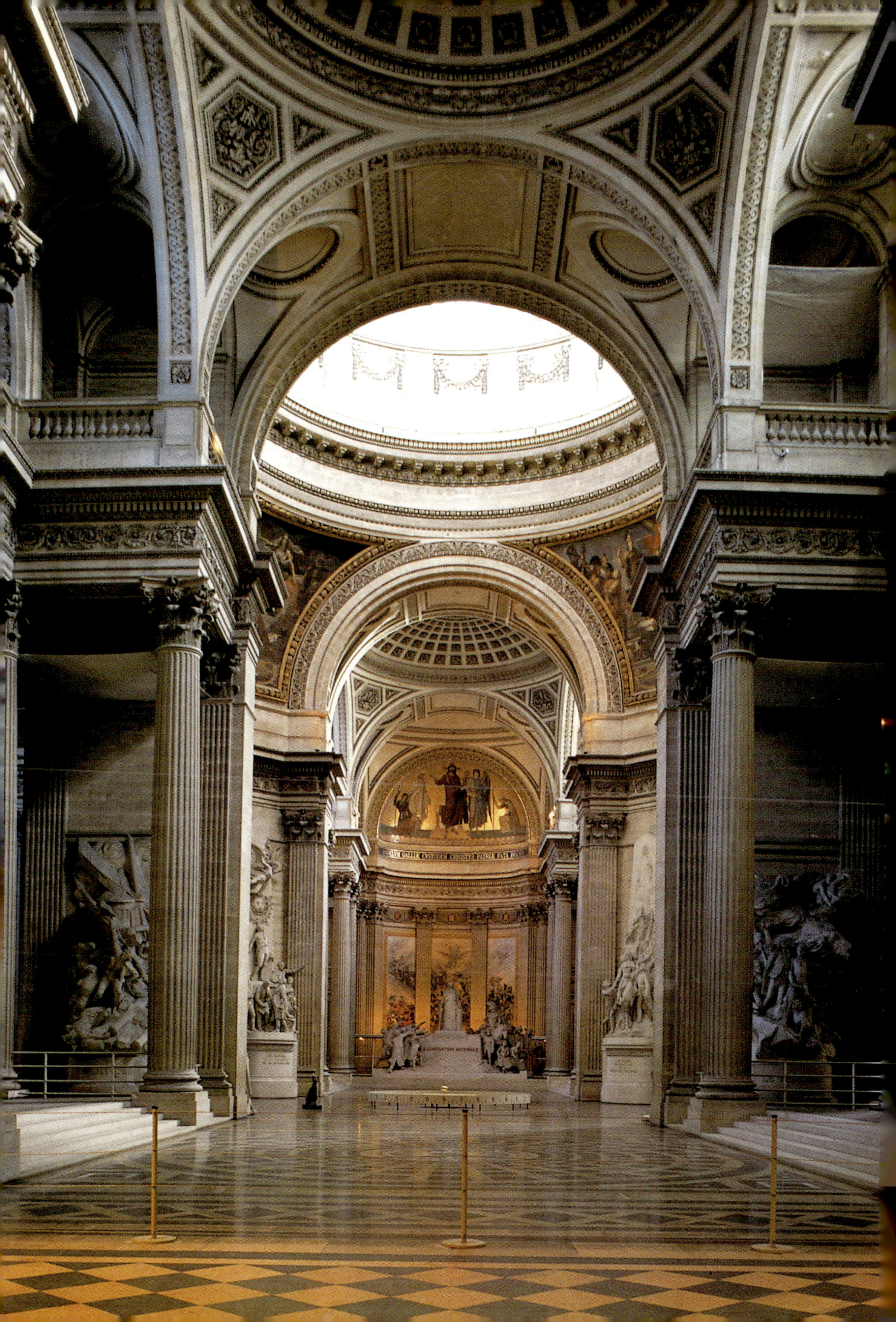

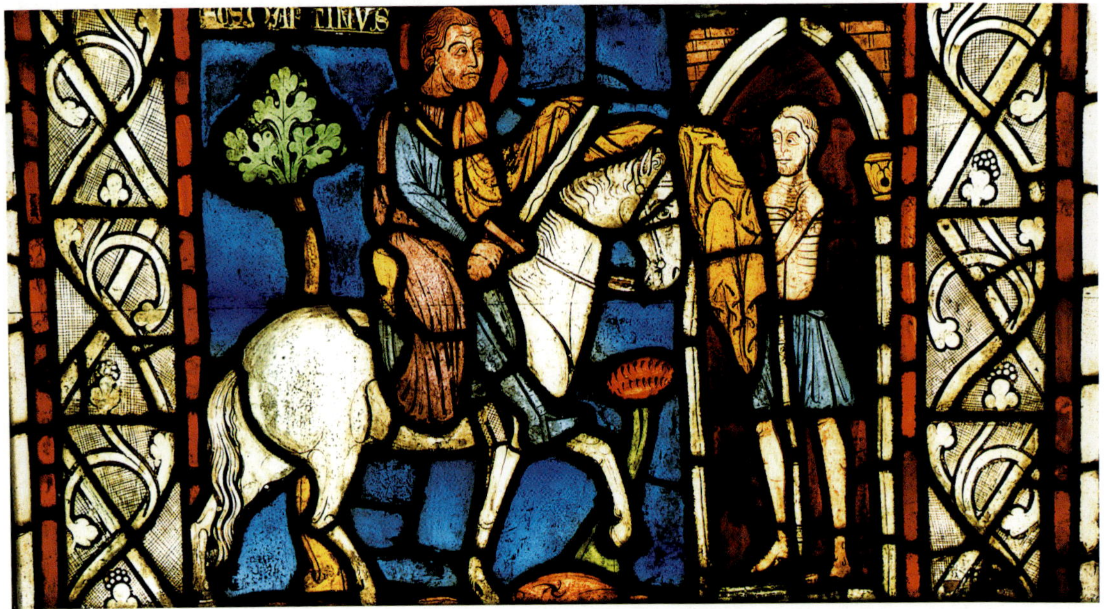

The Cluny Museum and Roman baths

The Parisian residence of the Cluny Fathers, which prefigures the city's private mansions, comprises a courtyard and garden and a main building flanked by two wings at the back. It was built by one of the Fathers, Jacques d'Amboise, between 1485 and 1498. The building served not only as a comfortable, richly decorated residence but also as a small château where its occupants could live in safety. The building's architecture combines typically flamboyant Gothic curves with the horizontal and vertical lines more reminiscent of the Classical style. In 1832, Alexandre du Sommerard rented part of the Hôtel de Cluny to house an important collection of works of art, objects and documents from the Medieval period. His son continued to build the collection and on his death left behind a museum containing some 10,000 pieces. Since 1977, part of the collection, comprising pieces from the Renaissance period, has been housed at the Château d'Ecouen. The Cluny Museum, renamed the Musée National du Moyen Age in 1991, boasts a number of masterpieces of Medieval art, including a collection of silver and gold pieces and enamels from the 7th to 12th centuries, the gold *altar front* from Basle cathedral (11th century), tapestries including those from the *Lady and the Unicorn* series (end of the 15th century) and the twenty-one heads of the *Kings of Juda* from the statuary of Notre-Dame, which were decapitated during the Revolution.

The Hôtel de Cluny was built next to the Gallo-Roman thermal baths of Lutetia, constructed at the end of the 2nd or beginning of the 3rd century AD between the Voie du Cardo (now the Rue Saint-Jacques) and the Route de Chartres (today, Boulevard Saint-Michel). Three of its rooms are still visible: the cold room (*frigidarium*), the only one still with its original vaults, the warm room (*tepidarium*) where visitors can see the baths and underground furnaces (hypocausts) and the hot room (*caldarium).*

In this room, dedicated to Notre-Dame de Paris, is a display of the twenty one heads of the Kings of Juda discovered by chance in 1977 during underground works (right).
A collection of stained-glass windows from the 12th and 13th centuries is exhibited at the Cluny Museum (above).

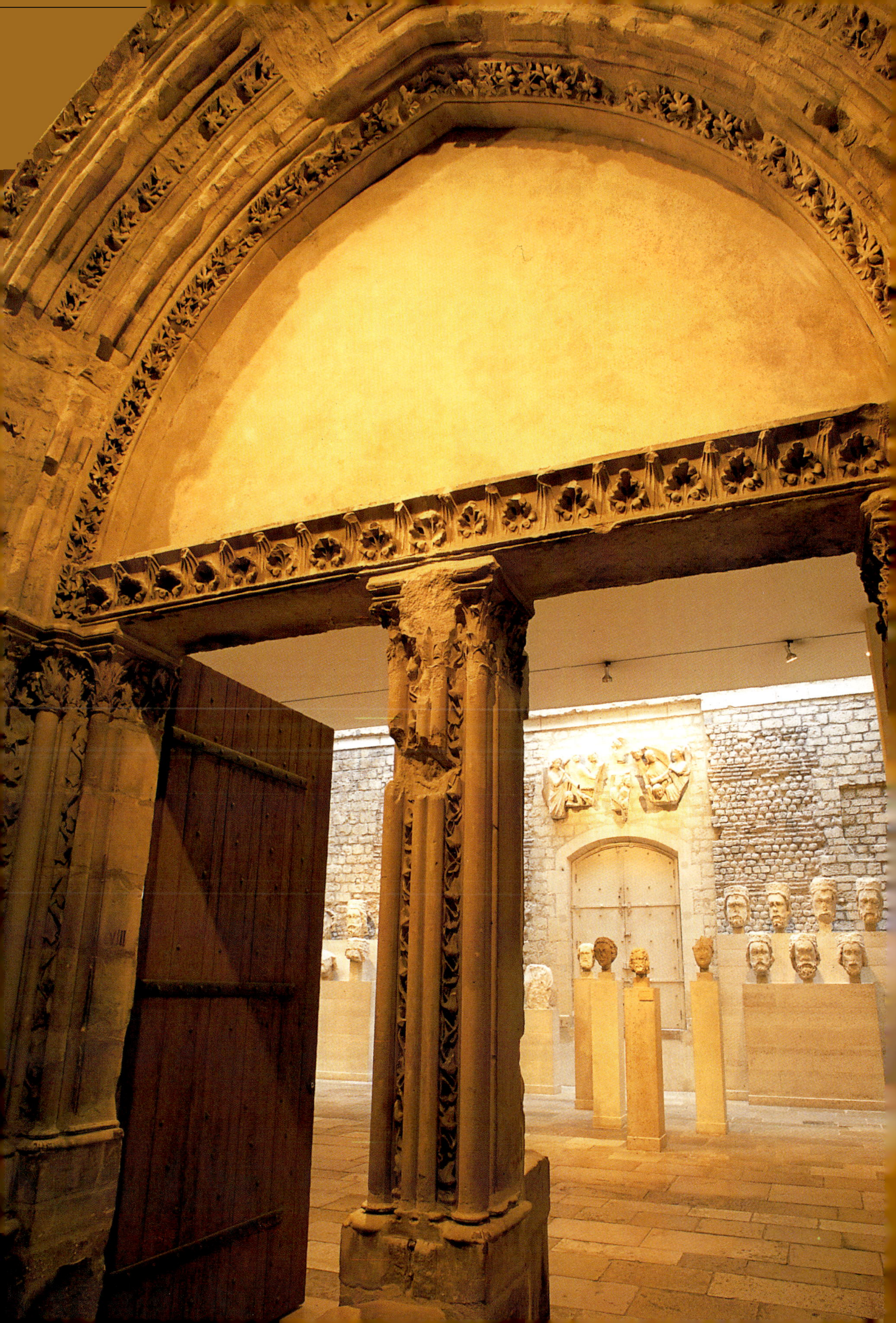

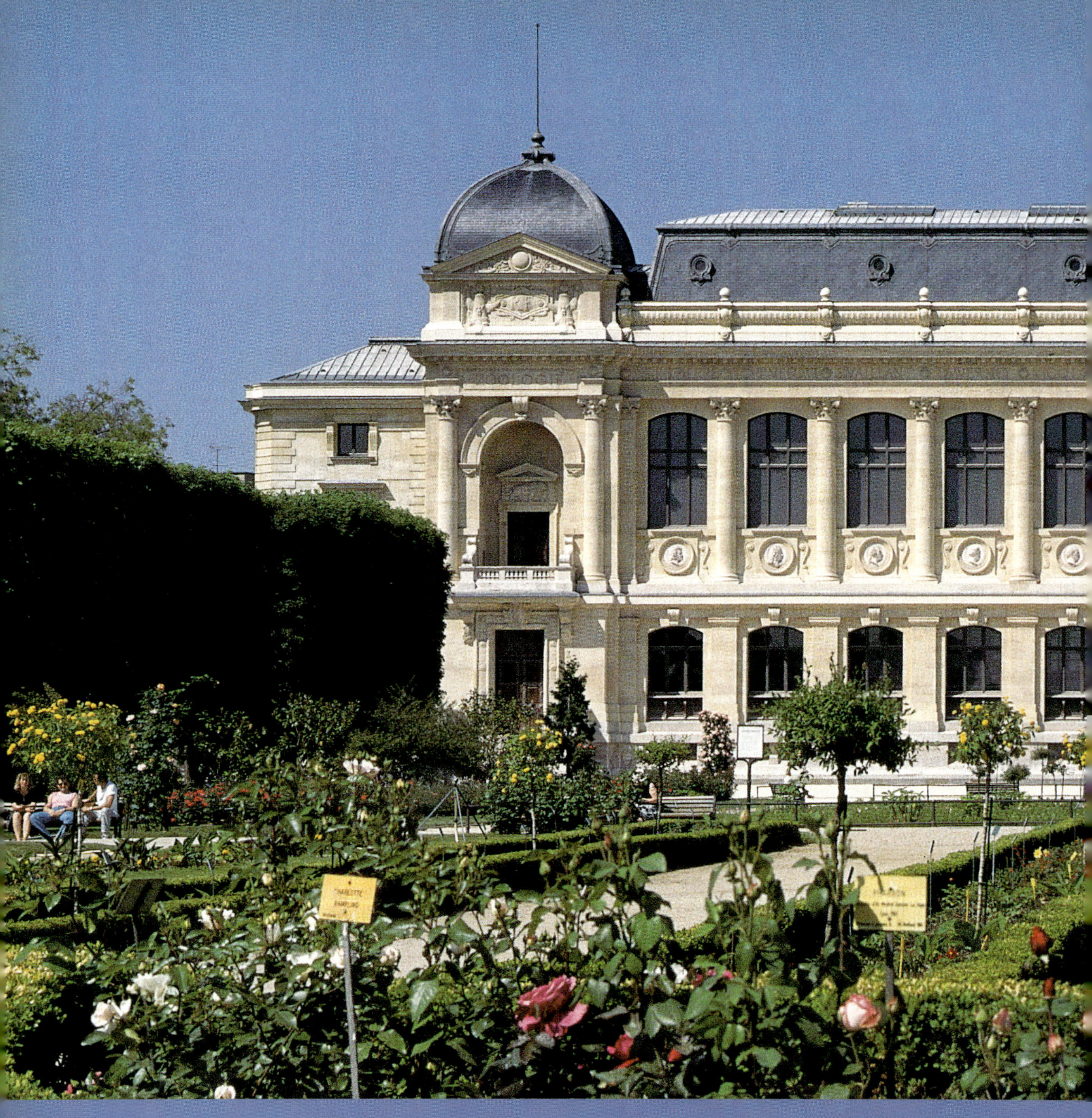

City life
5th arrondissement

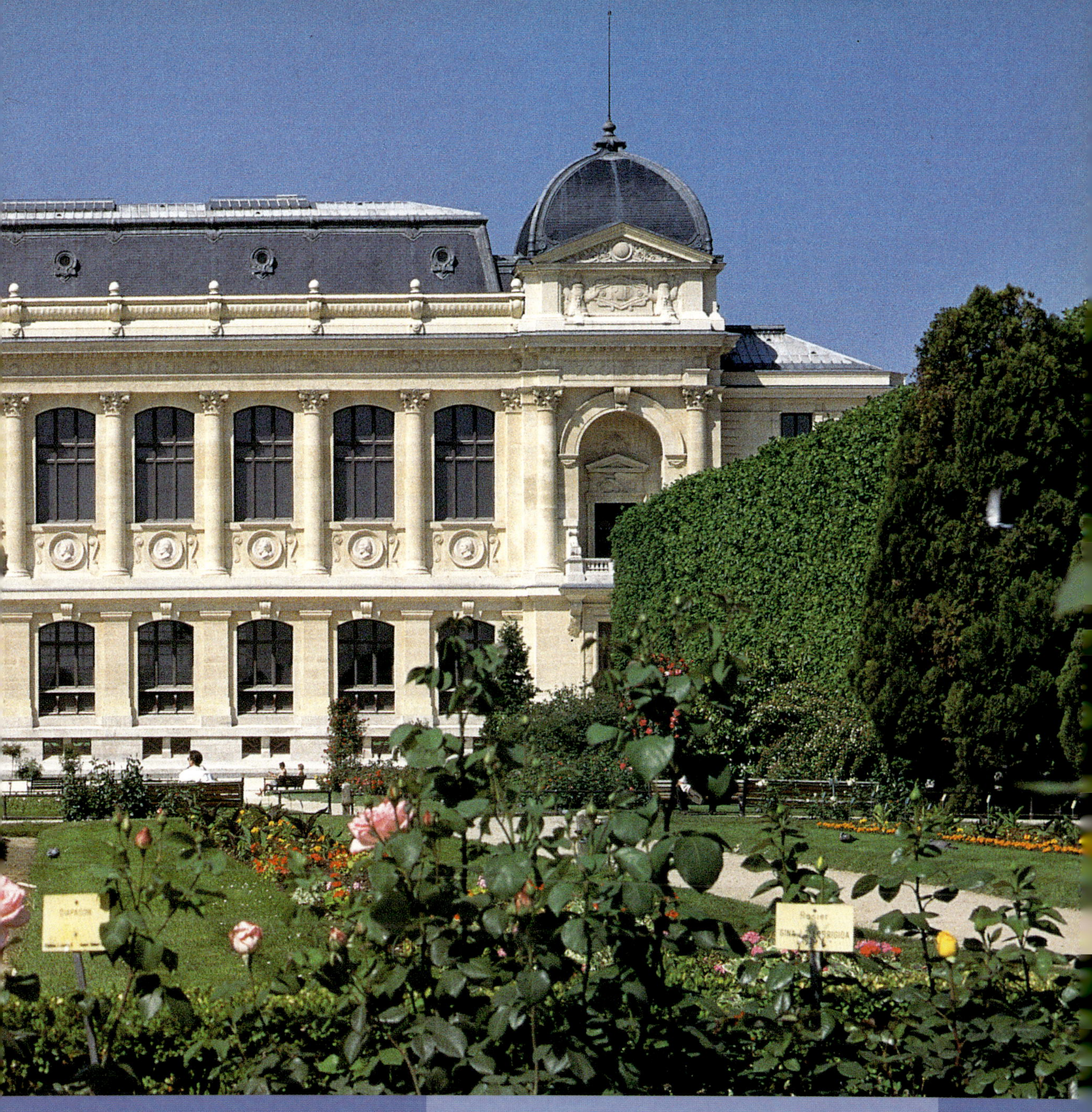

Jardin des Plantes

Jardin des Plantes
The Paris Mosque
Institut du
Monde Arabe

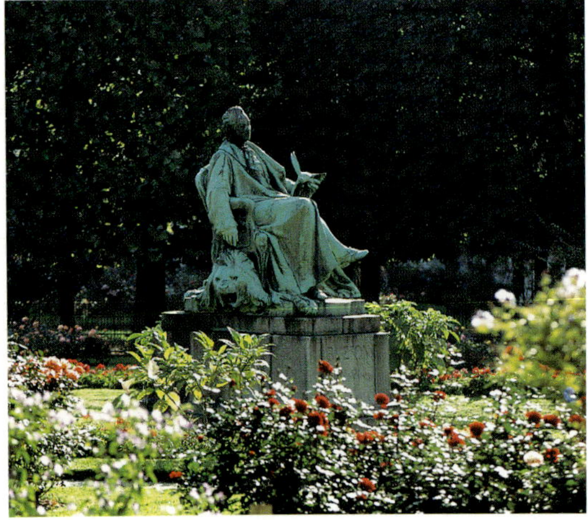

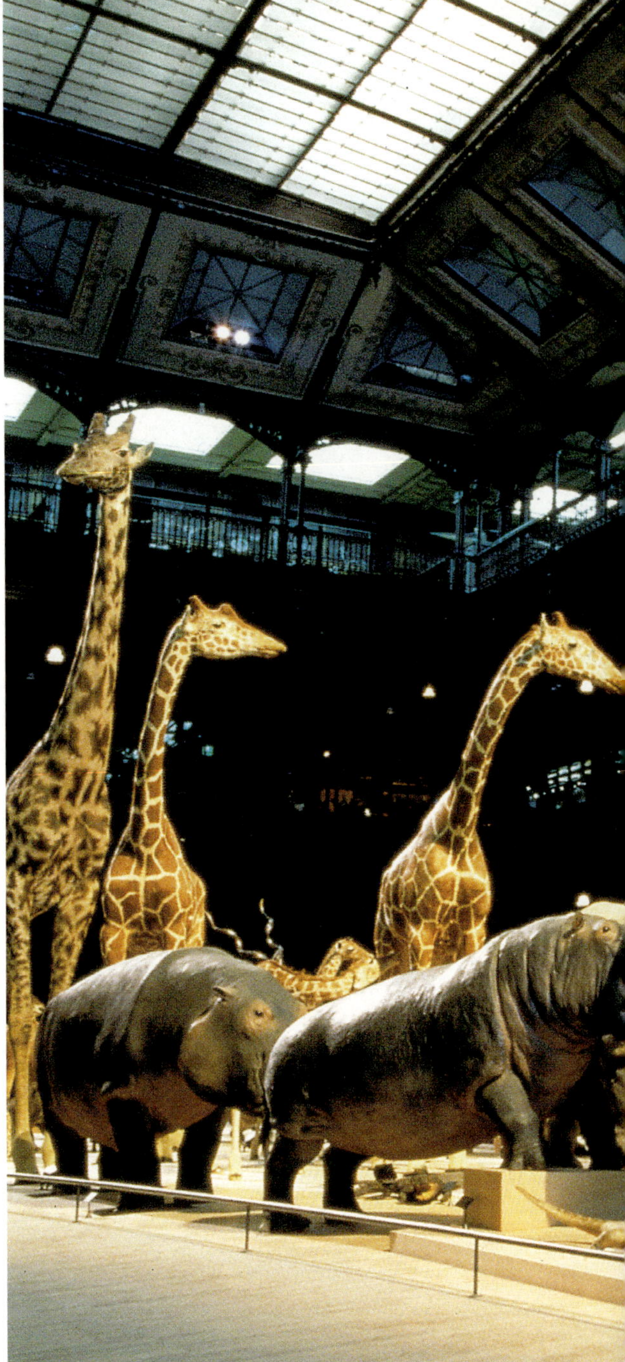

Jardin des Plantes

In 1626 the King decided to create a garden of medicinal plants in Paris for the use of medical students. Louis XIII placed his two doctors, Jean Héroard and Guy de la Brosse, in charge of the project. Later, Louis XIV's doctor Fagon, along with the botanist Tournefort and the Jussieu brothers, built up a precious collection of rare plants. However, it was Buffon, the King's garden steward and his partner Daubenton, who really extended and developed the gardens. The King's Garden was finally opened to the public in 1640 and under the Convention, became the Natural History Museum. Today, it is home to over twenty-five teaching chairs but is most famous for its gardens - these include a rose garden of around 180 different species and varieties, beds of iris, dahlias and cannas, shrubs located in its ecological park and some magnificent trees including the Lebanese Cedar planted by Bernard de Jussieu in 1774. Also popular with visitors are the menagerie, maze, Alpine garden and exotic greenhouses (tropical, Australian and Mexican).

The museum houses galleries devoted to Palaeontology, Mineralogy, Geology and Palaeobotanics.

The four floors of the beautifully laid out Grande Gallerie de l'Evolution, present the diversity of living things with exhibits ranging from micro-organisms magnified 800 times, to the largest animal species. The different environments of the earth are represented and retrace the history of evolution, via different theories that try to pro-

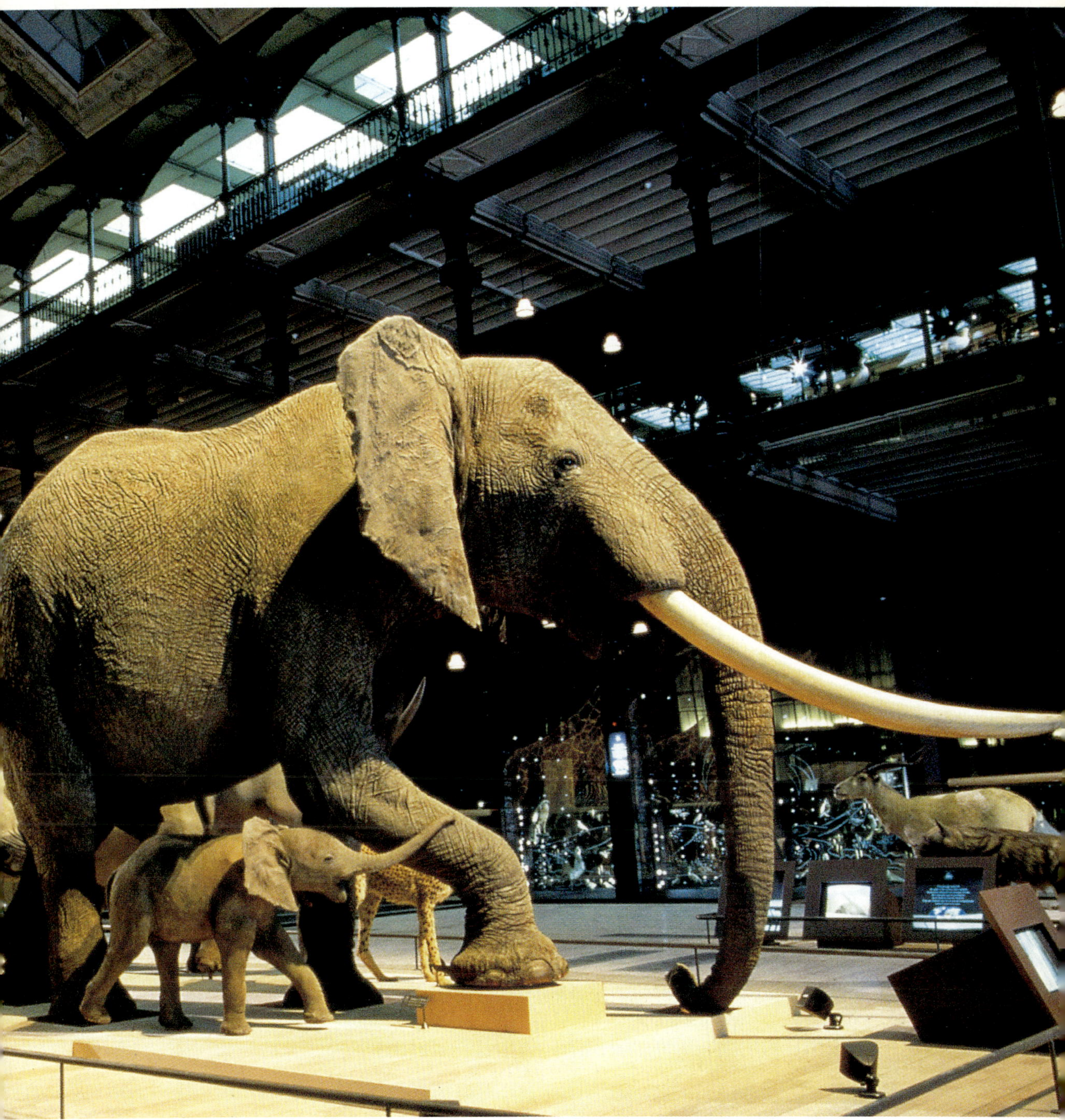

vide explanations, and man's place in the evolutionary process. Under the vast 1,000 m^2 glass roof which lights up the museum, visitors can also take a walk along the African caravan, which starts with the elephant and continues with a beautiful and spectacular display of stuffed African mammals.

The statue of Buffon, garden steward to the King from 1739-1788, is well-placed in the botanical garden which he personally helped to develop with new plants (top left). In the Natural History Museum, the Grande Galerie de l'Evolution presents a spectacular display of large, naturalised African mammals (above).

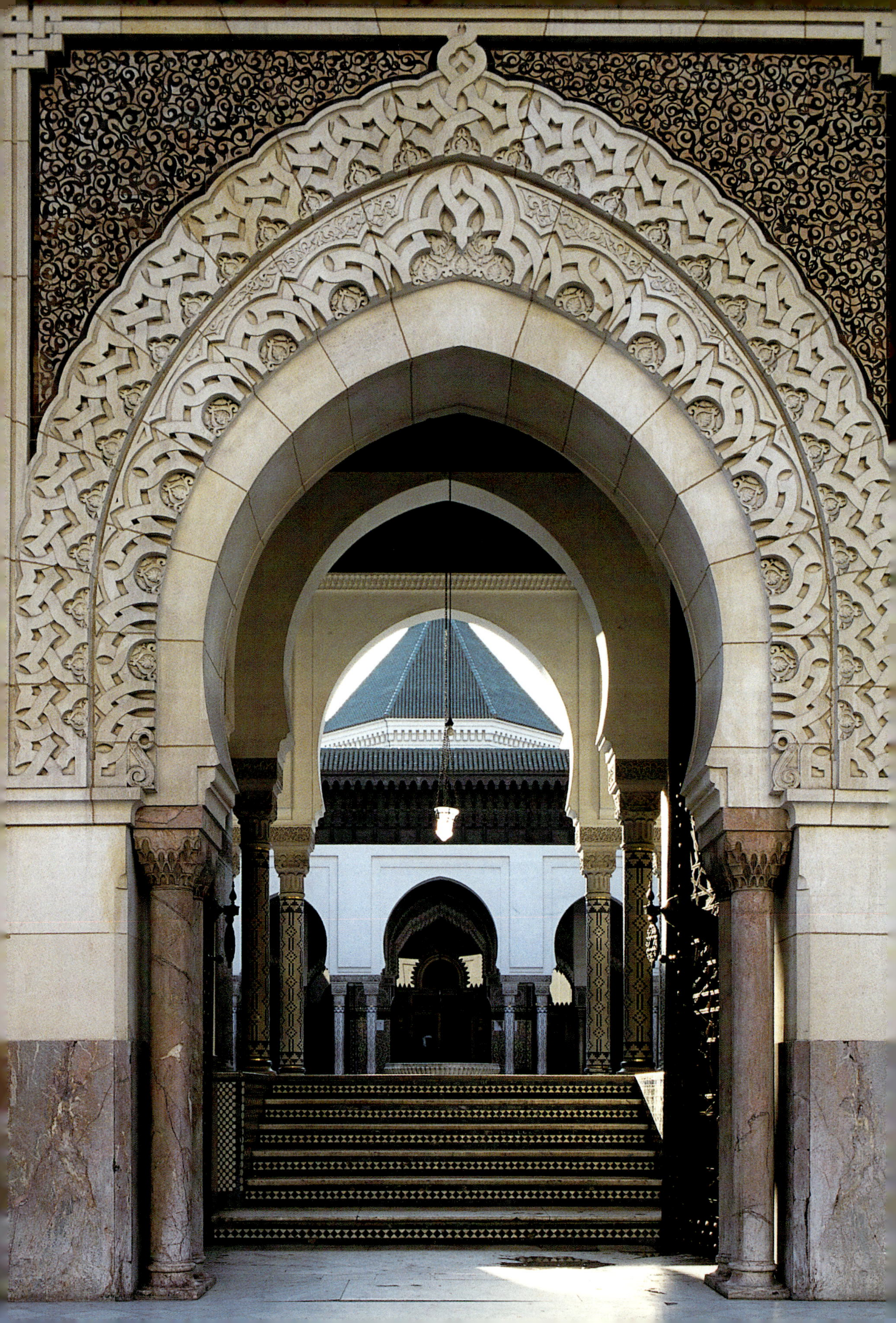

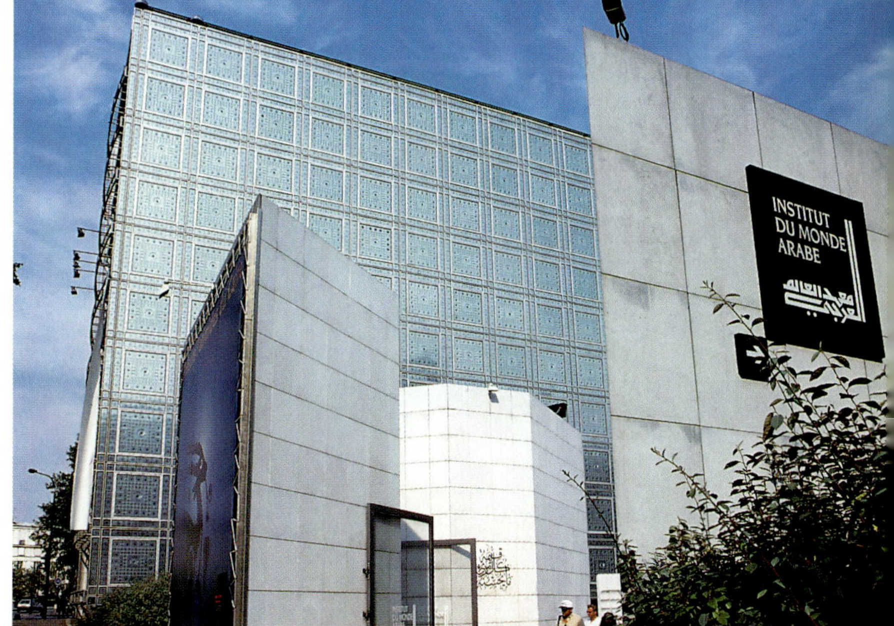

The Paris Mosque is open to the public every day except Fridays and Muslim religious holidays. Its Hispano-Moorish style is inspired by the Alhambra in Grenada (left). Located on the Quai Saint-Bernard, the Institut du Monde Arabe resembles the prow of a ship pointing towards the apse of Notre-Dame (right).

The Mosque

Built in Hispano-Moorish style between 1922 and 1926, in tribute to Muslim soldiers killed in the Great War, the Paris Mosque is a haven of silence and calm. The buildings, with their beautiful Moroccan-inspired decoration, overlook flower-filled courtyards and fulfil various different functions: there is the place of worship incorporating the mosque and its 26 m high minaret, the Institute for Muslim Studies, the Turkish baths and a café-restaurant where visitors can enjoy delicious pastries with a glass of mint tea.

Institut du Monde Arabe

In 1980, France and nineteen Arab countries signed the statutes of a foundation created to increase knowledge and awareness in France of the Arab-Muslim civilisation and promote dialogue between the Arab and European cultures. A site was allocated on the Quai Saint-Bernard and Jean Nouvel and Architecture Studio were put in charge of the building's design and construction. Started in 1982, the project was finally completed in 1987. To symbolise the purpose of the glass and steel edifice, the Arabic Moucharabieh tradition is combined with modern technology via the use of photoelectric cells which control its opening and closing. Inside, the use of white marble and the patio are representative of the Arabic culture.

Covering a surface of 26,900 m², the Institut du Monde Arabe comprises a museum, which frequently hosts major exhibitions, a media library, an auditorium with seating for 360 and on the top floor, a restaurant which gives a spectacular panoramic view of Paris. The Institut has been a great success, not only in terms of its architecture but also through its many popular events.

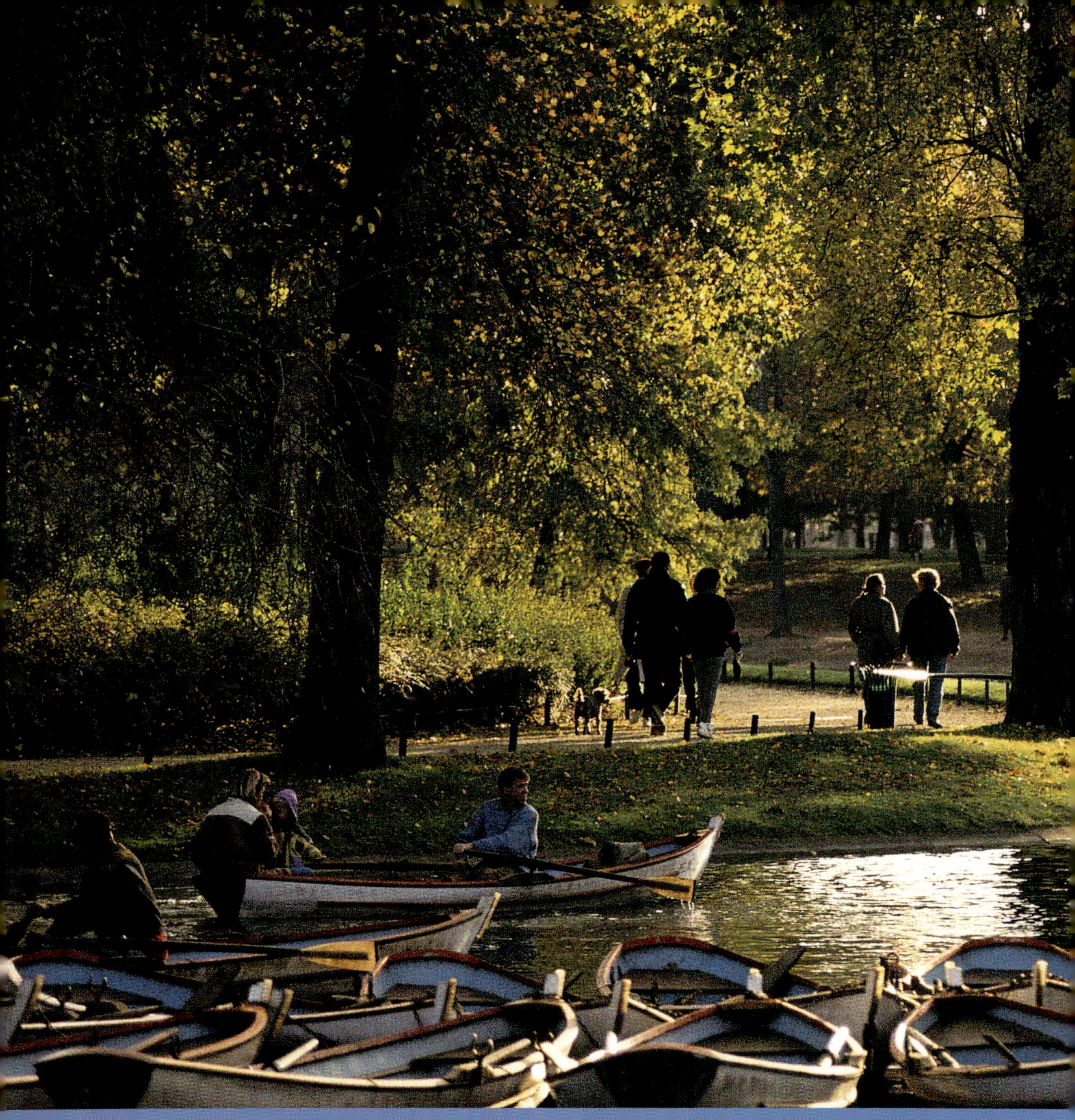

Paris Walks

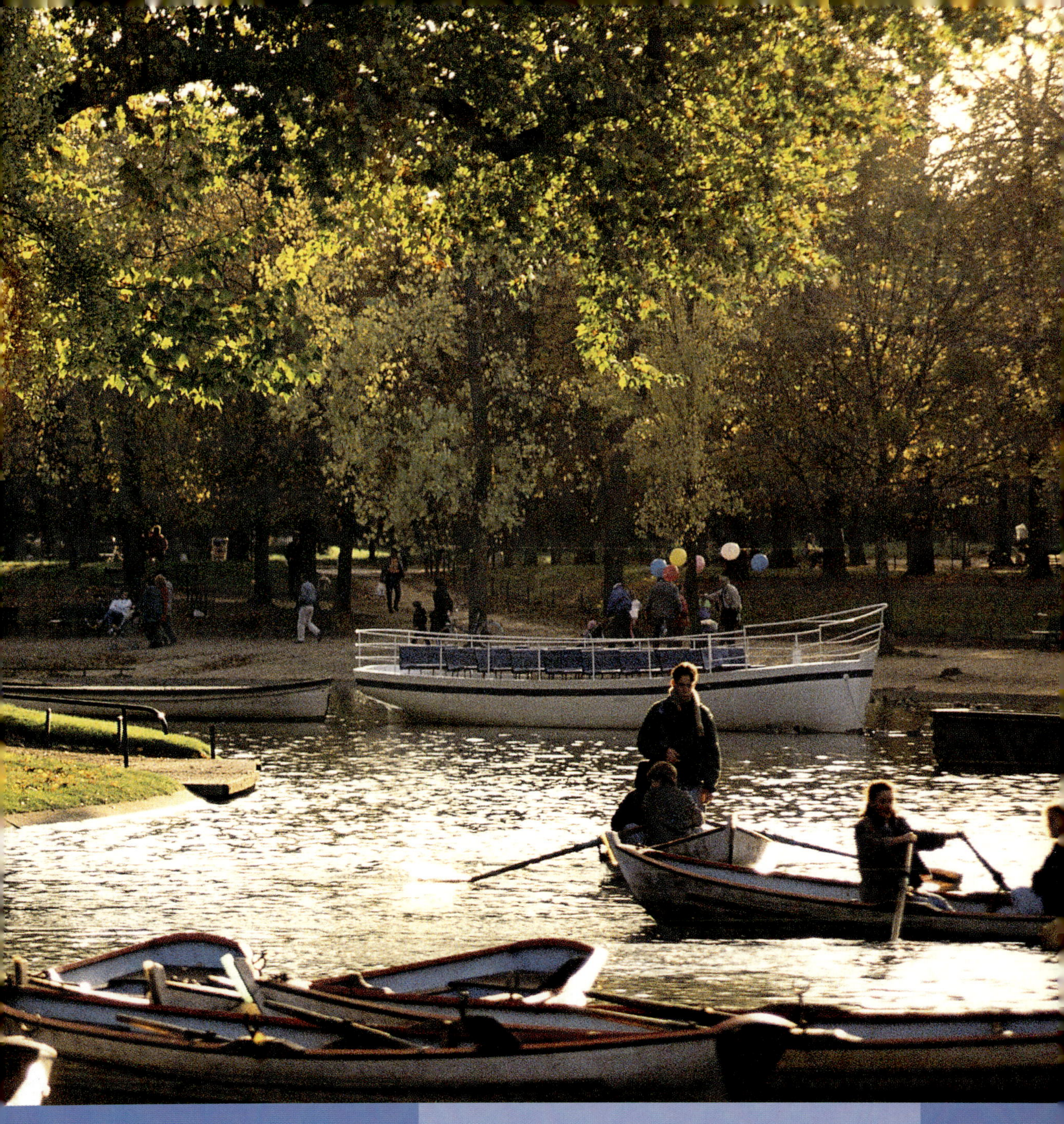

Vincennes
Père-Lachaise cemetery
Buttes-Chaumont Park
La Villette
Bois de Boulogne
and Bagatelle Park

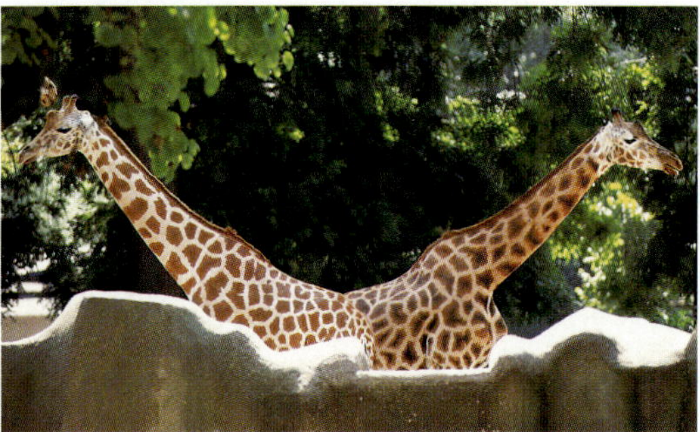

The giraffes at the Vincennes zoo can sometimes get up to mischief! (above).
This small temple decorated with Doric columns overlooks the Daumesnil lake in the Bois de Vincennes (right).

Vincennes

The wood

For a long time, the Bois de Vincennes was a favourite hunting ground of the Kings of France before becoming a military parade ground from 1796 to 1857. Then in 1860, on the initiative of Napoleon III and Haussmann, it was transformed into a vast landscaped park open to the public.

Today, its 995 hectares of forest (some 130,000 trees, the majority of which are oaks, beeches and maples), four lakes (lake Gravelle, Saint-Mandé, Daumesnil and Minimes) and 27 km of cycling, bridle and pedestrian paths are used for leisure and open-air activities. It is also home to various establishments, some of which occupy former military premises, such as the Théâtre de la Cartoucherie adjacent to the Parc Floral, the Institut Géographique National, Institut National des Sports, Institut de Recherches Agronomique et Tropicales, the Centre Technique Forestier Tropicale, the Georges-Ville educational farm, the zoological gardens and a racecourse. The Bois de Vincennes also hosted the Universal Exhibition of 1931. Along with the Bois de Boulogne, it is one of the capital's most popular areas for walking.

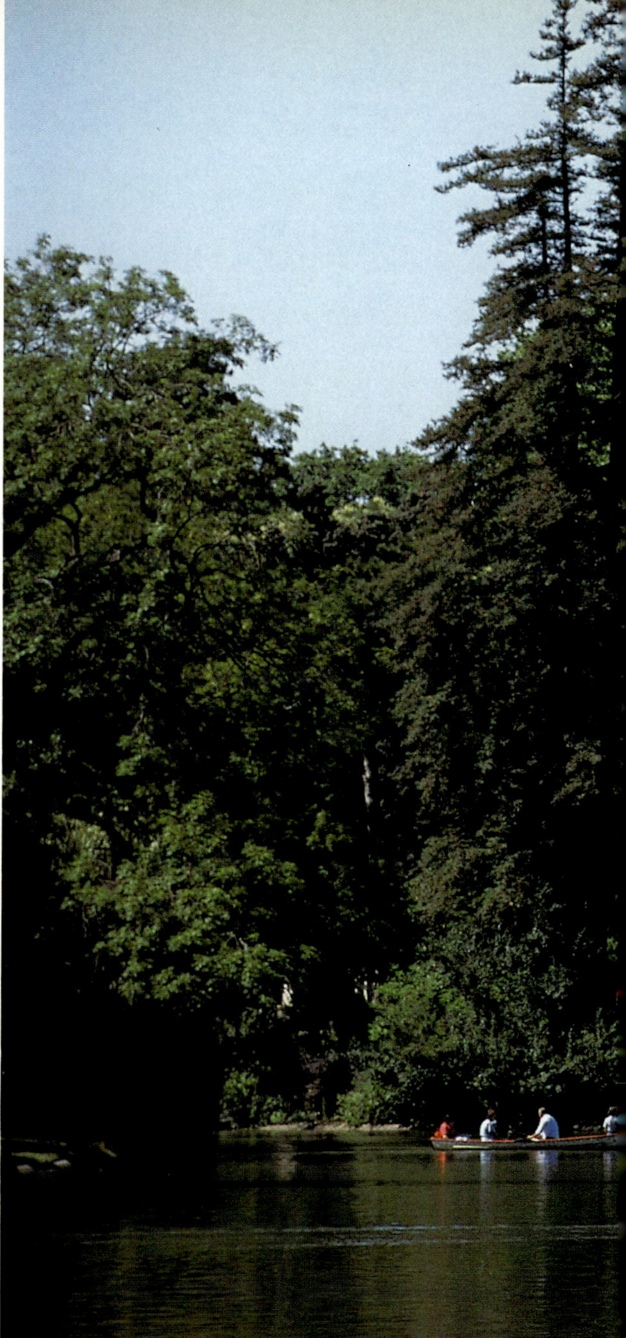

The château

Under the reign of Philippe Auguste (1180-1223) there was already a manor house on the site of the existing château. This had replaced the modest hunting lodge of his father, King Louis VIII. King Saint-Louis regularly stayed here and according to legend, would deliver justice under one of its oaks. The Sainte-Chapelle was started in 1400 and completed during the Renaissance by Philibert de l'Orme. The surrounding walls and keep (52 m high and flanked by 4

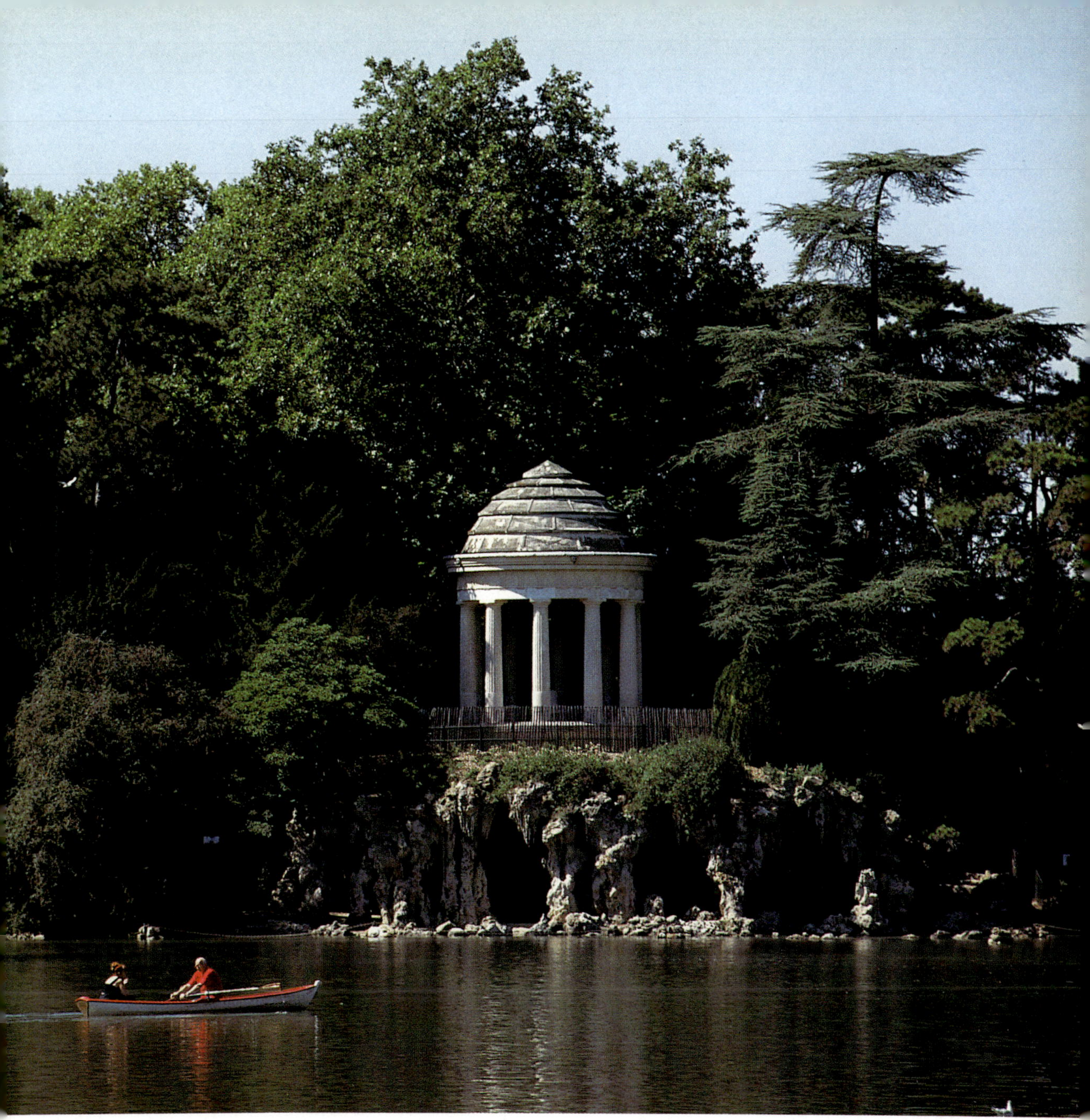

turrets at each corner) were built towards the 14th century. In the 17th century, Le Vau constructed two new wings, the King's pavilion for Louis XIV and Marie-Thérèse and the Queen's pavilion for Anne of Austria and Mazarin. Then in 1668, it ceased to be a royal residence and became a State prison. Between 1730 and 1756 it was home to a porcelain factory. Napoleon I then transformed the château into a fortress and arsenal, while the keep was still used as a prison. In 1804, the Duc d'Enghien, suspected of involvement in a plot against the Emperor, was shot in the château's moat. His remains are now in the Saint-Chapelle. After being severely damaged by German troops in 1944, the Château de Vincennes has undergone a gradual process of restoration. The original château was an immense building, flanked by nine towers, all of which were demolished under the Empire apart from the Tour du Village. The King's Pavilion now houses a historical museum, a museum dedicated to the First World War and historical army records.

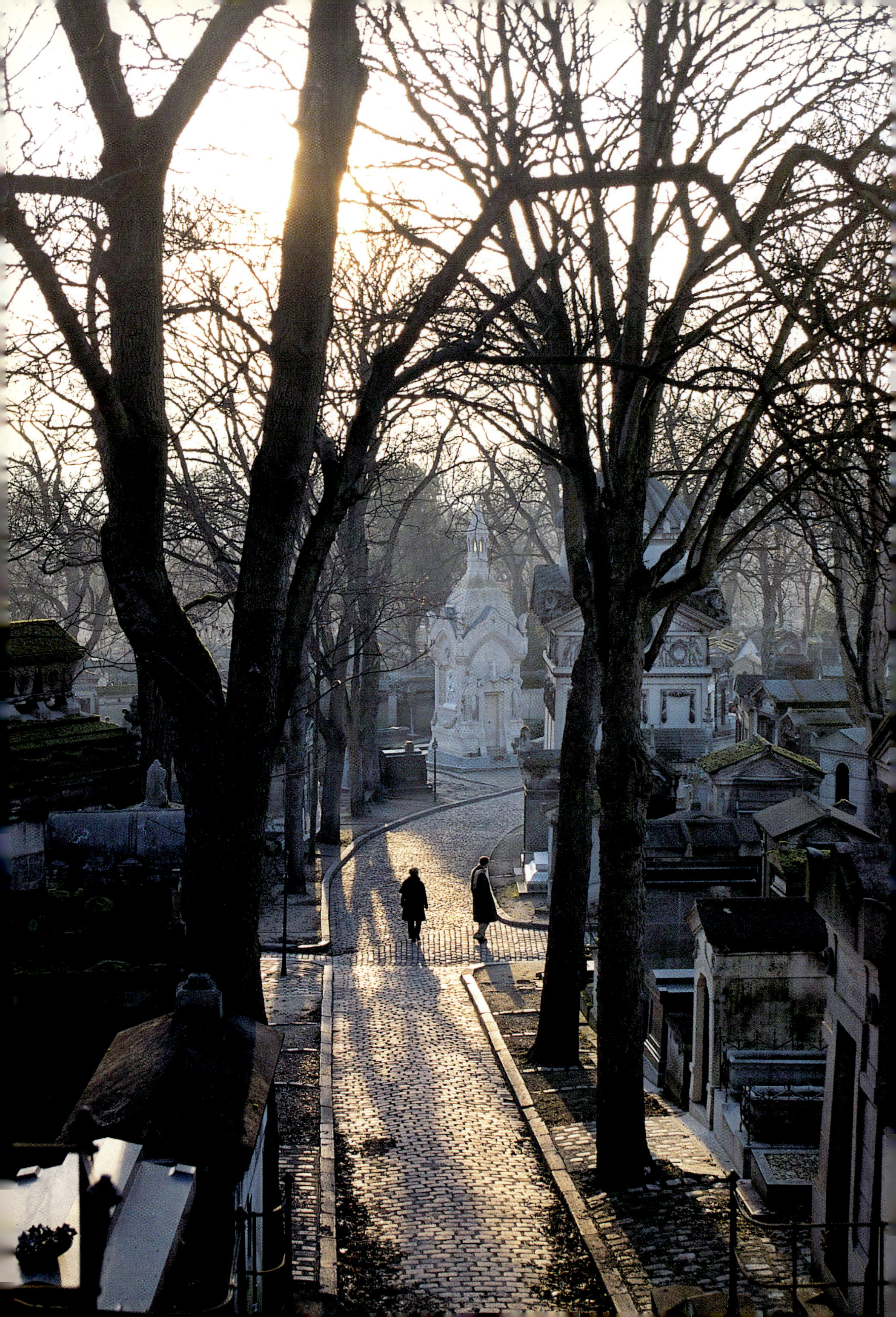

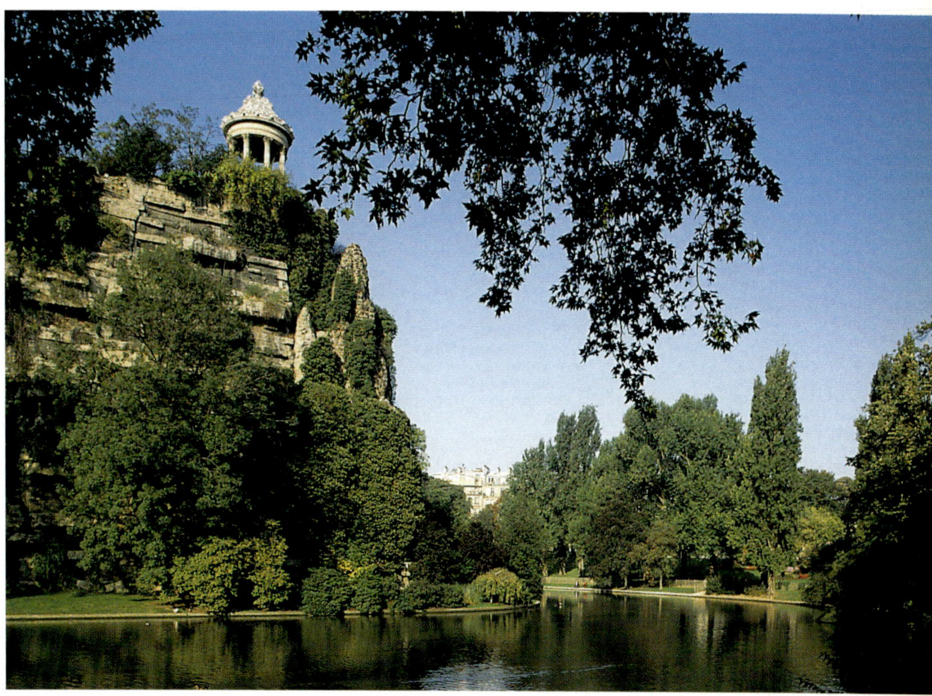

A path in the Père-Lachaise cemetery (left).
The little temple perched on top of the island in the Buttes-Chaumont lake, is a copy of the Temple of Sybil in Tivoli, Italy. This type of building is inspired by the follies popular in the 18th century (right).

Père-Lachaise cemetery

The most famous and largest of Paris' cemeteries was named after Père La Chaise, the confessor of King Louis XIV who had a house built on the site. Then in 1801, for reasons of sanitation and town planning, the Prefect Frochot passed an order forbidding burials inside churches, which until then had been the custom. Three cemeteries were created, the Montmartre, Montparnasse and Père Lachaise cemeteries. The third was designed by the architect Brongniart. Inaugurated in 1804, Père Lachaise cemetery is almost a "mini-city" in its own right, with its many passages, footpaths, "districts", places of pilgrimage and meeting places… not to mention its statues and busts of illustrious figures, its sometimes strange architectural styles, picturesque monuments and copses, which are perfect for a leisurely stroll. Père Lachaise cemetery has also been the scene of some bloody political events. During the Paris Commune in 1871, violent battles took place around the tombs themselves. On 28 May the same year, 147 federates were executed by firing squad by the Versaillais. The wall where the shooting took place has become a place of pilgrimage for political parties of the left.

Buttes-Chaumont park

Situated between Père Lachaise cemetery and La Villette, the Buttes-Chaumont park is one of the most beautiful in Paris. The area was restructured by dynamite blasting under the supervision of the engineers Alphand and Darcel and developed between 1866 and 1867 on the site of former gypsum quarries. Covering an area of 24 hectares, the park is a perfect example of the Haussmann style garden, with its rockeries, streams, waterfalls, stone balustrades and artificial grottoes decorated with stalactites. In the middle of a two hectare lake is an island, which can be reached by two bridges - the Pont de Brique and the Pont des Suicidés - and where an imposing rock stands. At its summit is a charming replica of the Neo-classical Temple of Sibyl. Among the park's impressive collection of trees are two ginkgo-bilobas, the oldest known species of conifer. The park was also the scene of some bloody battles in 1814, between Prussian and French troops and later in 1871 during the Paris Commune. Today, it is very popular with both walkers and sports lovers.

The nearby Amérique district, with its flower-filled cottages and villas and quiet streets is like a forgotten corner of the countryside in this bustling capital city.

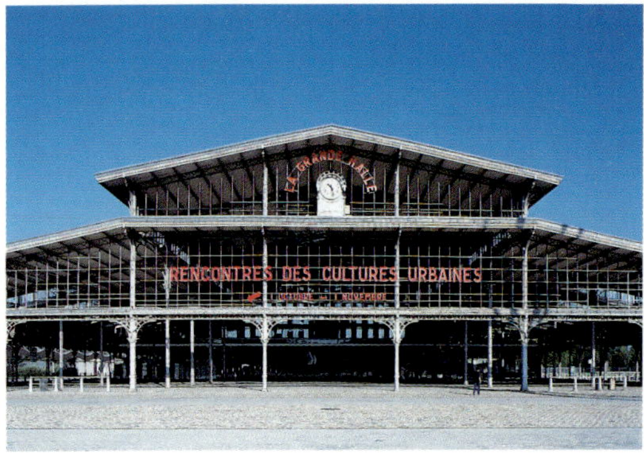

The Grand Hall at La Villette, built in 1867, escaped
demolition and is today the venue for a variety of cultural
events (above).
Located at the intersection of the Parc de la Villette
and the Cité des Sciences et de l'Industrie, the spherical
shaped Géode breaks the monotony of horizontal lines
in a spectacular way (right).

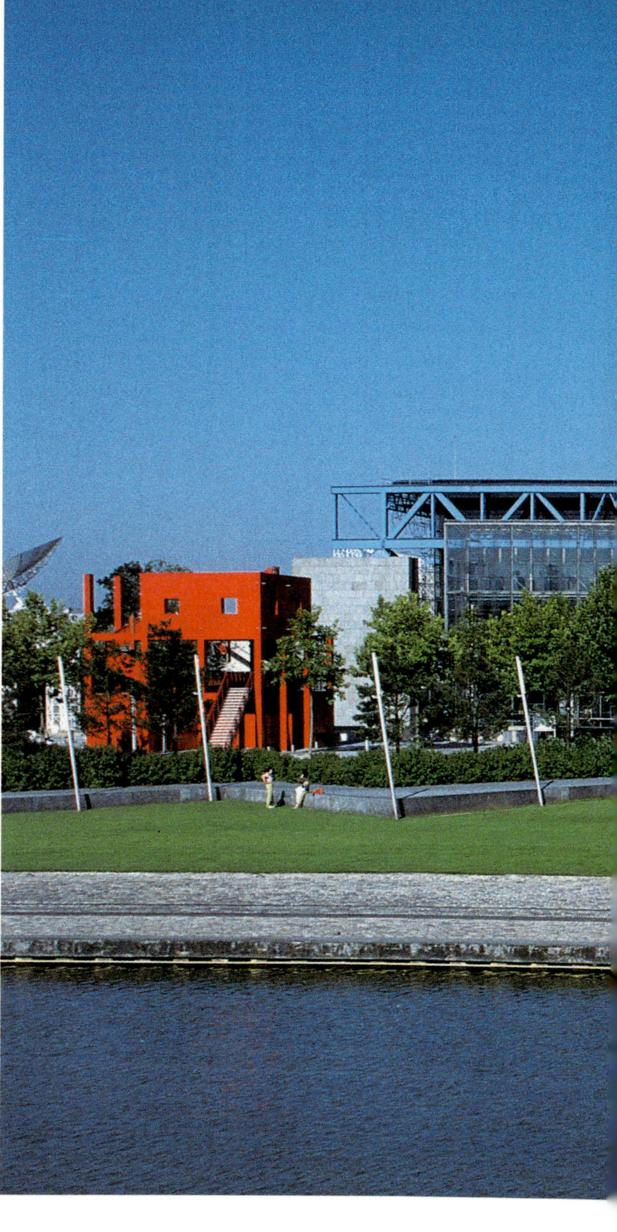

La Villette

The Cité des Sciences et de l'Industrie

In the 1960s, new abattoirs were built at the La Villette
site to replace the old ones dating from 1867. However,
the project was a financial disaster and when work was
completed in 1973, it was clear the buildings were obso-
lete. With the arrival of new refrigeration techniques that
enabled the transportation of meat, animals could be
slaughtered at the farm. To save the district, a decision
was made to replace the abattoirs with a Cité des Sciences
et de l'Industrie. Today, of the former 19th century abattoirs, only the Grand Hall has survived. This was the old
cattle market which has now been renovated into a multi-
purpose cultural centre for concerts, exhibitions and shows.
The complex's main building, surrounded by water-filled
moats and designed by the architect Adrien Fainsilber,
houses major exhibitions, interactive shows, model displays
and events linked to the universe of technology and the
environment. La Cité des Enfants and Techno-Cité offer
youngsters leisure and educational activities and an intro-
duction to new technologies. In the Géode, a vast 36 m
diameter sphere whose outer wall is covered in 6,433 steel
triangles which spectacularly reflect the sky and the surrounding landscape, is a 1,000 m² hemispherical screen.

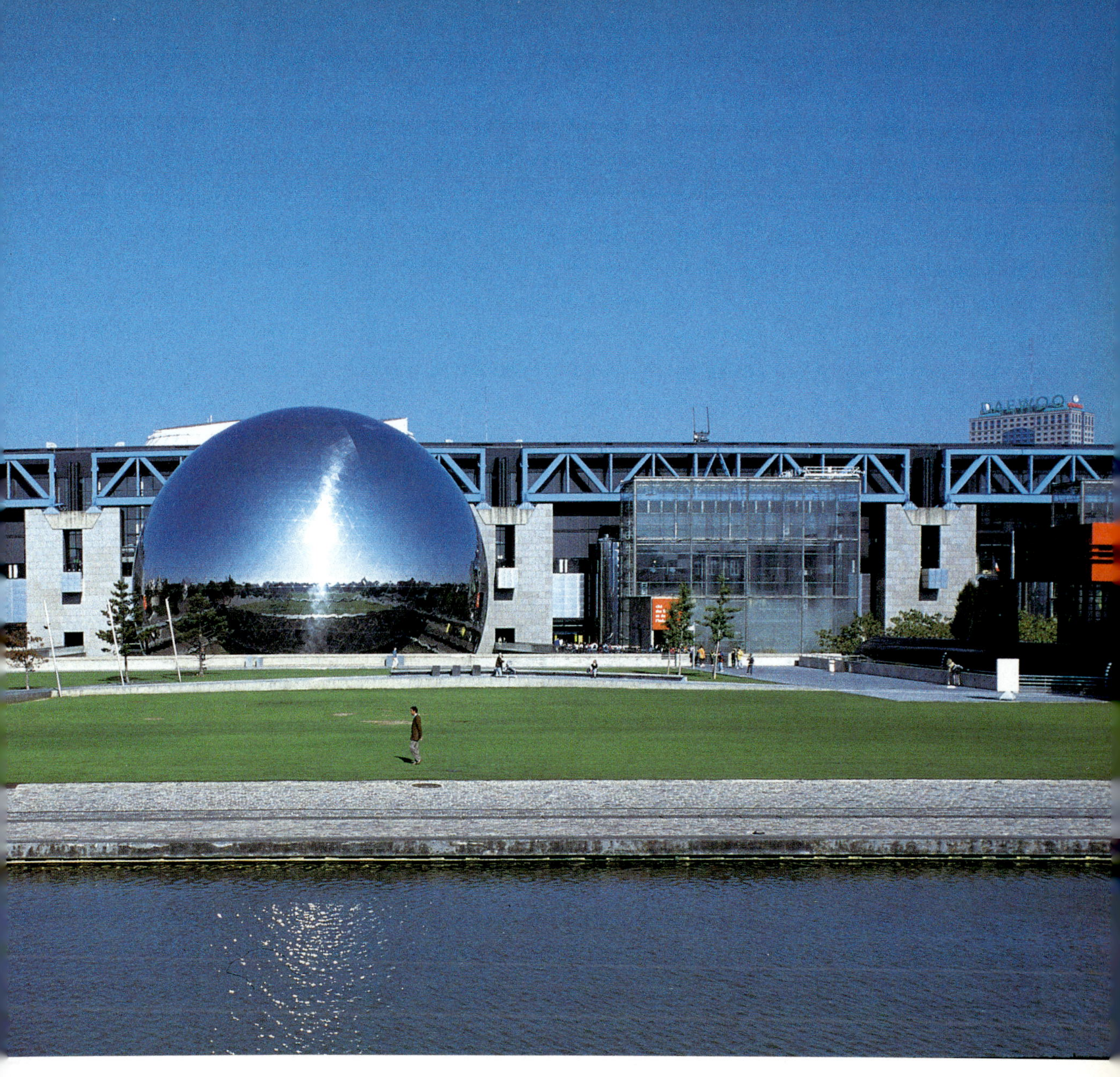

The *Cinaxe*, with its seats mounted on jacks, takes visitors on a thrilling simulated space flight or car race. The *Argonaute* submarine, grounded here after completing several trips round the world, gives visitors the chance to experience the cramped interior of this underwater craft. The *Zénith*, a multi-purpose structure, is a popular venue for rock and variety shows. The surrounding Parc de la Villette, designed by Bernard Tschumi as a "city-garden" and covering 35 hectares, is the largest public park in Paris. Here, strollers can wander around the various theme gardens (such as the Jardins des Frayeurs Enfantines, Jardins des Brouillards or Jardin des Bambous) with their 21 "follies", musical pavilions and restaurants.

The Cité de la Musique

The buildings of the Cité de la Musique, on either side of the Fontaine aux Lions designed by Christian de Portzamparc, house the Conservatoire National de la Musique et de la Danse, a concert hall and the Musée de la Musique. The latter displays a collection of over 900 musical instruments and takes visitors on a sound and vision tour of the history of music from the 17th century to the present day.

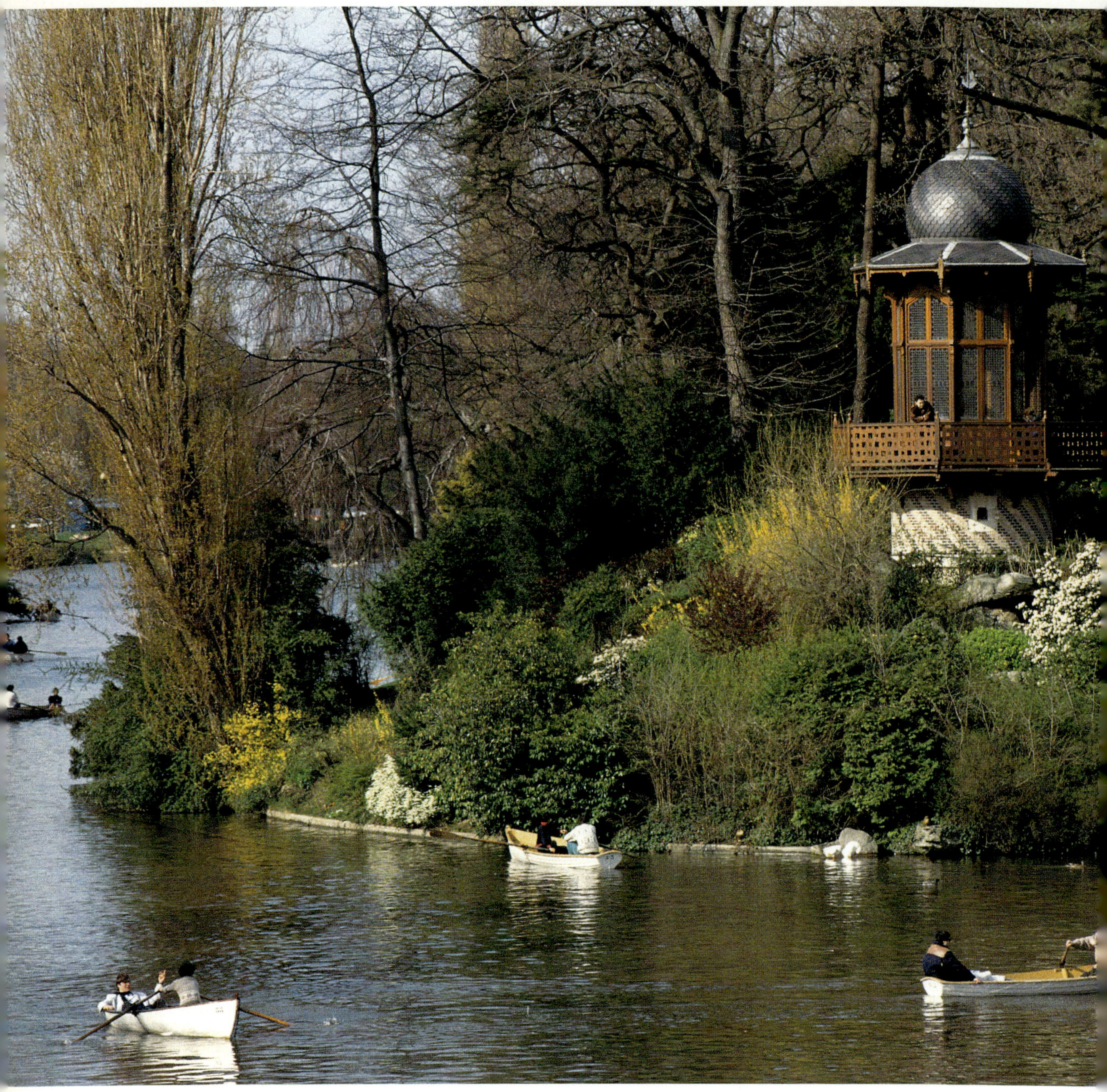

Bois de Boulogne and Bagatelle park

The Bois de Boulogne is what remains of the old Rouvray forest, named after the red oaks (Quercus Robur) which once covered the hills of north-west Paris. It was here in 1301 that Philippe IV le Bel decided to build an oratory dedicated to Notre-Dame de Boulogne. The Longchamp mill is the only vestige of the Abbey founded on the edge of the forest in the 13th century by Saint-Louis' sister and later destroyed under the Revolution. The Bois de Boulogne's reputation for illicit night-time activities is not a recent phenomenon. In the 18th century it was already a place for licentious behaviour among the Kings of France who used the Château de Madrid (built by Francis I and now disappeared) for illicit rendezvous. The nobility, not wishing to be left out, then built some splendid châteaux here, such

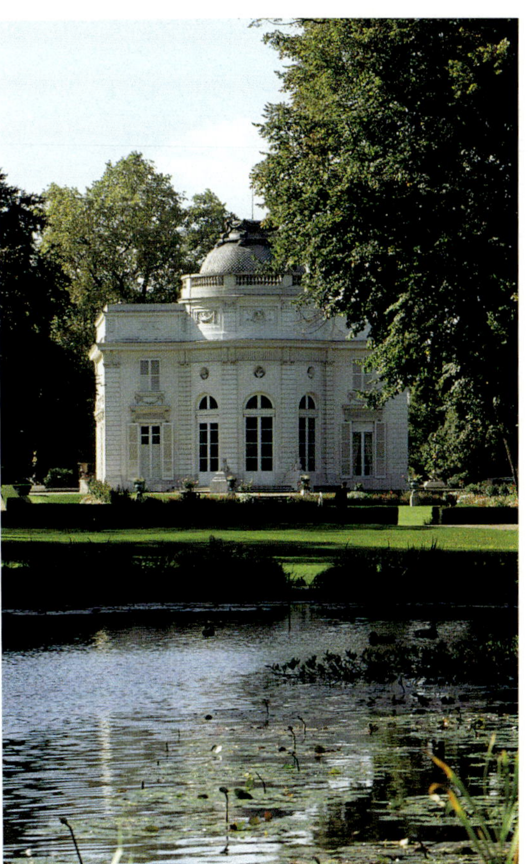

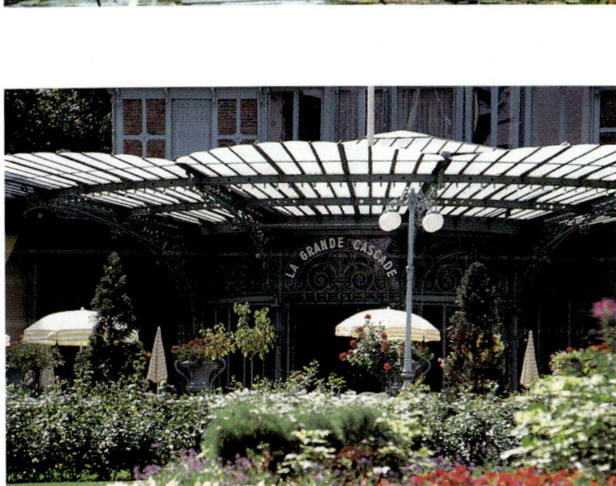

Boating on one of the two lakes in the Bois de Boulogne
is a favourite pastime of Parisians (left).
La Grande Cascade restaurant enjoys a high reputation (top).
Around the lakes of the Bois de Boulogne, walkers can find
various chalets and pavilions (above).

as La Muette, Neuilly and Ranelagh. The only one that
remains today is that of the Bagatelle. The forest was a
popular place for walking under the First Empire, then rav-
aged during the Prussian occupation between 1814 and
1815 before being redeveloped from 1852-1855. It was
redesigned by Alphand, who created two lakes, 95 km of
pathways, dug out rivers and planted 400,000 trees. Under
the Empire concessions were granted for the construction
of the Pré Catalan, the Jardin d'Acclimatation, the
Longchamp race course and later the race course at Auteuil.
Today, the Bois de Boulogne is a park covering 846 hectares
planted mainly with oaks - some are over 200 years old -
which is home to many species of mammals and birds.

Adjacent to the Bois de Boulogne is the Parc de
Bagatelle. The park and pavilion were built in 1775 by
the Comte d'Artois in just 63 days, following a wager with
Queen Marie Antoinette. Thomas Blaikie created an Anglo-
Chinese style garden, in fashion at the time, with grottoes,
waterfalls, rockeries and pagodas. At the end of the 19th
century, a patron of the arts, Richard Wallace - who is responsible for a hundred or so public fountains dotted around
the capital which all bear his name - built two new pavilions here along with the Trianon. The "Folie d'Artois" is
decorated with 18th century furniture and in its grounds
are a series of different types of garden including English
and French, gardens of iris, aquatic plants, dahlias and opposite the orangery, a magnificent rose garden containing
9,000 roses of over a thousand different varieties. The Parc
de Bagatelle, once the scene of many aristocratic and royal
celebrations under the Ancien Regime, is now a venue
for various prestigious events.

Monument

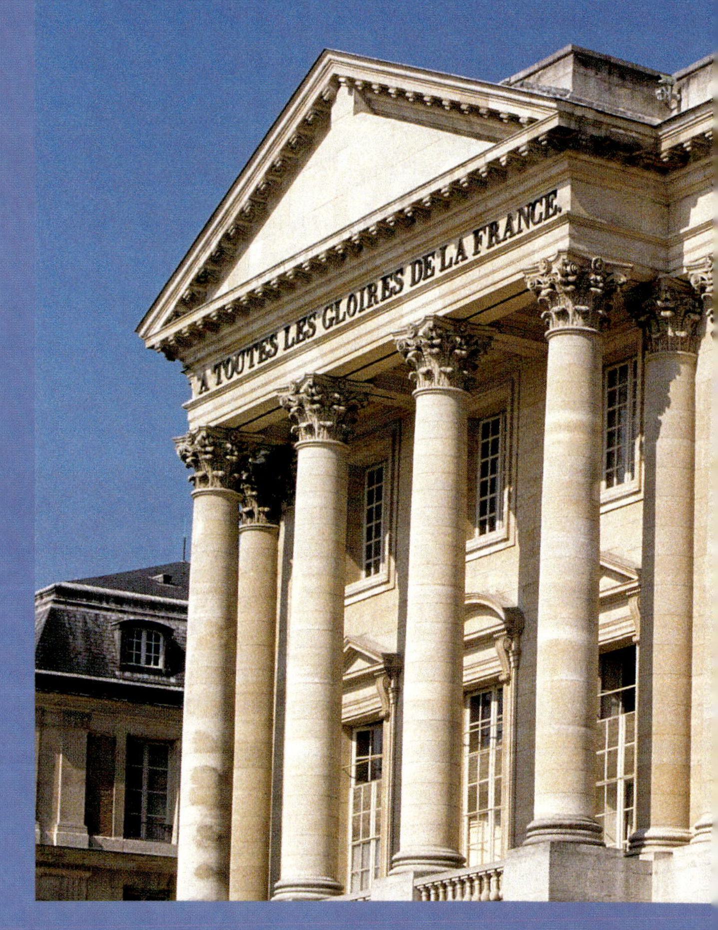

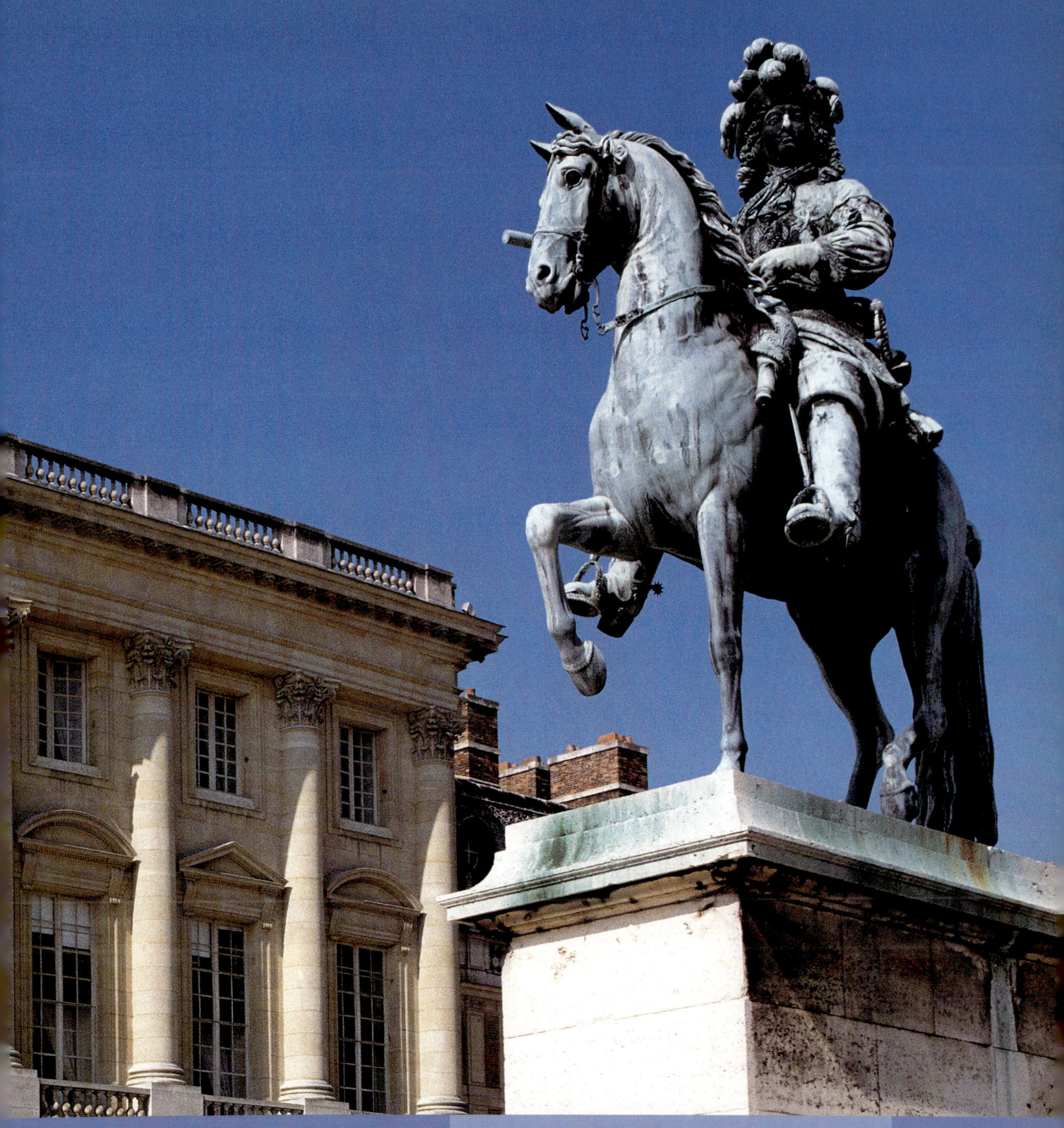

Versailles

The château
and gardens

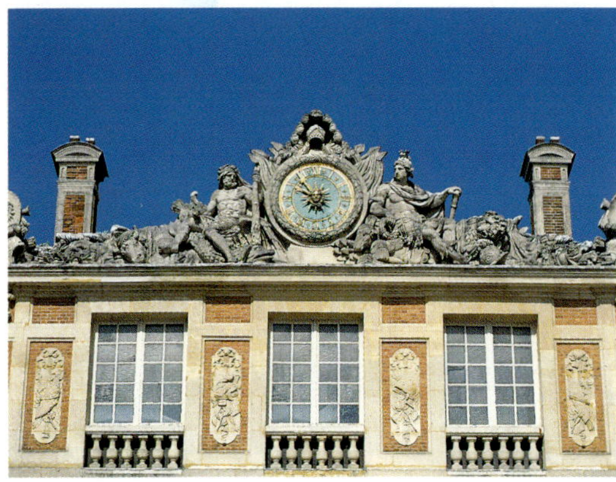

The elegant hunting lodge built by Louis XIII remains
the central element of the Château de Versailles (above).
Versailles palace was designed entirely in praise of Louis XIV,
the Sun King. The palace stands as a symbol of absolute
monarchy (right).

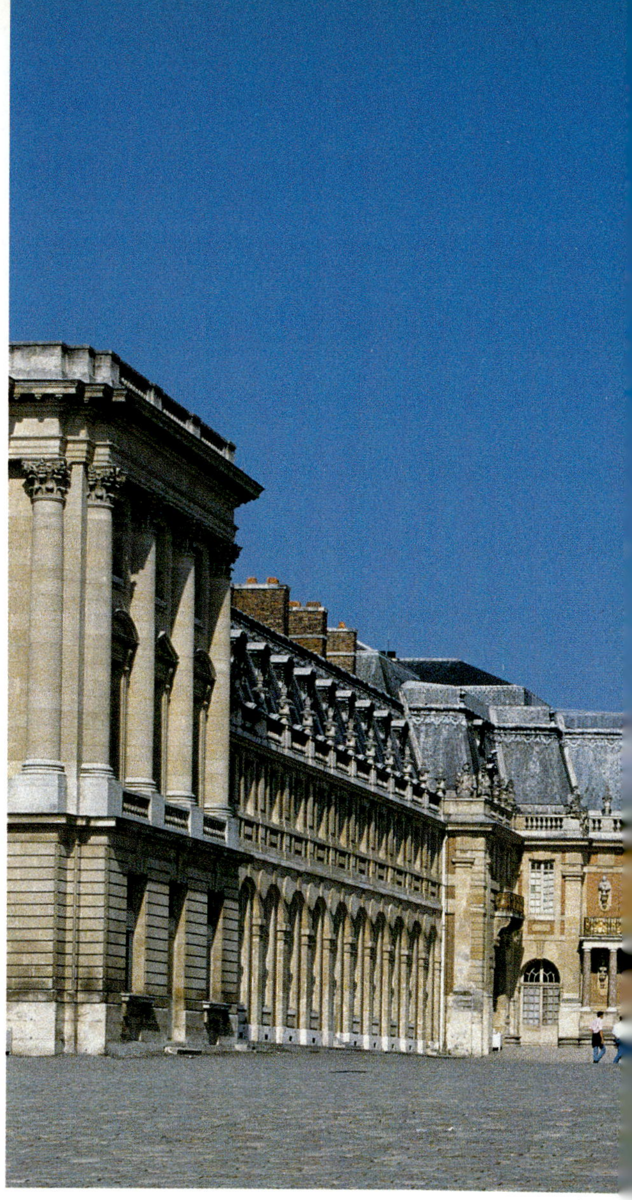

Versailles : the château and gardens

The reign of Louis XIV

When Louis XIV came to the throne in 1661 at the age
of 23, the young monarch decided to transform his father's
hunting lodge into a royal residence. The 40 hectare site
at Versailles had originally been purchased by Louis XIII who
enjoyed hunting in the area. Between 1631 and 1634, the
King commissioned Philibert Le Roy to construct a modest stone and brick building, which Saint-Simon derisively
called a "house of cards". Louis XIV placed Le Vau in charge
of the architectural work and gave instructions to preserve
the original building, making it the starting point of the
extensions. The painter Charles Le Brun was appointed for
the interior decoration and the gardener Le Nôtre brought
in to create the gardens.

The former château was preserved: on the eastern side
towards the town, it remained visible, opening out onto a
marble courtyard and inserted between the new buildings
to be used by the royal administration, while on the western
side towards the gardens, it was lost from view behind a new
façade. Between 1679 and 1684, the first floor terrace was
closed to receive the Hall of Mirrors. Located in the main central building, the State Apartments were specially designed for
official functions, to dazzle foreign visitors - they are decorated
in a profusion of gold and marbles, inspired by Classical mythol-
ogy and the planets moving around the sun. The Queen's
Apartments face south while those of the King, to the north.

In 1678, Louis XIV decided to make Versailles his main
residence. To accommodate the royal family, the edifice
had to be extended, with a south wing (1678-1682) and north

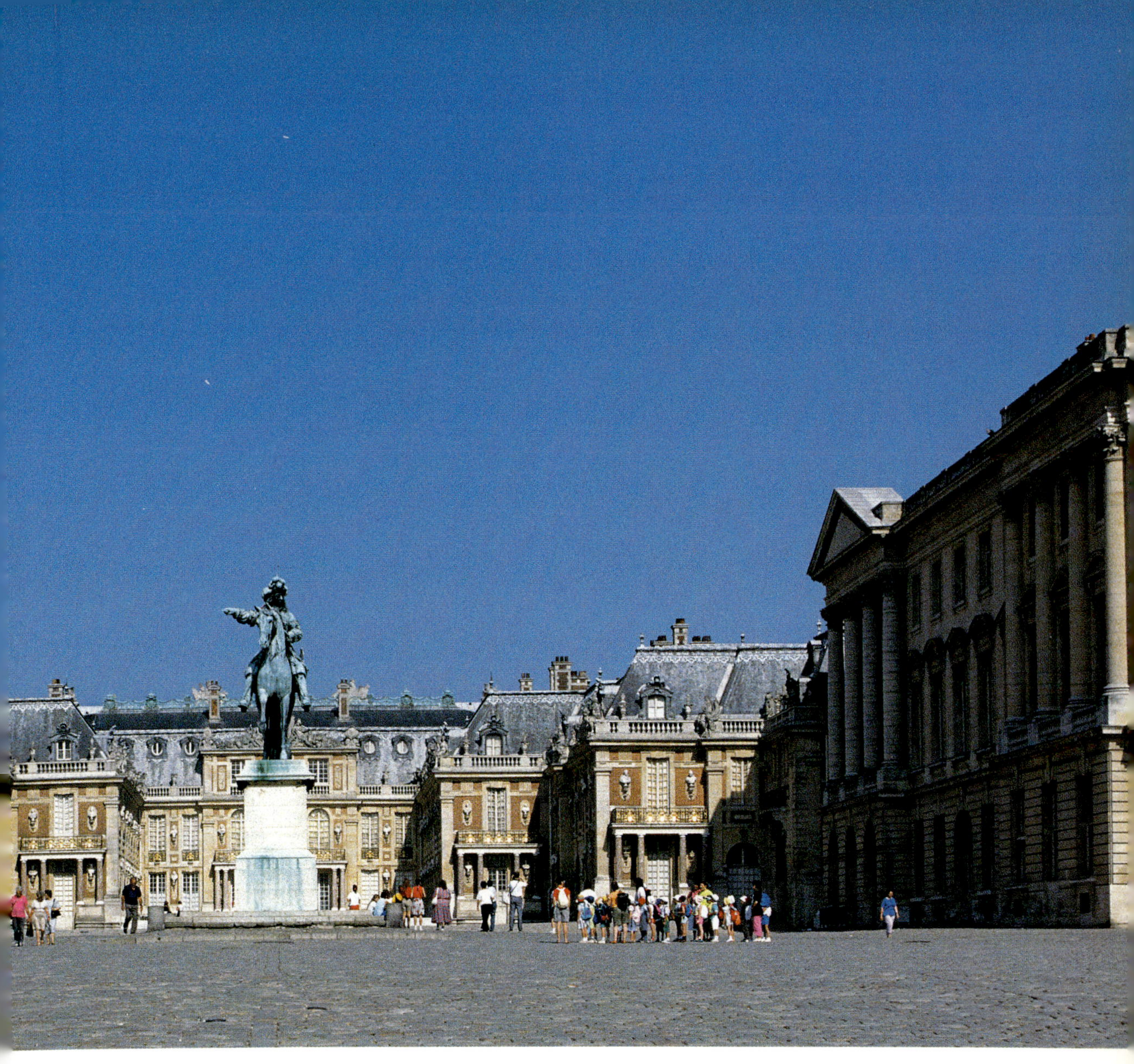

wing (1685-1689). On each side of the vast Place d'Armes preceding the palace, are two buildings: the Grand Stables and Small Stables, built between 1679 and 1681 followed by the Grand Commun in the following two years. In 1689, Mansart began work on the current chapel which was completed by Robert de Cotte and consecrated in 1710. The chapel's nave is linked to the royal apartments on the first floor while on the garden side, it is hidden by the façade. Only its apse is visible from the side facing the town.

From 1663, Le Nôtre designed a vast open park around the buildings covering about a hundred hectares, combining terraces and water features in a spectacular play of perspectives receding into the distance. In the main axis of the façade are the two Parterre d'Eau by Mansart, involving statues of the rivers of France, which were executed by the Kellers (1685-1695). Lower down, the Latone Basin leads to the Tapis Vert, decorated with vases and statues by students from the Académié de France in Rome. The Apollo Basin, which involves a statue of the god on his chariot, was designed by Le Brun (1684) and the Grand Canal, 1,520 m long and 120 m wide, is home to a whole fleet of different craft. To the south, below the terrace, Mansart built an orangery (1684-1686) and to the north, the Fountain of the Bathing Nymphs leads to the Allée des Marmousets,

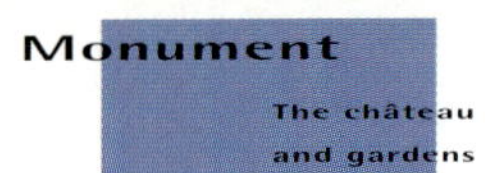

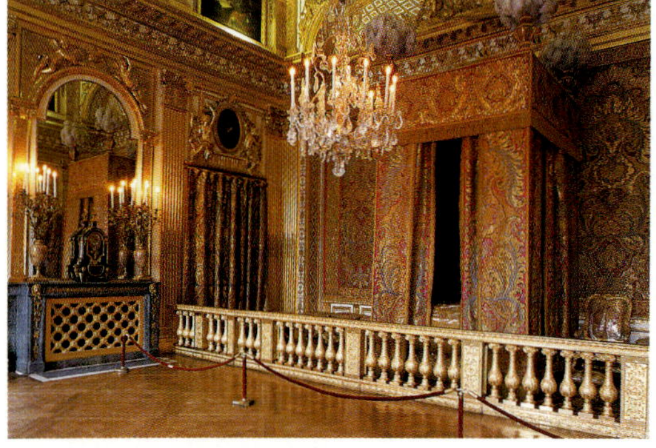

designed by Le Brun, and the Basin of Neptune. Some charming groves can be found nestling between the two East-West and North-South axes, where visitors can admire the Ballroom decorated with rockeries and the colonnade with its marble arches sculpted by Coysevox, with at its centre, the *Enlèvement de Proserpine* by Girardon (1699).

Between 1687 and 1690, Mansart built the Grand Trianon, an Italianate marble palace composed of two wings joined by a peristyle opening out onto the gardens. Louis XIV liked to spend time here, in the company of close family members.

The reign of Louis XV

On the death of Louis XIV in 1715, the château was abandoned for seven years, the Regent preferring to live in the capital. But at his coming of age, Louis XV decided to move back to the palace of his ancestors. The new King had the royal apartments refitted, with a preference for the smaller, more comfortable rooms, although he did preserve the ceremonial State Apartments. He then appointed his architect, Gabriel, to construct the opera at the far end of the north wing. Gabriel was also responsible for designing the Petit Trianon for Madame de Pompadour. The latter died before the works were completed and the building was inaugurated by the King's next favourite, Madame Du Barry in 1770.

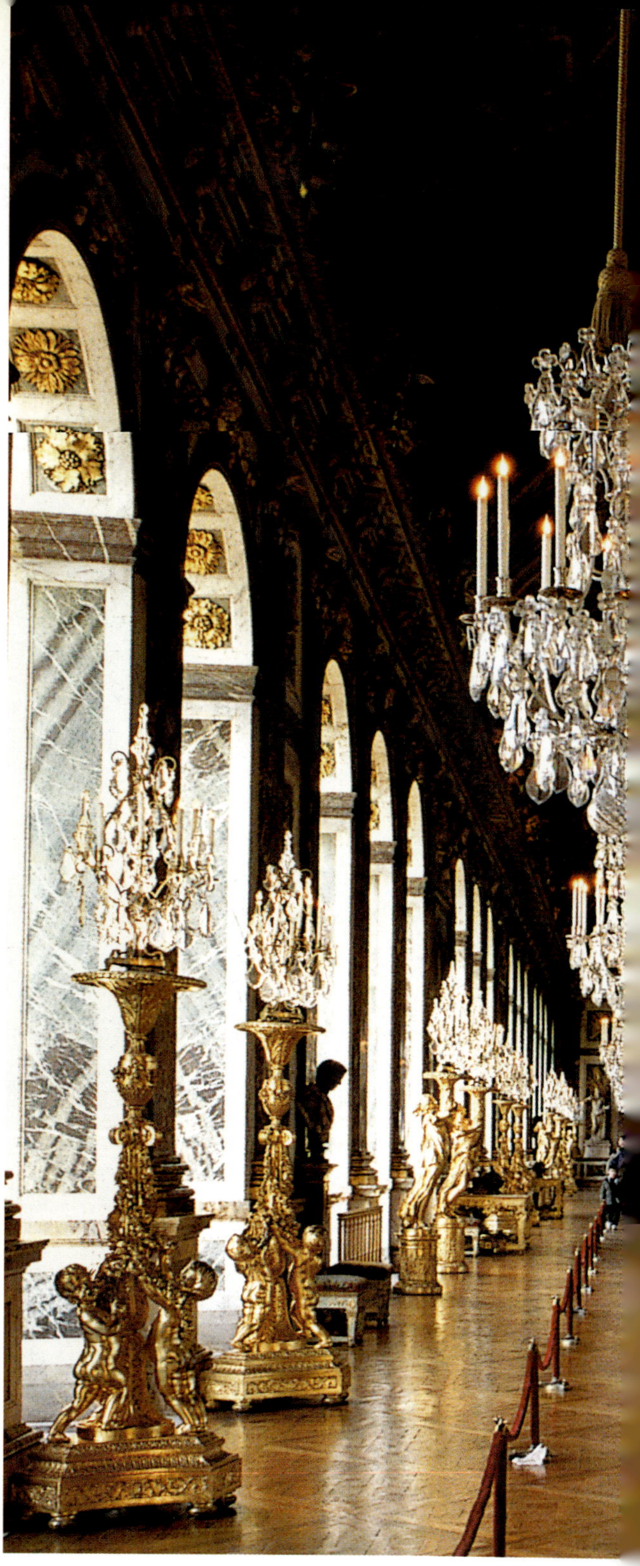

The reign of Louis XVI

On the death of Louis XV in 1774, Louis XVI gave his wife, Marie-Antoinette the Petit Trianon. She redesigned the grounds, built the gazebo and Temple

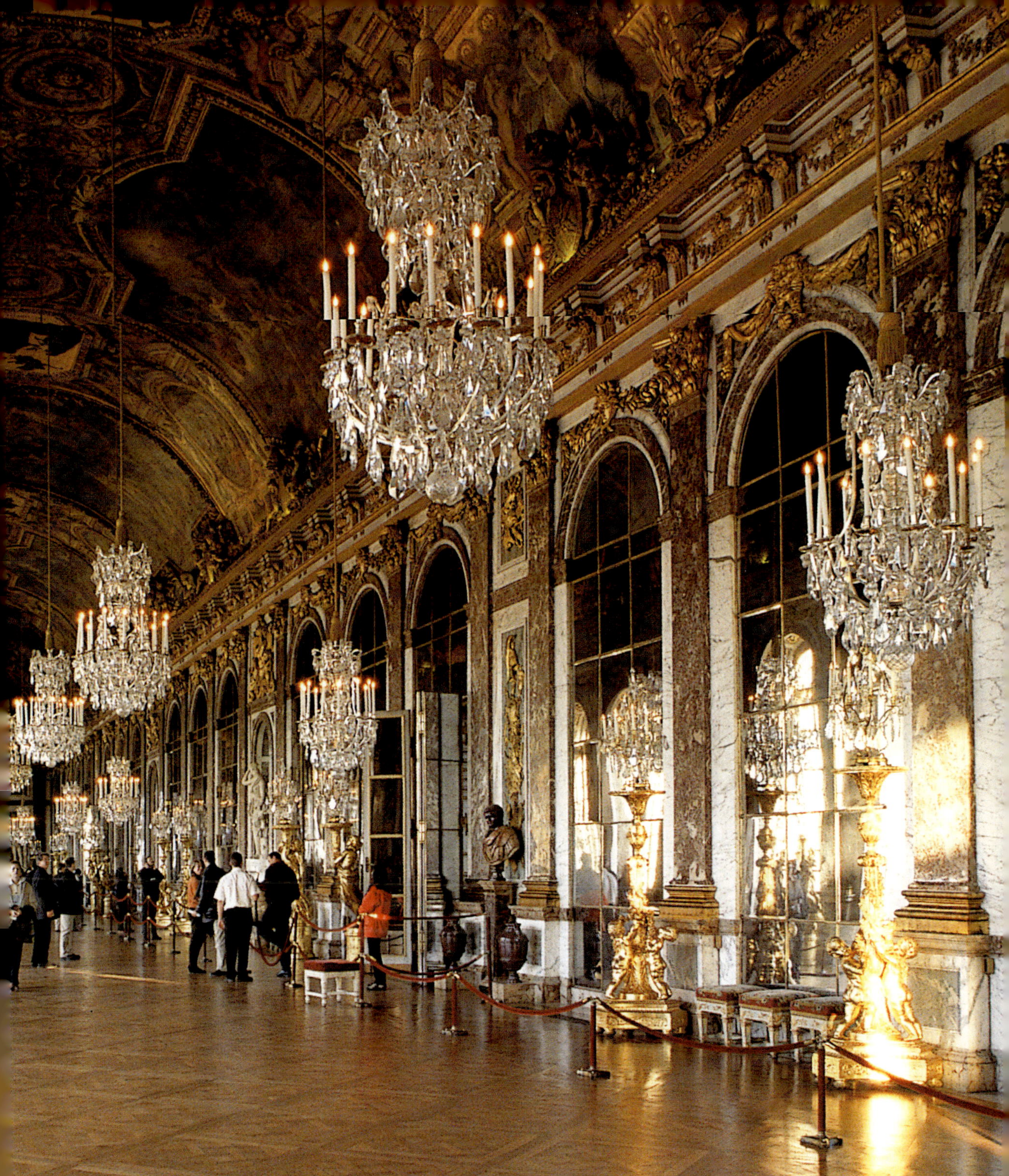

of Love and created Le Hameau, a kind of model farm and village comprising a dairy, dovecote and mill. She also built a theatre, where she enjoyed giving performances.

The King's chamber, where official ceremonies were held in the presence of various courtiers (top left). The Hall of Mirrors represented a real technical achievement for its time. It was the scene of many magnificent balls and functions given by the monarchy (above).

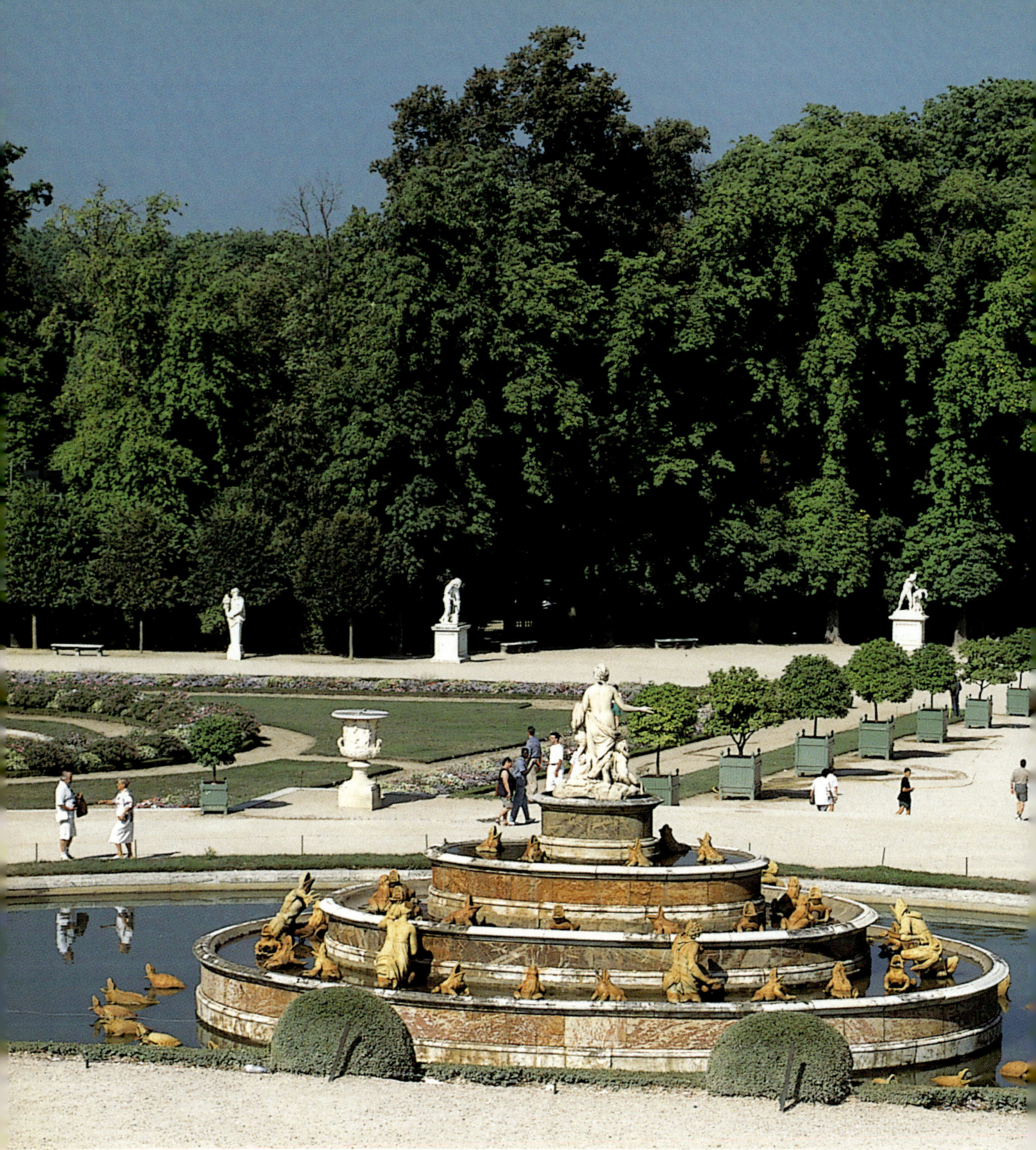

From the Revolution to the present day

The last event held by the monarchy in Versailles was the opening ceremony for the Estates General in May 1789. In October the same year, the rebels brought Louis XVI, Marie-Antoinette and the rest of the royal family to Paris. Versailles was abandoned and emptied of its furniture, the majority of which was sold. Napoleon showed no interest in the château and neither did the Bourbons, who had no desire to live there during the Restoration. It was Louis-Philippe who saved the palace and transformed it in 1837 into a historical museum devoted to "the glories of France". The Battle Hall contains a series of large

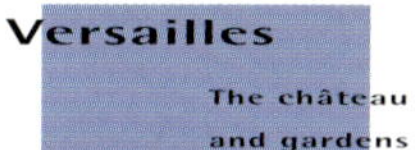

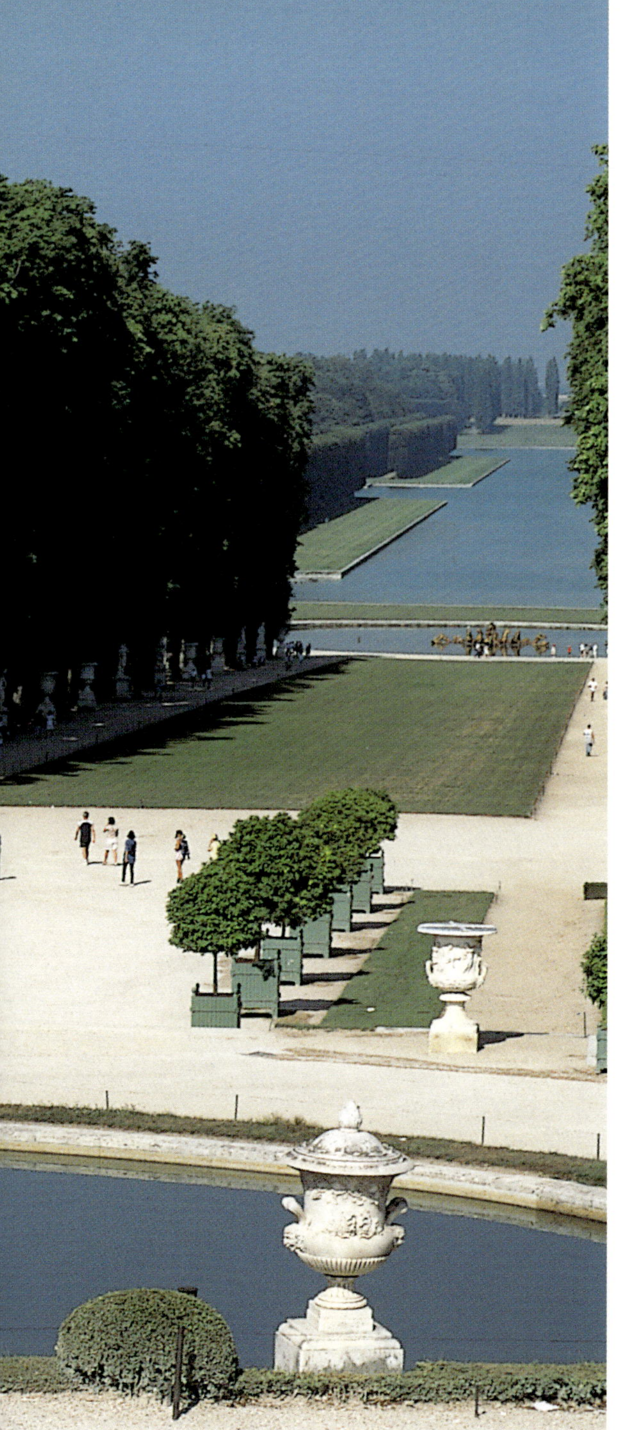

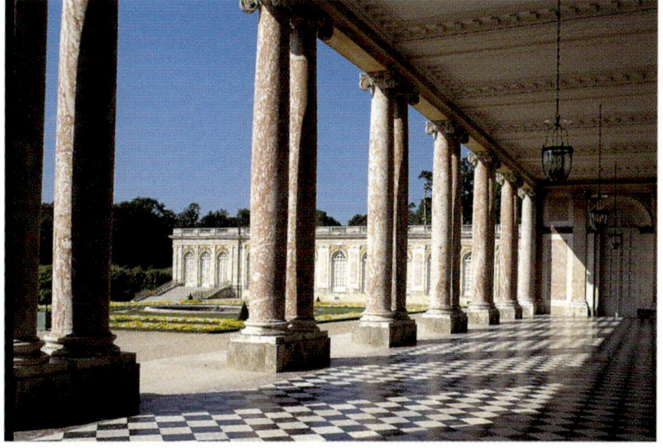

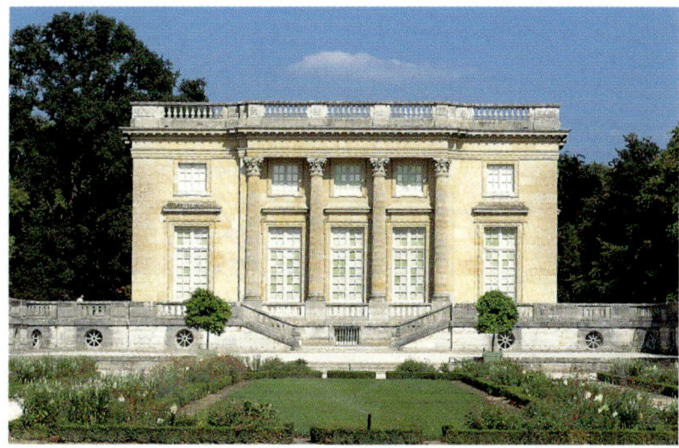

Surrounded by sea monsters, the Latone basin overlooks
the Tapis Vert and down towards the Grand Canal (left).
The Grand Trianon was built for Louis XIV who often
spent time here with close family members (top).
The Petit Trianon was built by Gabriel for Louis XV
who gave it to his favourite, Madame Du Barry (above).

canvases each representing a great battle in the history of
France. New rooms were opened under the reign of
Napoleon III. During the Paris Commune Versailles was
the seat of the government and in 1871, William I was
proclaimed Emperor of Germany in the Hall of Mirrors. It
was also here that the Treaty of Versailles was signed on

28 June 1919, the declaration of the Allies' victory over
Germany after the First World War. Since the proclamation of the Third Republic, the Senate and the Chamber
of Deputies hold meetings here when the two chambers
need to discuss important issues such as the revision of
the constitution.

Antiquity

3rd century BC. The Celtic tribe known as the Parisii settle on the Ile de la Cité. Their village is called Lutetia.

52 BC. The War of the Gauls. Julius Caesar's army conquers Lutetia.

The Gallo-Roman town grows and develops on the left bank.

Middle Ages

5th century. Following barbarian invasions and the fall of the Roman Empire, the Franks become the masters of Gaul.

508 AD. Clovis makes Paris the capital of the Frankish kingdom.

9th century. The Normans sail up the Seine and pillage Paris several times.

10th century. The Capetians make their home on the Ile de la Cité.

The reign of Louis VII (1137-1180). In 1163, Bishop Maurice de Sully begins construction of Notre-Dame de Paris cathedral.

The reign of Philippe Auguste (1180-1223). In 1190, a rampart designed to protect Paris is erected.

The reign of Saint Louis (1234-1270). In 1246, construction of the Sainte-Chapelle is started and Notre-Dame de Paris cathedral completed.

The reign of Charles V (1364-1380). A new surrounding wall is built on what is now the Grands Boulevards. The first municipal organisation in Paris is formed. Etienne Marcel is appointed the Provost of the merchants of Paris.

Renaissance

Reign of Francis I (1515-1547). The Louvre fortress is transformed into a Renaissance palace.

The Regency of Catherine de Medicis (1560-1564). The Queen commissions the construction of the Tuileries palace.

Modern times

The reign of Henry IV (1589-1610). In 1594, the king renounces Protestantism and enters Paris. Creation of the Place des Vosges and building of the Pont-Neuf.

Regency of Marie de Medicis (1610-1614). Construction of the Luxembourg Palace.

The reign of Louis XIII (1614-1643). Extension of the Louvre. Richlieu moves into the Palais-Royal.

The reign of Louis XIV (1643-1715). Parliament and the nobility start a rebellion against Mazarin and royal authority, called

The Fronde. As a result, Louis XIV sets up the government at Versailles. The Place Vendôme is created. Founding of Les Invalides. The Porte Saint-Denis and Porte Saint-Martin are erected, in the form of triumphal arches dedicated to royal victories.

The reign of Louis XV (1715-1774). Creation of the Place de la Concorde, Ecole Militaire, Champ-de-Mars esplanade and founding of the Sainte-Geneviève church, the future Panthéon.

The French Revolution (1789-1794). Storming of the Bastille on 14 July – Louis XVI and Marie-Antoinette are guillotined on the Place de la Concorde in 1793.

The Empire (1804-1815). Napoleon I creates grand monuments, inspired by classical Rome: the Vendôme column, the Arc de Triomphe du Carrousel, the Arc de Triomphe on the Champs-Elysées and the Madeleine. In 1814, English and Cossack troops occupy Paris.

The Restoration (1814-1830). The reigns of Louis XVIII and Charles X.

The July Monarchy (1830-1848). The reign of Louis-Philippe.

The Third Republic (1848-1852). Louis-Napoleon Bonaparte is elected President of the Republic.

The Second Empire (1852-1870). During the reign of Napoleon III and under the authority of the Prefect of Paris, Haussmann, the city of Paris is completely transformed: its old districts are razed to the ground, new avenues are built, parks and gardens designed and stations constructed. Charles Garnier is appointed architect for the new Paris Opera.

The Franco-German War (1870-1871). A French defeat leads to the Prussian occupation of Paris.

March to May 1871. The insurrection of the Commune represents a refusal of defeat and leads to large scale destruction of the city: the Hôtel de Ville and Tuileries Palace are burnt down.

A project is started for the construction of the basilica at Montmartre.

Contemporary era

The First World War (1914-1918).

1937. Universal exhibition and construction of the Palais de Chaillot at the Trocadéro.

Second World War (1940-1945). Paris is occupied by the Germans.

Proclamation of the 5th Republic (1958).

1969-1974. President Georges Pompidou starts the construction of the Georges Pompidou Centre, which is completed in 1976.

1981-1991. Major projects are undertaken by President François Mitterrand: the Louvre pyramid, the Institut du Monde Arabe and the Opera-Bastille.

Production: Marceau Presse, 3 rue de Provence, 75009 Paris

Editorial Co-ordination: Sophie Picon

Page format and graphics: Thierry Renard

Publishing secretary: Nathalie Garcia-Mora

Translation: LTA

Photogravure : Sele Offset, Turin

Printed by Rotolito Lombarda, Milan

ISBN : 2 85025 766 4

Registration of copyright: April 2001